African Traditional Law

THE CUSTOMARY LAW OF THE DINKA PEOPLE OF SUDAN

In comparison with
Aspects of Western and Islamic Laws

African Traditional Law

THE CUSTOMARY LAW OF THE DINKA PEOPLE OF SUDAN

In comparison with
Aspects of Western and Islamic Laws

by

John Wuol Makec

LL.B (Khartoum), LL.M (London)

Judge of the Court of Appeal (Judiciary) Sudan

formerly

Minister of Co-operatives and Rural Development and
Speaker of the Bhar el Ghazal People's Regional Assembly

AFROWORLD  PUBLISHING CO

AFROWORLD PUBLISHING CO.
31 Grenfell Tower,
Lancaster Road,
London W11 1TG,
England.

Copyright © John Wuol Makec, 1988

All rights reserved. No part of this publication
may be reproduced, stored in a retrieval system, or
transmitted in any form or by any means, electronic,
mechanical, photocopying, recording, or otherwise,
without the prior permission of the copyright owner.

First published in 1988

ISBN 0 948583 03 7 (Hardback)
ISBN 0 948583 04 5 (Paperback)

Design, typesetting and production
by Nuprint Ltd, Harpenden, Herts AL5 4SE.
Printed and Bound in England for
CPH Printing Ltd, London W11 4NS.

Contents

Acknowledgement   13
Foreword   15

Introduction   17

Part A
1. Recognition of custom as one of the sources of law in the Sudan   18
2. The need for development of the customary laws of the Sudan   20

Part B
1. The conditions which qualify a custom to acquire a binding force of law   21
2. The test of reasonableness of a custom   25

CHAPTER ONE

The Sources, Development and Objectives of the Dinka Customary Law   31

1. SOURCES
   1.1 Practice   31
   1.2 Courts' decisions   32
   1.3 Religious beliefs   33
   1.4 Principles of morality   33

2. THE DEVELOPMENT OF THE LAW   34
   2.1 Development in the field of civil law   34
   2.2 Non-existence of law enforcement agencies   34

3. THE LEGAL OBJECTIVES   35
   3.1 The rudimentary state of the criminal law   37

3.2	Attempts to resolve differences between customary rules through a unified code	38
3.3	The re-statement and the wide-scale codification of the customary rules	39

CHAPTER TWO

1. The Nature of Legal Sanctions in Dinka Law — 41

1.1	The positive character of man	42
1.2	Self-aggrandisement and the break-down of the positive character of man	42
1.3	The need for law	43
1.4	The need for legal sanctions	44

2. THE APPARENT ABSENCE OF LEGAL SANCTIONS IN DINKA LAW — 45

3. THE NATURE OF LEGAL SANCTIONS — 46
3.1	The fear of God	47
3.2	Mystical beliefs	49
3.3	Public criticism	51
3.4	The fear of revenge	51

CHAPTER THREE

The Family Law ('Lôôngē-Kôôcē Ruāi') — 54

1. *RUĪ* (MARRIAGE)
1.1(a)	Union between one man and one or more women	54
1.1(b)	The scope of the union	56
1.1(c)	Union for their lives	57
1.1(d)	Union between 'his successor and one or more women'	59
1.2	Why marry and produce children for the dead?	60
1.3	Marriage objectives	61
1.3(a)	Sexual cohabitation	61
1.3(b)	Procreation of the young	61
1.3(c)	Maintenance of the homestead	62
1.4	The requirements of marriage	62
1.4(a)	Consent (Gēm; Gam)	62
1.4(b)	Capacity in marriage (Dit)	63
1.4(c)	Bride-wealth ('Hok-thieek')	63
1.4(d)	The final marriage ceremony	65
1.5	Marriage as a social contract and not a commercial contract	65

2. ADULTERY *(AKOR)* — 67

3. DIVORCE *(PUOKĒ-RUĀI)* — 77
3.1	Puokē-ruāi (Divorce) reverses the marriage objectives	81

3.2	Puokē-ruāi must take place in court	81
3.3	Reasons why divorce must take place in court	82
3.4	Whether puokē-ruāi may be obtained with ease	86
3.5	Grounds for divorce (puokē-ruāi)	88
3.6	The legal consequences of puokē-ruái	90
3.7	The relation between the bride-wealth and the father's right to children	95
3.8	All claims must always be settled in a divorce suit	97
3.9	Procedure	97

4. THE CUSTODY OF CHILDREN AND MAINTENANCE ORDERS 99

5. DISTRIBUTION OF FAMILY PROPERTY AFTER DIVORCE 103

6. JURIDICTION AND CHOICE OF LAW IN DIVORCE CASES OR DISPUTES ARISING OUT OF MIXED MARRIAGES 105

6.1	Cases arising out of marriage or divorce between the Dinka and members of other tribes	105
6.2	Divorce cases or disputes arising out of marriages among the Dinka Christians	107
6.3	Divorce cases in marriages between non-Muslim Dinka girls or women and Muslim men	109

CHAPTER FOUR

Some Aspects of The Law of Property   118

1. PERSONAL PROPERTY   123

1.1	The transfer of title or ownership of property	123
1.2	The right of the original owner to trace his property into the hands of others	127
1.3	Exceptions to the right of tracing	132
1.3(a)	Impossibility of recovering the original property	132
1.3(b)	Circumstances where the law stops the right of tracing	134
1.4	The rights of innocent parties	136
1.4(a)	Where the property is obtained from the owner	136
1.4(a)	(i) Acquisition of property through marriage	136
1.4(a)	(ii) Acquisition of property through sale, discharge of debt or any other obligation	137
1.4(b)	Where the innocent party obtains property from a non-owner	137
1.4(b)	(i) Acquisition of property through a rogue	138
1.4(b)	(ii) Acquisition of property by a finder or by one who acquires it from a finder	139

2. INTESTATE AND TESTAMENTARY SUCCESSION … 140
   2.1 Who are the legal heirs? … 141
   2.2 The main principles to be observed in dealing with the deceased's estate … 141
   2.2(a) One must have a family … 141
   2.2(b) Property as a source of power for raising a family … 142
   2.2(c) Communal ownership of family property … 142
   2.2(d) The estate must remain within the family … 142
   2.3 The consequences of the above principles … 142
   2.3(a) Limitation imposed upon the testator's freedom of bequest … 143
   2.3(b) Duty imposed upon the trustee of the deceased's estate … 143
   2.3(c) Exclusion of daughters from inheritance … 144
   2.3(d) Exclusion of the divorced wife or wives from inheritance … 144
   2.3(e) Testate or testamentary succession becomes less common … 144
   2.4 Brothers and parents as alternative heirs … 145
   2.5 Property which constitutes part of the estate … 146
   2.6 Appointment of a trustee for the family … 148
   2.7 The impact of tribal or public rights upon succession … 149
   2.7(a) Rights which cannot be inherited … 149
   2.7(b) The estate may be inherited with restrictions imposed upon it through the rights acquired over it by others … 149

3. THE LAND LAW … 150
   3.1 Statutory provisions … 150
   3.2 Stagnancy in land development … 151
   3.3 The two land divisions and their usage … 152
   3.3(a) The importance of the *Toc* … 152
   3.3(b) The importance of *Baai* … 153
   3.4 Public and private interests in land … 153
   3.4(a) Modes of acquisition of title to land … 154
   3.4(a) (i) By occupation … 154
   3.4(a) (ii) By conquest … 154
   3.4(a) (iii) By gift … 154
   3.4(b) The nature of the individual's right or interest in land … 155
   3.4(b) (i) Possessory right … 160
   3.4(b) (ii) Usufruct … 162
   3.4(b) (iii) Ownership right … 163
   3.4(c) The ownership of things on and under the land … 166
   3.4(c) (i) The case of Guen-jang … 167
   3.4(c) (ii) The case of Aber (metallic ore) … 168
   3.4(c) (iii) The ownership of animals on land … 168
   3.4(c) (iv) The loss of title to land … 169

3.4(d)		Reserved lands for communal usage	179
3.4(d)	(i)	Restrictions on reserved lands for common usage	180
3.4(d)	(ii)	Claims of title as a cause of inter-tribal disputes over land	180
3.4(d)	(iii)	Claim of title arising from the original occupation of land	181
3.4(d)	(iv)	A community may exercise exclusive rights over its fishing areas	182
3.4(d)	(v)	Where permission to settle on a tribal land develops into an adverse claim of title	183
3.4(d)	(vi)	Rights enjoyed over the property of another person	185

CHAPTER FIVE

The Law of Obligations 186

1. AMUK (OR AMEC)   187
2. LIABILITY FOR ANIMALS – DAMAGES FOR PERSONAL INJURY CAUSED BY ANIMALS   192
    2.1 Whether the animals are classified; and if so, whether the keeper or the owner is liable for the acts of the animals in both cases   195
    2.2 Whether the liability for the torts committed by these animals is absolute or whether the mental element of the keeper or owner is a necessary requisite for his liability   196
    2.3 Exception   196
    2.4 The basis of liability for the acts of animals   197
    2.5 To whom is the keeper of an animal liable?   198
3. LIABILITY FOR HOMICIDE (*NAKE-RAAN*)   198
    3.1 Why homicide is classified under the Law of Obligations   198
    3.2 The basis of collective responsibility for homicide or certain torts   199
    3.2   (i) Collective responsibility   200
    3.2   (ii) Persons who are liable collectively for the tortfeasor's act   200
    3.2   (iii) The basis or philosophy of the principle of collective responsibility   202
    3.3 Whether the mental element is a necessary requisite for liability in homicide cases   205
    3.4 Cases where damages are mitigated   207
    3.5 Cases where relationship or a particular circumstance exists   208
    3.5(a) Where a person causes the death of a relative   208
    3.5(b) Where the wife causes the death of a person   208

3.5(c)	Where the wife kills her husband	209
3.5(d)	Where the husband kills his wife	209

4. DEFAMATION 209
    4.1   Duty of care owed to the public 209
    4.2   Damages for defamation 211
    4.3   What constitutes defamation in a locality 211
    4.4   The corrective element 213
    4.5   Distinction between defamation and insult 214
    4.6   Whether *mens rea* is necessary in determining liability 215

CHAPTER SIX

Procedure 216

1. THE GENERAL PRINCIPLES REGULATING THE OPERATION OF THE RULES OF PROCEDURE 218
    1.1   The functional role of the judge or the court during a trial 218
    1.2   The principle of conciliation 220
    1.3   Settlement of disputes outside the court 221
    1.4   Simplicity of procedure 222

2. THE CONSTITUTION OF CHIEFS' COURTS 222

3. JURISDICTION OF CHIEFS' COURTS 223

4. CAUSE OF ACTION AND RIGHT OF ACTION 227
    4.1   Cause of action 227
    4.2   Right of action 228

5. NON-RENEWAL OF DECIDED CASES (*BERĒ-PINYĒ LUOK*) 229

6. WHO ARE THE PARTIES TO A SUIT OR A CASE? 229

7. SURVIVAL OF ACTIONS 230

8. PAYMENT OF SUBJECT-MATTER OF THE SUIT INTO COURT 230

9. COMMENCEMENT OF JUDICIAL PROCEEDINGS 231

10. SUMMONS 232

11. THE HEARING 233
    11.1   The seating arrangements of the people 233

12. WHO MUST OPEN THE CASE? 235

13. THE DEFENCE CASE 236

14. THE JUDGEMENT 237

15.	APPEALS	238
	15.1 Time for appeal	240
	15.2 Rationale behind making appeals	241
16.	POWER OF REVISION	241
17.	EXECUTIONS OF DECREES AND ORDERS	243
18.	EXECUTIONS OF DECREES AND ORDERS IN OTHER TERRITORIES	244

Table of Cases   247

Glossary   248

Appendix   253

Index   280

Acknowledgement

My profound indebtedness goes to Professor N. J. Coulson, my tutor at the London University (School of Oriental and African Studies), from September 1978 to October 1980, during my post-graduate studies in law. I can never forget his very interesting and inspiring lectures and discussions on Islamic Comparative Law. I also cannot forget the enthusiasm which I derived from reading the inspiring writings and presentations in various conferences by Professor A. N. Allott of the School of Oriental and African Studies, in connection with the development of African Law.

Further, my deep indebtedness goes to Mr Isaiah Kulang Mabor, the former Commissioner of Bhar el Ghazal Province, whose desire to contribute towards the development of the customary law in this Province prompted him to convene the Conference where the customary law was re-stated and which is the cornerstone of my present work and other manuscripts not yet published.

My acknowledgement further goes to my colleagues, the judges, among whom are His Honour Donato Mabior Mawien, Gordon Abyei Makuac, Martin Majier Gai, Abdel Atti Abdel Wahab el Assad, and Dr Akolda Mayen whose assistance during the preparation for the Re-statement of Bhar el Ghazal Customary Law, Local Order, 1975, was very useful.

My indebtedness extends to Mr Paul Marial Dot, whose knowledge of anthropology was very useful when he proof-read my manuscript. Similarly, my thanks go to Mr Ambrose Wol Dhal, a distinguished journalist, whose comments were very inspiring and useful indeed; further, I thank a countless number of friends and those who had the opportunity to read my work for the encouraging comments they made. Among this group, I must not forget the sincere appreciation of my work expressed by Mr Justice Henry Riad Sikla (Justice of the Supreme Court of Sudan). I must also acknowledge, among this group, the valuable and inspiring comments advanced by Mr Kwesi Krafona, the Ghanaian author and publisher. His precious comments are a reflection of his sincerity as a true Pan-Africanist, who strongly believes that African cultural identity must be demonstrated through writings of this nature.

Further, my gratitude goes to Mr Siir Anai Kelueljang, the Sudanese poet, for the great efforts he exerted towards the preparation of the manuscript for publication. My gratitude also goes to my wife, Veronica Nyabuot Makuac, for her untiring devotion to the preservation of all my research papers, which include the present work. I thank all the typists who took part in the typing of the material for this work at various stages. Among them, I must particularly mention Mr Simon Deng and Miss Aisha Ali Suggh el Ahumeer.

Foreword

This original and authoritative book could not have been published at a better time. It has come at a time when knowledge of the personal laws[1] and cultural values of the indigenous Sudanese communities in particular, and indigenous Africans in general, is in great demand.

In the colonial days African laws were declared either inapplicable or non-existent by the colonialists who, for their convenience, imposed the doctrine of 'extra-territoriality' whereby the application of the laws of their native countries was extended to the colonies in place of, and in total disregard of, the cultural values and legal principles of the indigenous people. Because of this, African laws, customs and usages, where recognised, were relegated to an inferior status vis-a-vis European or Islamic laws and remain largely unwritten, under-rated and under-developed. If the African is to be given a proper legal standard, derived from African culture and equal to any in the world, African lawyers must quickly recognise the importance of the traditional laws, review, codify and develop them.

Thus the publication of this book by the eminent Sudanese judge is timely in that it sets an excellent example for other African jurists to emulate. As custom is recognised in the Sudan as one of the important sources of law in the country, this book was written not only to illustrate the Dinka Law but to supplement the Re-statement of the Bhar el Ghazal Customary Law Act, 1984, which the author, in his capacity as Speaker of the Bhar el Ghazal People's Regional Assembly, helped draft and enact, and which comprises three codes,

---

[1] See footnote at pages 22–23 for the definition of 'personal law'.

namely, (1) the Dinka; (2) the Luo; and (3) the Fertit Codes of Laws (see Appendix).

The significance of this book is that it is the first of its kind which comprehensively deals with the substantive law and rules of procedure and demonstrates the wisdom and rationality underlying African traditional laws.

Judge Makec has done a pioneering job and it is hoped that his magnificent and brilliant example will be followed by other African legal scholars and practitioners for the benefit not only of posterity but all those, the world over, who are interested to know the true nature of African laws, customs and usages. His book, written from the perspective of an African well-versed in Western and Islamic laws, and in the customs of his people, is not only scholarly, it is a landmark in the development of African jurisprudence. It is for these reasons and in order to facilitate the proper study and teaching of African laws that I decided, without hesitation, to publish it.

KWESI KRAFONO, BA (HONS), MSc (LONDON)
London, January 1988

Introduction

In general, few people in the Sudan have been interested in the development of the customary laws of the country. Even the Sudanese jurists who might be expected to initiate their development have been regrettably silent. The reasons for this lack of initiative and the overwhelming need to develop these laws will be discussed later in this Chapter. However, a few writers,[1] mainly non-indigenous, have attempted to take up the initiative, thereby drawing the attention of the Sudanese people to the importance of undertaking more research in the field of customary law for the benefit not only of the ordinary people of Sudan but of interested jurists and scholars at home and abroad.

As there are different ethnic groups in the Sudan, so are there different customary laws applicable to each group. In writing this book, however, my main concern is not with the customary laws of the Sudan as a whole but with the development of the customary law of the Dinka people – one of the largest indigenous ethnic groups in the country. But for illustrative and comparative purposes, I shall be making some references to other African legal systems, including the

---

[1] A few of these writers are:
— C. d'Olivier Farran (1957) *Sudan Law Journal Reports,* pp.143–227 (published as a book: *The Matrimonial Laws of the Sudan,* Butterworths, London 1963.
— Cliff F. Thompson (1965) SLJR 474, *The Formative Era of the Law of Sudan.*
— Dr Francis Deng (1965) SLJR 535: *The Family and the Law in African Customary Law*; also in *Houston Law Review,* Vol. 4.
— P. P. Howell: *A Manuel of Nuer Law*, Oxford University Press, 1954 (based on the works of P. Evans-Prichard: *The Nuer,* Oxford, 1940; *Kinship and Marriage Among The Nuer*, Oxford, 1951).

customary laws of some other Sudanese tribes, as well as to some aspects of Western and Islamic jurisprudence.

This Chapter will deal essentially with preliminary issues which ought to be considered in the discussion of customary law. For example, it is necessary to know at a preliminary stage that custom has been recognised by the general Territorial Law (i.e. State Law) as one of the main sources of laws applicable in this country. Without this recognition it would be a waste of time writing about the Dinka Customary Law, unless one intended to contribute something in the anthropological field. With this recognition the need becomes imperative to develop the customary laws into a common law of the Sudan, and so Part A of this Chapter will discuss these issues. Part B will discuss the main conditions which a custom must fulfil before it can be recognised as having a binding force of law. In this respect, we shall treat separately one of the controversial features of customary law – the test of 'reasonableness', because it is this test which enables a court to determine whether a customary rule is admissible or not.

PART A

1. *Recognition of custom as one of the sources of law in the Sudan*

Custom is not only recognised as law by the 'Original Communities', it also forms one of the major sources of law in modern Sudan. By 'Original Communities' is meant the communities which still strictly adhere to their original customs and have not wholly or substantially been influenced by foreign ideas. Under section 5 of the Civil Justice Act 1983[2], under the heading 'Law to be Administered', it is provided that:

> 'where in any suit or other proceeding in a civil court any question arises regarding succession, inheritance, wills, legacies, gifts, marriage, divorce, family relations, or the constitution of wakfs, the rule of decision shall be ... any custom applicable to the parties concerned, which is not contrary to justice, equity and good conscience, and has not by this or any other enactment been altered or abolished and has not been declared void by the decision of a competent court.'

---

[2] which still retains the provisions of section 5 of the Civil Justice Ordinance 1929.

NB: The order of the contents of (a) and (b) of section 5 has been reversed under the Civil Justice Act 1983.

There were other statutes in the past (now repealed) which also recognised the application of customary law: The Chiefs' Courts Ordinance 1931 and The Native Courts Ordinance 1932. Section 7 of The Chiefs' Courts Ordinance provided that a Chiefs' Court shall administer:

(a) the native law and custom prevailing in the area over which the court exercises its jurisdiction provided that such native law and custom is not contrary to justice, morality or order;
(b) the provision of any ordinance which the court may be authorised to administer in its warrants or regulations.

The other Act which recognised the application of customary law was The People's Local Courts' Act, 1977. Section 13 of this Act provided that

'A people's local court shall administer the custom prevailing within the local limits of its jurisdiction provided that it is not contrary to justice, morals or public order. It shall administer the provisions of any other law, the administration of which is authorised by its warrant of establishment or the regulations accompanying the same.'

However, despite the repeal of these statutes, the status of custom as one of the sources of law in the Sudan has not been diminished but emphasised by section 5 of the Civil Justice Act 1983. Further, local courts' warrants issued from time to time by the Chief Justice authorise those courts to apply the local custom applicable to the contesting parties.

Apart from statutes, there are judicial decisions which have, from time to time, given recognition to custom as one of the sources of law in the Sudan. One example may suffice here. In the case of *Gilbril Barbare* v. *Reen Abdel Massin Khalil*[3], a plea for the application of the Non-Mohamedan Marriage Ordinance (which deals with the cases of non-Sudanese Christians domiciled in the Sudan who are not covered by the other ordinance – Excepted Communities) was raised by the defendant's (appellant) advocate to be applied to the family dispute between the parties. The plea was rejected by the Court of Appeal. The Court referred back the case to the Province Court (which was the court of first instance) to ascertain a common custom between the parties and to apply it.

The essence of the decision of the Court of Appeal was that the

---

[3] (1966) Sudan Law Journal Reports 53.

indigenous Sudanese must be governed by their own custom and not the custom or personal law which only governs personal matters of non-Sudanese who are domiciled in the Sudan. Custom is therefore a major source of law in the Sudan.

2. *The need for development of the customary laws of the Sudan*

The ease with which it is possible nowadays for one community to migrate from their land to settle in the territory of another community in the Sudan, and the constant influx of people from the rural areas into the towns, poses serious problems – social, economic and juristic. However, we are here only concerned with the significance of juristic relations which may develop between members of different communities and even between members of the same community in a different tribal area.[4] There may be marriages between members of different communities who have different customary laws, or marriages between persons who have a common custom. In disputes arising from such marital relations, the question for the judge is: what law must be applied in a personal matter where the parties have different customary laws? If the judge or the court is tempted to apply the provisions of section 6 of the Civil Justice Act, 1983 (formerly section 9 of the Civil Justice Ordinance 1929), he or it may be drawn to certain conclusions which are altogether alien to both parties and therefore unacceptable. For example, the judge may apply the English Law rather than the customary law of the parties.

The case of *Gibril Barbare* v. *Reen Abdel Massin Khalil,* already cited, may serve to illustrate this point. Gibril Barbare is a Southern Sudanese Christian and his wife is from a different community. To comply with the provisions of section 9 of the Civil Justice Ordinance, 1929, the appellant's advocate requested that the provisions of the Non-Mohamedan Marriage Ordinance be applied in this case. The Court of Appeal declared that the Non-Mohamedan Marriage Ordinance was inapplicable and referred the case back to the Province Judge to determine a common custom. Even though there was no common custom between the parties, the Province Judge had previously ordered the defendant (appellant) to pay maintenance allowance to his divorced wife. But the Judge did not state what law he applied. He may have either resorted to the provisions of section 9 of the Civil Justice Ordinance, 1929 or the provisions of the Non-Mohamedan Marriage Ordinance or he made his own decision according to what he thought was just. Nothing is reported again as to

---

[4] This aspect forms a part of Farran's discussion in the *Matrimonial Laws of the Sudan* (1957) SLJR.

what law the Province Judge later applied since it was obvious that the parties had no common custom to be administered.

Again, among members of the same community, judges who have no knowledge of their common personal law and who may be indifferent in ascertaining it may make judgements which members of that community may regard as unprecedented. The case of *Pan Akoc Majok* v. *Manoah Pabeek in 1965*,[5] serves to illustrate this point. Manoah eloped with Aluel Akoc, the sister of the plaintiffs, in Khartoum. The brothers of the girl did not want to marry her to Manoah. The dispute went to a civil court in Khartoum. The court ruled that since the parties (i.e. the spouses) were mature and had mutually consented to marry each other, they were so entitled. It is apparent in this decision that the court applied the English Law, and the marriage was upheld. But the spouses were Dinka and therefore had a common custom which should have been applied to do justice to the case. The family of Pan Akoc Majok was greatly disturbed by this decision and disowned the girl forever. However, the cases which pose more complicated legal problems are mixed marriages between Muslims and non-Muslim southerners, about which more will be said later in Chapter 3.

It is not only in cases of marriage that a blatant miscarriage of justice may occur, it may also happen in cases of tort and crime. In such cases, if the judge is ignorant of the custom of the communities or the parties involved, and has no means of ascertaining it, he may come to an arbitrary decision of his own, which may be at variance with the custom of the parties.

Such problems, which judges in the Sudan are likely to encounter and be thoroughly embarrassed by them for want of legal authority, serve to illustrate the urgent need to ascertain, codify and develop the customary laws of the country. These processes applied to the different customary laws of the different ethnic groups in the country will enable us finally to evolve a common law for the whole of Sudan. This is the task that lies ahead for the Sudanese jurists and indeed for other African legal scholars who are concerned to create a common law for their tribally heterogeneous people.

PART B

1. *The Conditions which qualify a custom to acquire a binding force of law*

The conditions which qualify a custom to acquire a binding force of

---

[5] Unreported case.

law are almost the same universally. For this reason, it is necessary to deal in general with these conditions before coming to the discussion of the Dinka Customary Law proper. It is also essential to define 'custom' before discussing the conditions which give it a legal force. In this respect references will be made to the definitions and explanatory views of various legal authorities who have already dealt with the subject-matter.

In the case of *Bamboulis* v. *Bamboulis*,[6] Lindsay, C. J., stated:

> 'Custom is established usage which by recognition in Sudan Court of Law acquires the force of law. The section (i.e. section 5 of the Civil Justice Act 1983) envisages that such custom can be altered or even abolished or declared void. The Ecclesiastical Rules of a Church and the Civil Laws of foreign countries are, in my view, incapable of being altered, abolished or declared void, and are clearly not contemplated by the wording of the section to be within the meaning of the word "custom". "Custom" in its context refers to local custom originating by usage in the Sudan, and is not applicable to imported rules of law of foreign origin.'

However, in *Kattan* v. *Kattan (1957) SLJR 35* this definition was heavily criticised. Although the matter before the justices in this case did not require a detailed consideration of the definition given in *Bamboulis*, the learned justices expressed the view:

> 'We feel the occasion justifies the statement that this restricted interpretation of s.5 of the Ordinance (1929) (now repealed but its provisions still retained by s.5 of the Civil Justice Act 1983) adopted in *Bamboulis* v. *Bamboulis* is no doubt novel and certainly not the view which has always been taken by the Sudan courts with regard to this section.'

In other words, the justices favoured a wider definition of custom. And Chief Justice Bennet said that

> 'The section had been interpreted as to a large extent letting in the church law[7] of the parties where there was no appropriate lex domicilii or natural law.'

---

[6] Cases in High Court and Court of Appeal (1954) p.76.
[7] The judicial interpretation of custom under S.5 of the Civil Procedure Act, 1983 (formerley S.5 of Civil Justice Ordinance, 1929) covers the Church Law (or Law of a Religious Community) and the Personal Law (i.e., the National Law of Personal Status) of persons domiciled in the Sudan. In *Abdulla Chercheflio* v. *Maria Bekryorellis, AC/App/12/1934*, for example, it was held by Gorman, J. (Justice):

Introduction

In fact, the controversy over the definition of custom relates more to its scope than its meaning. Chief Justice Lindsay advocated a restrictive definition while the Sudanese courts have always favoured a wider definition to include the canon law or personal laws of other communities who are domiciled in the Sudan. The parties in the above cases were non-Sudanese domiciled in the Sudan and it was important to determine the scope or the extent of the 'custom' so as to ascertain whether the canon law or the personal laws of such communities fell within the provisions of section 5 of the Civil Justice Act, 1983. And the Court said they did. But it must be stated at this stage that whether or not the canon law or personal laws of non-Sudanese who are domiciled in the Sudan can be defined as custom is not the subject of discussion here. In these pages we are only concerned with the customs of the Sudanese in general and the Dinka in particular.

A further definition of custom may be derived from the 7th edition of *Osborn's Concise Law Dictionary*, by John Burke, page 108, according to which custom

'is a rule of conduct obligatory on those within its scope, established by long usage. A valid custom has the force of law. Custom to the society is what law is to the state (Salmond). A valid custom must be of immemorial antiquity, certain, reasonable, obligatory, not repugnant to statute law, though it may derogate from the common law.'

'It has been decided in this Court (i.e., Court of Appeal) that where parties are domiciled in a country other than the Sudan which possesses a national law of personal status that such law is to be regarded as a body of custom applicable to parties within the meaning of S.5: the law of domicile is in these matters adopted by the law of the Sudan as their personal law. But where the parties are domiciled in the Sudan or in a country with no national law of personal status then, it has been held, it is the customs of the religious community to which they belong which are to be looked to and comprise their personal law.'

Also, in *Islamic and Customary Law in the Sudan, Sudan in Africa*, Khartoum University Press, 1985, 2nd ed, p.279, Natale O. Akolawin, the author of the article, states:

'The content of Islamic Law, as administered by the Sudan Sharia Courts today, is primarily personal. Customary Law is also personal, except when administered by the Chiefs and Native Courts Ordinance, 1931 and 1932 respectively.'

In his book[8], Dias has this to say:

'When a large section of the populace are in the habit of doing a thing over a very much longer period, it may become necessary for the courts to take notice of it. The reaction of the people themselves may manifest itself in mere unthinking adherence to a practice which they follow simply because it is done; or again it may show itself in a conviction that a practice should continue to be observed, because they approve of it as a model of behaviour.... The more people follow a practice, the greater the pressure against non-conformity. But it is not the development of a practice as such, but the growth of a conviction that it ought to be followed that makes it a model of behaviour.'

From these varied but not too dissimilar definitions, we can determine the conditions that have to be fulfilled for a custom, usage or practice to be recognised by a court of law as having the force of law. These conditions have been enumerated by Mr Salt and Sir Carleton Allen and reproduced by Dias in his book[9] as follows:

(a) The custom must be of immemorial antiquity. The onus of proving its antiquity is bestowed on the person who asserts the application of the custom. The proof becomes easier, however, if its origin cannot be remembered. The burden of rebutting it lies upon the party against whom the custom is to be applied.
(b) It must have been enjoyed as of right.
(c) It must be certain and precise.
(d) It must have been enjoyed continuously.
(e) It must be reasonable.

Of the above conditions, the last one (i.e. that the custom must be reasonable), about which more will be said later, is the most controversial because of the vagueness of the concept and its tendency to lend itself to subjective interpretations.

In addition to these conditions, Dias argues that for a custom to be recognised as law, 'it must not be incompatible with other custom within the locality.' This condition may be applicable to societies which have evolved a commom custom or law, but in the Sudan and indeed in other African countries where the customs are not homogeneous among the different tribes, this condition is certainly

---
[8] R. W. M. Dias, *Jurisprudence*, 2nd ed., Butterworths, London, 1964, p.142.
[9] Ibid. p.142.

Introduction

not applicable and cannot disqualify a local custom. It is a condition which may only apply in a locality where there is only a single community or several communities who have a common custom.

Mr Salt (in Dias's book) also advanced a proposition similar to the one given by Chief Justice Lindsay that the application of a local custom may be restricted in its scope:

> 'It (the custom) must be local, which means... it has for its scope a class of persons limited by inhabitancy and a right whose subject matter lies in the same defined district. But, if the ambit of the rule is widened in respect of the class of persons or the subject matter of the right, it cannot subsist as a local custom but must be a rule of common law, or else it is not law at all.'[10]

But as stated before, this restricted scope of custom is not the one favoured by Sudanese courts who have always defined custom in a wider sense so as to include, for instance, the canon law of persons domiciled in the Sudan. The persons governed by canon law may be regarded as a class but their inhabitancy is not defined. Also, certain tribal communities such as the Nuer, the Dinka and the Luo do have many customs in common, but they cannot be regarded as one class of persons limited by inhabitancy.

In fact, custom, once established, can never be restricted, altered, abolished or declared void except by Statute or a court decision. In other words it must not conflict with a judicial decision or a statutory rule. This only shows the inferior position enjoyed by custom compared with a judicial precedent which constitutes a general territorial law. However, a custom may also enjoy a superior status if it becomes a statute by an Act or Ordinance. The main difference between a custom and a general statute is that the former's application is confined to a defined community whereas the latter forms part of the general territorial law and is applicable throughout the length and breadth of the Sudan.

In conclusion, despite the diversity of definitions and qualifications of custom, there is no doubt that a general consensus of opinion on some of them exists.

2. *The test of reasonableness of a custom*

It has been stated that a custom which is capable of acquiring a force of law must be reasonable. This concept requires a more elaborate

---

[10] R. W. M. Dias, *Jurisprudence* 2nd ed., Butterworths, London 1964, p.142.

discussion because of its significance. In the Sudan the corresponding concept of 'reasonableness' of a custom is its conformity with 'justice, equity and good conscience.' According to Dias, 'this is a condition which the courts have used in such a way as to gain a great measure of control over the admission of local customs.'[11]

Difficult problems are posed by this concept of 'reasonableness' and its equivalent concepts in the Sudan Law. If a custom is accepted and obeyed or strictly adhered to by a community which practises it, it is to them reasonable or it conforms with justice, equity and good conscience. But in the Sudan it is the judges who determine whether a custom is reasonable or not, or whether or not it conforms with justice, equity and good conscience. The question therefore is: is it fair to subject the fate of a custom of a community to the decision of a judge? This doubt arises because there is usually a tendency on the part of the judges to be subjective in their determination of what is or is not reasonable, or what does or does not conform with justice, equity and good conscience. In agreement with this view, Mr Natale Olwak said: 'Of course a judge tries to determine a suit before him in accordance with the rules of law he knows, and in accordance with the sense of justice. And, as we shall see later, 'justice, equity and good conscience' were eventually equated with English Law.'[12]

It is to be noted that these concepts were being equated with English Law by the English judges who worked in the Sudan and by the Sudanese judges who took over from them after Independence. These vague concepts give the person making the judgement the discretion to approach a custom by applying a subjective opinion. The question is: is it the English Law alone which can satisfy the requirement of these concepts? Of course not, and rules of other legal systems could also be equated with these standards.

The reasons why the judges in the Sudan equate the English Law with justice, equity and good conscience is that it is the law in which they were trained and which they know best; and so they can apply it on the pretext of it being in conformity with these concepts. There is also another reason why the English judges applied the English Law under this pretext: it was their law, and so they had to equate it with these concepts. The Sudanese judges adopted (and still adopt) the English Law because of their orientation to that legal system. But where the validity of an African custom is determined by Western notions, it means that the judges are given undue liberty to import alien cultures to dilute African systems. Such importation of alien

---

[11] R. W. M. Dias, *Jurisprudence* 2nd ed., Butterworths, London, 1964, p.141.
[12] (1968) SLJR p.232.

cultures into an African personal law is likely to produce adverse results. It will be shown later that the institutions of *Polygamy, Levirate,* or *Muta,* are regarded by many Westerners (judging through their own concepts) as unreasonable and therefore not in conformity with the principles of justice, equity and good conscience, since they take their notions as the universal standards by which the fate of any custom is to be determined. I do not of course assume that all Western writers or judges maintain the same ideas. There are a good many of them who look at these customs objectively and express their appreciation. But human frailty naturally leads one to judge one's own practice as better than that of others. One may instinctively believe it to accord with justice, equity and good conscience, and be sincere in asserting it.

> 'There is in each one of us an underlying philosophy of life which gives coherence and discretion to our thought and action. This philosophy of life is an outcome of inherited instincts. Traditional beliefs and acquired conviction and what one may consider just and equitable or in accordance with good conscience is necessarily limited by the above factors.'[13]

D'Olivier Farran discussed these concepts in his article published in the Sudan Law Journal Reports in 1957. His views are interesting and need to be referred to briefly here. He observed the vagueness of these concepts now under discussion. He also indicated the human tendency to apply the subjective test in judging the concepts or customs of others. He referred to divorce in Islamic Law as one example where Westerners judge the values of others through their own concepts. He said:

> '... by Islamic Law the power of the husband to divorce his wife is virtually unrestricted and it is this fact rather than the potentially polygamous character of the union which has shocked many Western observers, including the English Judges, who, as we have seen, showed a deep antipathy to the Mohamadan Law of Marriage.'

It is therefore obvious that such a custom which allows no restrictions on divorce may be regarded as unreasonable or, in terms of Sudan Law, inconsistent with justice, equity and good conscience. But Sharia Law is supposed to be an immutable law (promulgated from the Divine Authority) and so an English judge would find it

---

[13] Natale Olwak, (1968) SLJR p.232.

difficult to declare it unreasonable, if he were dealing with such a case, although the custom would hurt his conscience.

Further, in his discussion in the same article, Farran anticipated that legal problems might arise where certain cases governed by custom from Southern Sudan eventually reached the Civil Judges in Khartoum or other parts of the Northern Sudan. Such cases might relate to 'ghost marriages' or the custom of *levirate*. Fearing that such judges might be shocked by such customs and declare them unreasonable or inconsistent with justice, equity and good conscience, he gave a word of caution:

'They (i.e. the judges) will obviously have to exercise great caution before rejecting even what appears to them to be an extremely exotic form of customary marriage – e.g. those between two women or between a woman and a "ghost" as already mentioned – on the ground of it not being a legal marriage or on the ground of it being contrary to justice, equity and good conscience.'

It is not only Westerners but also Muslims who would express shock about such Dinka marriages. Further, Muslims, Westerners, the Dinka or other African communities would be shocked by the Zande (i.e. the Avungara) custom where a father marries his daughter. Again the Dinka and some other communities would be shocked by the Muslim custom where a person marries the daughter of his paternal uncle. Similarly, Muslims and many other African communities would be shocked by the ways Westerners express sexual love. To go still further with another example of human prejudice, almost all communities in the world would condemn the Hindu custom of *Suttee* referred to by Farran, where a widow was burnt alive on her husband's funeral pyre, on the ground that it is immoral or inconsistent with justice, equity and good conscience.

In conclusion, the survey I have just made shows that the noble objective expected to be achieved by subjecting a custom to the test of 'reasonableness', or to the test of its conformity with 'justice, equity and good conscience' in order to conclude that it does or does not qualify as law, may fall to our preference for the subjective test. The subjective test often carries with it a great deal of prejudice. It brings about the idea of judging the concepts or values of other communities in the light of the concepts or values of one's own community. This human tendency may promote what may be described as 'the survival of the fittest'. This means that some customs may be eliminated or strangled by judges under the pretext of their non-conformity with justice, equity and good conscience or on the ground of their being immoral. Such situations may arise where there is, for example, a sensitive competition between two customary laws within one state. The legal system with more judges entrenched in its upper echelons may enjoy a 'fitter' position, because those judges who adhere to this particular legal system may try their best to combat the other system on the basis of these vague concepts. Of course it may be difficult to destroy that legal system (i.e. customary law) totally since it would be impossible to declare all its rules as unreasonable or inconsistent with justice, equity and good conscience. But if such judicial decisions become numerous, they are likely to erode deeply into that law, and may even destroy it.

I do not support the abolition of the use of these concepts in testing a custom as to whether it is capable of acquiring a force of law. But it requires a great amount of integrity and sense of fairness on the part of a judge to reach a just conclusion on whether or not a particular custom under consideration should be admitted and applied in a case before him. In my view a judge must consider many important issues, such as:

1. The amount of social value a particular custom serves or the amount of social value attached to it by the community concerned. This social value may have had a long historical background and so the custom must not lightly be declared void. Some are connected with sacred beliefs and a judge must be very cautious in attempting to reject them.
2. Whether the application of such custom or its practice produces or is likely to produce harmful or detrimental consequences to the members of the community; or whether its harmful consequences can also extend to affect members of other communities. An example of a harmful or detrimental custom may be the Hindu custom of *suttee*, which has already been mentioned. Since it causes the death of another person, it is definitely 'inconsistent with justice, equity and good conscience'.
3. Whether such a custom impedes or is likely to impede in any way the social and economic progress of the community concerned or whether it is detrimental to the welfare of the society.
4. If, as in (1) above, the custom has a great amount of social value attached to it by the community to the extent that it would lead to disobedience or crisis in the society if a court rejected it or declared it unreasonable or inconsistent with justice, equity and good conscience, it is my opinion that it should not be within the powers of a judge to make such a decision. It is a matter which

ought to be referred to a law commission which, if it agrees with the judge or judges, should refer the same to the legislature to decide.

Since a custom affects the beliefs of the community which practises it, if it is to be annulled, the legislature must adopt, through the representatives of the community concerned, a procedure by which consultations with many prominent members of the community can be made before the decision is made (by the legislature). I do not intend to suggest that every custom which a court or a judge considers 'unreasonable' should be referred to the legislature, but the determining factor in declaring such a custom unreasonable should be the degree of reaction to be expected from the society. If a judge or a court were to reject the custom of *levirate*, I believe the Dinka community would never recognise or obey such a ruling because of its long history and the sacred aspects attached to it.

These are some of the considerations I would expect a judge or a court of law to make before it condemns the custom of a community as unreasonable. A judge must appreciate the sensitivity attached to certain customary rules or personal law, and this requires a great deal of caution on his part before making a judgement contrary to the belief of a community. I must emphasise that the list of factors a judge or a court must consider before it declares a particular custom 'unreasonable' is not exhausted. However, a judge or a court must be capable of judging what customary rule may be rejected without provoking a communal anger and disobedience to the decision.

CHAPTER ONE

The Sources, Development and Objectives of the Dinka Customary Law

One cannot properly study the Book of the Old Testament without reading the Book of Genesis, nor can one properly study the New Testament without beginning with the Birth of Jesus Christ. It is therefore necessary for a proper understanding of the Dinka Customary Law to start with its origins.

1. SOURCES

There are four sources of the Dinka customary law: practice; judicial decisions; religious beliefs; and principles of morality. These will be discussed in turn.

1.1 Practice

Practice is the first source of the Dinka Customary Law. It has been mentioned already that a custom grows out of repeated practice over a long time. In the words of Salah El Gorashi,

> 'The origin and foundation of the Dinka Customs and Laws is of great interest... The origin of their laws appears to have been experience, so applied as to suit the tribal mode of life; and this experience, and the customs based thereon, is of such antiquity that it is almost hopeless from lack of any written records to trace back to their origin.'[1]

In English law, 'immemorial antiquity' is ascribed to a custom if that custom has existed since before 1189. This is the first year of the

---

[1] Ref. file BGP/66–B–1 p.102.

reign of Richard I, and the start of the Plea Rolls. The date was established to accord with the period of limitations set by the Statute of Westminster, 1275, for the bringing of writs of right.[2]

The Dinka Law does not fix a period from which 'immemorial antiquity' starts. The Dinka people are contented with the fact that the custom has been in practice constantly from immemorial time. It is even doubtful that the character of the custom being 'immemorial' is strictly essential for the acceptance of a custom as a rule of law. But it is a feature which gives it a more authoritative force. A Dinka court, applying a rule of custom to a particular case, will try to ascertain, in case someone raises a doubt about its validity, whether such a rule has been in practice for a long time or not. If it is shown by some members of the court or sometimes by a member of the public that *Ke long dan theer* ('it has been our law for a long time' – i.e. for an indefinite time) it will be adopted in the settlement of the dispute before the court. The question of the rule being unreasonable does not arise for if it were unreasonable it would not have survived. It would have been rejected long ago, so it is taken for granted that it is reasonable.

In Dinka society it is not the practice of one person or a small group of people that makes a custom. It is rather the repeated practice of the whole community. For example, in the case of a civil wrong done, if a particular solution is adopted, usually by the elders of the people, and it is accepted both by the aggrieved party and the wrongdoer; or if it is a solution which prevents either party from taking the law into his hands by revenging, that solution acquires the semblance of legality. It will then be repeated in solving similar cases. If its application acquires a wide acceptance for a long time or for an indefinite time, it will be regarded as a custom with a binding force. It is in fact the acceptance of it as law which strictly gives it a legal force and not essentially its 'immemorial antiquity'. The condition that a practice or a custom must have been of immemorial antiquity is only essential when someone or one of the contesting parties expresses a doubt as to the validity of the rule or when its reasonableness is being questioned.

1.2 Courts' decisions

Although the Dinka Law is called a customary law it is not to be understood that its source or origin is a practice of immemorial antiquity. The decisions of the courts have contributed to the development of the law. Despite the fact that there was no formal system of judicial precedents which existed in the modern sense, the decisions of the courts constitute a valuable contribution to the law.

---

[2] R. W. M. Dias, *Jurisprudence* 2nd ed., Butterworths, London, 1964, p.141.

Judicial decisions were and are still kept in memory by the chiefs and are applied in similar cases. Before the advent of modern government, *Banybith* (i.e. the spiritual leader) played various roles. He was a religious leader, an administrative ruler and a judge. Besides *Banybith*, the elders of the people also used to form ad hoc courts. Judicial decisions made by those courts used to serve as guiding rules in subsequent cases.

Since the establishment of Chiefs' Courts, made possible by the Chiefs' Courts Ordinance 1931, enacted by the British Government, there has been a rapid expansion of the law through an increase in judicial decisions. With the advent of modern government, it has become easier for judicial decisions to spread from district to district because of conferences and inter-districts' courts convened regularly to solve border disputes and conflicts between the people of those districts. These gatherings furnished a useful forum for the exchange of views on judicial matters. New rules were being added to the law from time to time. For example, rules became firmly established regulating the payment of cattle as *awac* for the impregnation of a girl; and that where a married woman has committed adultery for the second time after the payment of *akor*[3] cattle in the first case, the husband is not entitled to obtain *akor* cattle for the second time. Further, through courts' decisions the number of cattle for *apuk* (i.e. compensation) was raised from 10 head of cattle to 30 head.

1.3 Religious beliefs

Religious beliefs also constitute a source of Dinka Law. Some aspects of the religious beliefs of the Dinka people, such as the prohibition of incest and adultery, will be discussed in the next Chapter. Further, the decisions of *Banybith*, whether made in court or outside the courts, were also respected as law, since he was thought to be the representative of God on earth. His decisions were and are still regarded as having a divine force behind them.

1.4 Principles of morality

Moral principles were and are still treated as a source of the Law. The rule against causing death to a human being or the commission of theft was derived from the principles of morality. Generally the rules against crime are based on morality.

---

[3] *Akor* means, in the first place, the act of adultery; in the second place, it means damages paid to the aggrieved husband for the offence committed by the adulterer.

2. THE DEVELOPMENT OF THE LAW

2.1 Development in the field of civil law

Law may be divided into criminal law and civil law. Of course, there are various classifications of the law. However, for the purpose of the discussion here, it is the classification into criminal law and civil law which is relevant.

Criminal law deals with crimes while civil law deals with civil wrongs. The distinction between a crime and a civil wrong is always very difficult to draw. Vague definitions have sometimes been advanced in an attempt to draw a distinction. One of these definitions, which is often referred to, states that:

> 'a crime is an act which injures the community while a civil wrong is an act which injures the individual, and an act which injures both the individual and the community is both a civil wrong and a crime.'[4]

There is no need to go into the juristic analysis of the distinction. For the purpose of the subject under discussion, it is sufficient to know that criminal law protects the community against criminal acts. It inflicts penal sentences on a person who commits a crime in order to deter potential offenders. There are other reasons for the imposition of penalty but they are not relevant here. On the other hand, civil law essentially awards damages to persons who are aggrieved by a civil wrong. The same act may in fact be a crime and a civil wrong.

While I do not intend to assert that the Dinka do not have a criminal law, I must state that they have developed the civil law more extensively. Whenever a wrong (damage or injury) has been done the invariable question is: what remedy should be awarded to the aggrieved party? Once the aggrieved party receives damages or compensation, justice is done and the accused is free. The frequency of claims for damages led to a rapid and extensive development of the civil law. Conversely development failed to take place in the field of criminal law. This may be the result of two main factors: the non-existence of law enforcement agencies and the objectives of the law.

2.2 Non-existence of law enforcement agencies

The execution or the enforcement of the provisions of criminal law requires the existence of certain institutions which I call the law

---

[4] Lord Esher, *Mogul Steam Ship Co* v. *McGregor Gow and Co.* (1889) Queen's Bench Division, p.606.

enforcement agencies. There must be judges[5] to try criminal cases. There must be police to prevent the commission of crime, to apprehend criminals and present them to the courts for trial. There must be prison warders to take custody of convicts who have been sentenced to terms of imprisonment, or to execute death sentences. There must be prisons and cells where these convicted prisoners or detainees who are waiting for trial can be confined. Without these institutions and facilities, it is unlikely that the criminal law can achieve its full objective. To impose penal sentences in circumstances where these institutions and facilities are non-existent would produce the opposite result. The *Banybiith* and the elders of the people who were judges could not impose penal sentences for the reason that such sentences would not promote the peace but would rather result in more breaches of the peace. Clearly, the application of the provisions of criminal law cannot be carried out efficiently without the existence of these institutions.

3. THE LEGAL OBJECTIVES

The other reason why development has taken place in the field of civil law and not in the field of criminal law is to be found in the objectives of the law itself. This one-sided development is not a characteristic feature of the Dinka Law alone, but is universal in African law. The objectives of African law are generally identical. I will therefore refer to the views of writers on African law as a whole. The objectives of the law are paraphrased by Taslim Oluwale Elias, as follows:

> 'Let us examine the general ideas held about the aims of the law in African societies before we attempt to analyse the basic concept of liability for civil and criminal wrong.... It is commonplace to describe African law as positive and preoccupied with the maintenance of the social equilibrium of the community.... It has also been claimed for it that its chief aim is compensation for the wrong as opposed to the European idea of punishment of the wrongdoer; the aim of African law, so the argument runs, is restitution, not retribution...'[6]

These views of T. O. Elias have been expressed by other writers in comparing the aims of African law with those of European laws. Elias observes:

---

[5] This requirement has not been in any way lacking in Dinka society.
[6] T. O. Elias, *The Nature of African Customary Law*, Manchester University Press, 1965, pp.130–144; 155–161.

'Writers on African Law are perfectly right to stress that its essential characteristic is the maintenance or restoration of the social equilibrium of the community and that this pervades the whole fabric of African Law.'[7]

A further aim of the law is the maintenance of peace in society. After the payment of compensation in cases of homicide, conciliatory measures are always undertaken in order to establish a permanent peace between the two sides involved in blood feud.

'... The purification or peace-making ceremony of killing a goat and/or sheep (Note: in the case of the Dinka, it is a bull) after payment of compensation for the murdered is designed, either by itself or in addition to the taking of an oath, to effect lasting reconciliation between the families of the murderer and the murdered.'[8]

Again, in the words of J. H. Driberg:

'... African Law is positive and not negative. It does not say *Thou Shalt Not*, but *Thou Shalt*. Law does not create offences, it does not make criminals; it directs how individuals and communities should behave towards each other. *Its whole object is to maintain an equilibrium, and the penalties of African Law are directed, not against specific infractions, but to the restoration of this equilibrium.*'[9]

The objectives of the law can now be summarised as the maintenance of peace or equilibrium and the restoration of the status quo through the payment of damages.

In conclusion, the development of the civil law can be stated to be a consequence of two factors: (1) the non-existence of the agencies and facilities that are necessary for the efficient operation of the criminal law; and (2) the objectives of the law which are geared to the maintenance of equilibrium and peace among the people. These factors have given precedence to the development of the civil law with the result that the criminal law has remained rudimentary.

---

[7] T. O. Elias, *The Nature of African Customary Law*, Manchester University Press, 1965, pp.130–144; 155–161.
[8] Dundas, quoted in *Readings in African Law*, Vol. I, Frank Cass, London, 1970, p.178.
[9] J. H. Driberg, *The African Conception of Law* (extract published in *Readings in African Law,* Vol I, p.163).

3.1 The rudimentary state of the criminal law

It is not true to say that the Dinka have no criminal law. What has happened is that the civil law has been more extensively developed than the criminal law. The advantage obtained by the civil law over the criminal law is a consequence of the reasons already stated. Due to this extensive development of the civil law, the existence of the criminal law cannot be felt. Moreover, a Dinka court does not bother to analyse or express whether the case before it is a criminal case or a civil case, nor does it expressly state that its decision constitutes either a penalty or a civil award of damages. But if one goes deeper into the law, it becomes obvious that courts always pass penal sentences which appear on the surface to be civil remedies. In many instances there is a punitive element in the award of damages which appears to be solely a civil remedy. It is hard to grasp the distinction because the part of compensation (or damages) which should be treated as a fine goes to the aggrieved party. In foreign legal systems (such as Western legal systems), the fine usually goes to a third party – the State. But in Dinka Law and African law in general, the fine, together with the compensation, goes to the aggrieved party; hence the difficulty in distinguishing the punitive part of the court decision. I think that the absence of a centralised system to receive the fines justifies making the fine a part of the award of damages.

The existence of the punitive element in compensation or in the award of damages will become apparent later. The courts have, from time to time, increased the amount of compensation or damages to deter wrongdoers from the commission of certain acts. In Yirol district, the courts established a precedent that a person who steals a cow must pay three cows to the aggrieved party. Compensation is tripled. This precedent was established to combat the high rate of cattle theft in the area. An example of the application of this rule is the case of *Jacob Mabor Agany*,[10] where each cow stolen from him was returned to him with two additional cows. Surely, this was not for the maintenance of equilibrium or the restoration of the status quo alone, for which the recovery of the stolen property or its value would have been sufficient.

Awac or *awuoc* is a Dinka term which stands for both a criminal act and a civil wrong. Where a court orders a person who has done wrong to pay something to an aggrieved party as damages or compensation, it often employs the term *apuk*. In this respect it becomes obvious that the law which is being put into operation is the civil law, although it is possible that the punitive aspect may be involved without being

---

[10] CR/251/71; Yirol Town Court.

stated; for example, where the amount of damages ordered to be paid is excessive. But when the term *awac* or *awuoc* is employed by the court it signifies that the court is passing a penal sentence. In cases where payment is ordered for raping a girl or a woman, or the impregnation of a girl, such payment is often termed as *awac* or *awuoc*. In such cases it is the criminal law which is put into operation, although it may be stated that the civil law is also being applied at the same time.

The difference in the number of cattle paid in cases of rape and other offences committed with respect to girls or free women demonstrates the operation of the criminal law. For example, where a girl is eloped with or made pregnant, the wrongdoer is ordered to pay one heifer as *awac*.[11] But in the case of rape he pays five cows. The degree of gravity of the offence of rape makes it different from other sexual wrongs committed against girls or free women. A more serious sexual offence is the act of adultery, and for this the offender pays six cows and one bull.

In conclusion, criminal law is a part of the Dinka Law. However, it has not been developed to the same extent as civil law, for reasons already stated. I may add that the sentence of fine (which goes to the aggrieved party) is the only one a court may pass in the circumstances where there are no prisons and law enforcement agencies like the Police and where there is no central system of administration. Any other sentence such as imprisonment or the death sentence cannot be passed. The views on African law, which I have previously referred to, explain why the customary law did not develop on the criminal side.

3.2 Attempts to resolve differences between customary rules through a unified code

The Dinka may be assumed by others to be a single tribe which maintains a complete uniformity of rules of law. This assumption is not true. The Dinka consists of several sub-tribes. Although the law is generally the same from district to district, there are minor differences.[12] These have often confronted the courts with difficult problems of conflict of rules where there are no rules governing their conflict. Such differences increased as the courts of each district began to expand the rules or add new rules to the customs in order to

---

[11] In the case of impregnation, he pays *awac* if he refuses to marry the girl.
[12] These minor differences did not in fact rest on general principles but mainly on matters related to the quantity of material or number of animals to be delivered in discharge of particular obligations according to the prevailing local circumstances.

overcome the surrounding problems. For example, the number of cattle to be paid to an aggrieved husband was four cows and one bull in the Lakes District, while it was eight cows and two bulls in Gogrial and Tonj Districts. The two districts of Tonj and Gogrial raised the number of *akor* cattle with the aim of combating the offence of adultery more effectively. Further, the number of *arueth* cattle payable, in Tonj and Gogrial, to the husband by the wife's relatives was four cows for every ten cows he had paid to them as bride-wealth at the time of the conclusion of marriage. In Rumbek *arueth* was and is still three cows for every ten cows the husband pays as bride-wealth. But the Atuot of Yirol District did not use to pay *arueth*, although it has recently started to be introduced in Apaak area. At Aliab the husband was not entitled to recover the bride-wealth cattle he had paid when the death of the woman dissolved the marriage. But in the Dinka areas of this region, when the marriage is dissolved by the death of the wife, the husband is entitled to recover bride-wealth cattle.

Owing to this lack of uniformity in the application of some of the most important rules, Chiefs' Conferences attended by various District Commissioners of the then Bhar el Ghazal Province, together with the Heads of Departments in the districts, were held in the past in Wanh-alel in Tonj District. But these Conferences were only confined to the chiefs of Tonj and Gogrial Districts. However, through these Conferences, the two districts have been able to overcome some of their major differences in the application of the customary rules regulating adultery, divorce, redemption of children and the recovery of bride-wealth property after divorce or the dissolution of marriage. However, the codification of the customary rules during those Conferences was very limited, being confined to the Family Law.

3.3 The re-statement and the wide-scale codification of the customary rules

On the 10th of April, 1975, another conference was held under the Chairmanship of the Province Commissioner, Mr Isaiah Kulang Mabor, with my assistance, to review and codify the unwritten law. This was the most expanded conference ever held in the history of Wanh-alel conferences. Not only did it bring the chiefs and elders from all seven districts of Bhar el Ghazal Province, but it was attended by all the Heads of Departments in Wau town, together with the Assistant Commissioners and Inspectors of Local Government in the districts. The re-stated customary rules were subsequently codified. This conference made two major achievements: firstly, the codification (though it did not embody the whole of the Dinka Customary Law) covered a wider range. For example, it substantially embodied the Personal Law; Tracing of Property; the Transfer of Title to Property; Recovery of Damages for Personal Injuries; Damages for Trespass to Property; Payment of *apuk*; Succession; Defamation and so forth. Secondly, the conference achieved the unification of the rules which are of common application in the courts today.

Some relevant points may be mentioned about the coming into existence of the Code of the Dinka Customary Law.[13] Firstly, the previous codification was repealed. Secondly, the codification of the customary rules during the Conference was mostly a re-statement of the law which already existed. That Conference cannot be equated with a legislative organ which has the power to bring new laws into existence. It was the ideal forum for ascertaining and re-stating the customary rules of law already applied in the courts. It brought together the chiefs and the elders who are a good 'store' of the unwritten rules. After the re-statement, the rules were codified. They were later passed as a Local Order by the then Province Council. The Code was passed as Part II of The Re-statement of the Bhar el Ghazal Region Customary Law Act, 1984.

Finally, since the Code[14] does not embody the whole of the Dinka Customary Law, it is open to any future conference at Wanh-alel or elsewhere to re-state all the other customary rules which were left out during the last Conference, which thereafter could be incorporated into the new Act.

We have already discussed the lack of initiative on the part of the authorities concerned to develop the customary law, although it is one of the recognised sources of the general territorial law. This lack of initiative has caused a general outcry from academic writers. We have also seen the great efforts made by administrators, from the last stages of the colonial era to the early sixties, to develop the customary law by re-stating it first at the various district levels and then by providing a unified code. All the writers and the former administrators who showed concern for the development of the customary law had a consensus of opinion on its codification. Now, with the passing of the Re-statement of the Bhar el Ghazal Region Customary Law Act, 1984 (Act No. 1), there is a step forward in the fulfilment of their efforts to prepare the ground for a unified code of customary law. We also hope that the passing of this Act will serve as a stimulant to other parts of the Sudan and Africa to follow suit.

---

[13] This Code is the part (i.e. Part II) of the Restatement of Bhar el Ghazal Customary Law Act, 1984.

[14] Or Part II of the Restatement of Bhar el Ghazal Region Customary Law Act, 1984.

CHAPTER TWO

The Nature of Legal Sanctions in Dinka Law

Having dealt with the objectives of the law, we now have to consider whether there are legal sanctions for its enforcement and observance, and, if there are, what their nature is. It is important to know this, in view of the fact that the criminal law has not been sufficiently developed, and it is the criminal law which always makes provisions for the establishment of the machinery and legal institutions which are necessary for the enforcement and observance of the law. Before considering this issue, there is a preliminary question to be answered first, and that is whether it is necessary to have legal sanctions at all?

The answer is founded upon the dilemma in which man finds himself in his attitude toward law. This attitude reflects the nature of man which must also be discussed in order to find an answer to the question. In the words of Jeremy Taylor,

> 'A herd of wolves is quieter and more at one than so many men, unless they all have one reason in them, or have one power over them.'[1]

The above quotation depicts man to be worse than a pack of wolves. Commenting on it, Egon Guttman said:

> 'This statement in the Hobbesian tradition maintains that man without the application of some superior force to keep him in control is the most anti-social creature in nature.'[2]

---

[1] Jeremy Taylor, *Works*, cited by Egon Guttman in a series of public lectures on *Crime, Cause and Treatment*, delivered at the University of Khartoum, 1957.
[2] Ibid.

In this respect, man may be described as lawless, brutal, greedy and so on. But before we are inclined to believe this description of man, we have to explain his positive character towards law and then determine whether there is in him a concurrent negative character which necessitates the existence of legal sanctions to control him.

1.1 The positive character of man

We can state in general terms that man is a progressive social being. By this statement is meant that mankind has two instinctive objectives. The first objective is to live in society. The second is to progress economically, socially, politically, educationally and so on. It may be stated that progress or development is a product of living in society. All the necessities of life cannot be achieved unless people live together in a society where there is interdependence. For example, a farmer depends on the blacksmith or the manufacturer of agricultural implements for his tools, while the blacksmith depends, for his food, on the farmer.

It is generally believed that, of all the animals on earth, man is the most intelligent creature. He plans for his future and the future of his offspring. Where one or more members of the same society are in danger of some kind, their neighbours or kinsfolk come to render collective assistance. All human beings are aware of the fact that co-operation is strength. This positive character of man does not only make men contented with living in society, it urges them to set up institutionalised bodies or organisations so that each member finds himself under an obligation to discharge certain duties for the welfare of the whole society. Man needs property, and this constitutes his wealth. He needs good food and decent accommodation for protection against the weather, disease and other dangers. Besides, he also needs to procreate. These few examples in the life of man justify the statement that he is a progressive social being. They also indicate his positive character towards order, for without this positive character he may not be able to achieve all the interests which are necessary for his progress in society.

1.2 Self-aggrandisement and the break-down of the positive character of man

In seeking to live and progress in society, man may not always achieve his aims without clashing with the interests of another. The magnitude of the clash or the conflict of interests may be due to scarcity of property and the desire to have more of it. The desire to have more material posessions leads to the development of malicious and selfish attitudes. Some individuals may therefore strive to progress at the expense of others. Such attitudes lead to physical conflicts, since the person whose interest is being jeopardised by the wilful and selfish attitude of his neighbour will try to defend it physically.

Because of these selfish and malicious attitudes which produce conflicts of interest, society may regard certain acts as anti-social, for example, theft, murder, adultery and rape. These conflicts of interest and the desire to commit acts which are deemed to be anti-social leads to a situation of lawlessness in which the lives and properties of people are put at risk. According to Hobbes,

> 'Nature hath made men so equal in the faculties of the body and mind... From this equality of ability ariseth equality of hope in the attaining of our ends. And therefore if any two men desire the same thing, which nevertheless they cannot both enjoy they become enemies; and in the way to their end, which is principally their own conservation, and sometimes their delectation only, endeavour to destroy or subdue one another... where an invader hath no more to fear than another man's single power; if one plant, sow, build or possess a convenient seat others may probably be expected to come prepared with forces united to dispossess and deprive him, not only of the fruit of his labour, but also of his life...'[3]

The desire for wealth and comfort at the expense of others easily undermines the positive character of man. The struggle which derives from the conflict of interests tends to justify the assertion that man is the most notorious creature on earth. His superior intellect may often create a more brutal form of anarchy than wolves are cabable of.

1.3 The need for Law

As life in society consists of this bitter struggle, it is imperative to have a set of rules with which to establish and regulate harmony between these conflicting interests. Without these rules to regulate human conduct, it would be impossible to live in society, as it would be the strongest or the most intelligent who survived. The society of men would be worse than a pack of wolves. If these rules are accepted and obeyed, they become the law of the society. In other words, there cannot be anything called society if there is no system of law which regulates the interests of people.

---

[3] Thomas Hobbes, *Leviathan*, ed. by M. Oakeshott, Basil Blackwell, Oxford, 1960, pp. 141–2.

1.4 The need for legal sanctions

In the light of the conflict of interests, the law cannot however achieve its objectives unless there is a system within itself which compels obedience to it. Such obedience to the law may be procured by a system which inflicts some physical or mental suffering on violators. This system may be called the legal sanction. The legal sanction may inflict fear on the people and the fear induces obedience to the law.

In the early stages of development of human society, the existence of legal sanctions may not be apparent. But, as society progresses and becomes more and more complex, these sanctions become apparent. For example, in its advanced stage of development, society will establish legal institutions for the enforcement of the law. There will be the judiciary consisting of trained judges to administer the law. There will be the police to prevent, among other things, the commission of crime and, if necessary, use force to bring offenders under legal control. Penal law, which creates offences and provides the type of punishment for each offence, may be established. For example, punishments may comprise of death, amputation of the limb (Islamic Law), stoning a person (Mosaic law), imprisonment, fine, detention in reformatory schools and so forth.

All these penalties (i.e. legal sanctions) are partly responsible for obedience or allegiance to the law. In the absence of legal sanctions, the law would certainly be like a crocodile without teeth and people would violate the legal order with impunity.

I do not intend to assert that obedience or allegiance to the law solely depends on the existence of legal sanctions. I do not further intend to go into the jurisprudential analysis of the subject matter. But, suffice it to say that, the existence of legal sanctions induces obedience to the law. Experience shows that criminals or wrongdoers often calculate their chances of committing criminal acts or ommissions without being exposed to legal penalties. To achieve this objective, the criminal may try his best to conceal his acts or omissions from others. If the chances are well gambled so that he or she commits the offence without being discovered, the possibility of escaping the penalty becomes very high.

In conclusion, therefore, the foregoing argument may be summarised as follows: that, on the one hand, because of the necessity of interdependence, man must live in society. But, for society to continue to exist in harmony, there must be laws to regulate the conduct and interests of every individual. If these laws were obeyed absolutely, the attitude of man towards law might be described as positive, in which case there would be no need for legal sanctions. The only importance of the law would be to serve as a guide to one's rights and duties in society and the limitations thereon, in order to avoid conflicting claims of interests or duties. But, on the other hand, it is commonly observed that a positive and a negative attitude towards law exists concurrently in man, and this is due to conflict of interests. In short, an individual member of society needs the law when it suits his interest but chooses to violate it when it obstructs the attainment of his interest.

Man therefore has an ambivalent attitude to the law. However, owing to the existence of this ambivalence or dilemma, it is necessary to have legal sanctions to regulate his conduct in society. This answers the preliminary question as to why there should be legal sanctions for the operation of law. These sanctions may not be of a uniform nature in every legal system, because each may develop its own sanctions according to the peculiar circumstances prevailing in the society and the objectives that society expects to achieve by law.

2. THE APPARENT ABSENCE OF LEGAL SANCTIONS IN DINKA LAW

While it is necessary for there to be legal sanctions to induce obedience or allegiance to the law, the Dinka Customary Law, like other customary laws, does not apparently have legal sanctions. What then induces obedience to it?

Although it appears on the face of the Dinka Law that legal sanctions do not exist to command obedience to it, this is, in fact, not true. It is true that direct physical sentences like the death sentence and imprisonment do not exist in the law. But the fact that there are no police, professional judges, prisons or cells to accommodate convicts and detainees does not mean that legal sanctions do not exist in the law. As has been mentioned already, the Dinka Customary Law, like other African legal systems, did not develop the kind of penal sanctions which would require the creation of the necessary institutions and the machinery for its observance, but developed the area of civil law in which remedy for the wrong was the main objective. However, despite the stated objective, and the fact that sanctions which are similar to those which the State laws provide do not exist, the Dinka Customary Law has more effective sanctions to induce obedience and to enable society to maintain a strong sense of discipline. But there are no external signs of the existence of such sanctions. This is the factor that misleads many people to conclude that there are

---

[4] But this does not, of course, mean that there are no good men in society who respect the operation of the law even if it works against their interests.

no sanctions in the Dinka Law.

This apparent absence of legal sanctions is not a peculiarity of Dinka Customary Law alone, it is a general phenomenon of all African legal systems, something inherent in almost all the legal systems of the 'original societies'. Because of this, some Europeans have sometimes been tempted to conclude that African communities or societies have no law. They associate the existence of legal systems with the existence of institutionalised sanctions. In *The African Conception of Law*, J. H. Driberg draws attention to this conclusion of European observers on African law:

'European observers have often doubted the existence of law in African societies, because generally the paraphernalia which we associate with law are absent. Without the prisons and the police force it is assumed that there can be no sanctions such as would give the requisite validity.'[5]

In his disapproval of this assumptive conclusion, Driberg went on to say that

'The penal sanctions are the least important of them all; chiefly the law is positive and not negative and because it is solely interested in maintaining the social equilibrium.'

While I concur with Driberg in his disagreement with the opinion of those observers, I would add further that the sanctions and the law are not necessarily one and the same thing. The law exists first, but because of the fear of its being violated by some members of the community, then sanctions, as a mechanism to enforce its observance, follow. It is even more misleading to convey the impression that in legal sanctions lies the validity of the law. Sanctions are only aimed at compelling people, through fear, to obey the law but not to give it validity.

3. THE NATURE OF LEGAL SANCTIONS

As the objective of African law is not punitive but restitutive, Africans developed totally different sanctions from those Europeans expected. These were and continue to be (a) the fear of God, (b) the fear of supernatural powers, (c) the fear of public criticism and (d) the fear of revenge.

---

[5] J. H. Driberg, *Readings in African Law,* Vol. I, Frank Cass, London, 1970, p.166.

3.1 The fear of God

The fear of God serves as a more effective sanction than the sanctions prescribed by secular law which may easily be tampered with. God is referred to as the Creator and Most Powerful Father of mankind. What He does is always right. He is the Fountain of justice and the law. Justice and the law must therefore be respected and feared as people respect and fear God.

There is a Dinka saying which is attributed to the hyena, which goes like this:

> 'Justice (or the law) comes from God. Even the fox, my cousin, if he has a right, will receive justice from me, although he once inflicted grievous harm on my limb.'

General statements of principle or wisdom such as this are often ascribed to animals to demonstrate the impartiality of the author, in order the more effectively to regulate the conduct of society. Animals have no interest in human affairs and the statements said to have been made by them are deemed to have been made without prejudice and should therefore be adopted as guiding principles. The statement attributed to the hyena implies that justice must be applied indiscriminately, even to one's enemies.

As the custodian of justice and the law, God also holds the key to its observance. The sanctions which He imposes upon wrongdoers or society are deemed to be indirect. For example, where there is a general catastrophe or pestilence in society, it is regarded as an indication of the wrath of God. It may be interpreted that society as a whole or some members of it have become impious or Godless. Impiety or Godlessness may be measured by the high rate of crime or the failure of the elders and the *Banybiith* to perform their duties by seeking God's audience through ritual sacrifices and ceremonies. For example, where offences have been commonly committed by members of the society or where fighting results in bloodshed or death, ritual performances have to be conducted 'to remove the blood' and to avert God's anger; otherwise, He will punish the society. This fear of God's anger creates collective responsibility in the prevention of crimes and other acts which are regarded as anti-social, because the punishment that God might impose would affect the people collectively. For example, if there is a long drought which destroys crops or prevents cultivation, it may be regarded as God's punishment for certain serious crimes or bloody conflicts for which there has been a failure to offer sacrifices as a means of invoking God's mercy.

In Dinka custom, where people move with their cattle to set up camp in a new place or move to make new homes on new agricultural land, the first thing the elders do is to slaughter a sacrificial bull. The new land, if it has not been named before, will be named after the colour of the sacrificial bull. In the prayers that are conducted before the slaughter of the bull, God is asked to protect the children (i.e. the people) from diseases and enemies, as well as from internal conflicts, and to let them live in peace. Also, in the first day of a new cattle camp, milk is collected from various units of families. Then, in the evening, the elders move ceremonially around the cattle camp saying prayers and invoking God to keep away wild animals, diseases and enemies from the people and the cattle. During this ceremony the elders pour some of the milk in predetermined places around the camp, and then sprinkle the cattle and the people with the rest of the milk, calling upon the names of their ancestors who are supposed to mediate with God for their protection.

This society, in which the *Banybiith* and the elders regularly conduct prayers for the welfare of the people, is described as *pan mac ne long* (i.e. the land or society which is ruled through the will of God or God's laws), and the degree of discipline maintained in it is very high. The youth are not expected to stage fights among themselves or against external enemies, unless, in the latter case, it is approved by the elders, especially the spiritual leaders. Such approval is deemed to have God's recognition. But no offences can be committed nor can fights be staged near holy shrines for fear of arousing God's anger and punishment. Any offences committed near holy places are considered as disrespectful either to God or to deceased ancestors. Even if one meets with one's enemy within the territorial jurisdiction of a holy shrine, one is not expected to fight or quarrel.

From this brief account of the Dinka attitude to God, one can imagine how powerful religious sanctions are in Dinka society, as compared with secular sanctions imposed by criminal law. In secular law one may evade a sentence if one puts up a good defence or if the prosecution fails to obtain sufficient evidence to prove the guilt of the accused. But there is no expectation of the possibility of evading a religious penalty since God is both the Witness and the Judge. In the words of J. H. Driberg, 'It is this religious nexus which gives African law an authority sufficient to dispense with the mechanics of enforcement'.[6]

Before the advent of modern government, the administration of justice was run by the divine priests already referred to as the *Banybiith*. They were prophets who represented the will of God on

---

[6] J. H. Driberg, *Readings in African Law*, Vol. I, Frank Cass, London, 1970, p.167.

earth. They still do. The word *Banybith* has often been mistakenly associated with magic by foreigners, and in Arabic it is referred to as *kujur*. This is, in fact, a total misunderstanding. *Banybith* is not a magician but a prophet in Dinka thought. He does not make use of esoteric medicine or drugs as magicians often do. Unlike a magician, he does not claim the power of a daignostician to know the causes of illness or death. His prayers are directed not to the gods adored by magicians but to God, the Omnipotent and Merciful. Because of his close special relationship to God, the *Banybith* is given a special place and respect in Dinka society. Consequently, the judicial orders and decisions passed by the *Banybüth* enjoy maximum respect in society, and if they are disobeyed or obstructed, it is feared that God will directly or indirectly punish the society or the particular culprit.[7]

3.2 Mystical beliefs

Along with the fear of God, numerous mystical beliefs have been developed to induce obedience to the law. The fears produced by these beliefs were, in fact, developed as a matter of policy in order to combat certain immoral acts effectively. To illustrate this point, let us take, for example, the belief which has been developed to combat the offence of adultery. It is believed that adultery produces a kind of 'impurity' which exacerbates sickness, so that an adulterer or adulteress must never go near sick people. Even people who are not sick fear the presence of an adulterer or adulteress because 'sickness' is suspected to be in his or her body although there are no obvious signs of it. If he or she attends the sick or passes near the sick, purification rites have to be performed after his or her departure. To do this a flame of fire is passed over his or her foot-steps or over any piece of ground which came into contact with any part of his or her body. Fire, as the belief goes, removes the ingredient of impurity. Whether this belief is rational or not, it has served a useful purpose in controlling the incidence of adultery in Dinka society. People are fearful of being stigmatised as 'impure' or rejected by society and so, generally, they refrain from committing the offence of adultery.

Another illustration is the belief developed to combat the evil of sexual cohabitation between blood relatives. Sexual cohabitation between blood relations, whatsoever the degree of cohabitation, is strictly prohibited. The evil produced by such a relationship is known

---

[7] In his notes prepared on the customary laws of the Aweil Dinkas, Capt Stubbs briefly discussed the sanctions for the obedience to the law. He said: 'Sanctions enforcing the observance of the moral code were fear of direct punishment from God and the burden of providing a sacrificial beast for purifying ceremony.'

as *akeeth* (i.e. incest). *Akeeth* is believed to be fatal to the offspring of this kind of sexual union and purification rites have to be performed by the elders to avert the evil. Apart from it being fatal, the children of *akeeth*, if they survive, are generally believed to be weak physically. However, no purification rites can be conducted until the woman has confessed the name of the man or all the male relatives who have had sexual intercourse with her. Purification rites are tied up with a public confession of the act as a means of indirectly inviting public condemnation of the offence. Besides the fear that one's offspring might die, it is socially humiliating for one to be exposed to the public to confess one's immoral conduct.

A further illustration concerns the offence of homicide. It is wrong or 'sinful' to kill a person in cold blood or to kill a person and then deny it. It is believed that God punishes such a killer. It is a new attitude these days for a Dinka to kill a person and then deny it. It is the result of the influence of foreign ideas. Although, nowadays, a killing may be denied before a court of law or before the relatives of the deceased, the killer must still confess it somehow to his very close elderly relatives in order for them to perform (secretly, if they intend to conceal the killing) purification rites. These sacred rites are conducted in order, as it were, to 'turn away the eyes' of the deceased soul from the killer.[8] The soul of the deceased is appeased when *apuk* (i.e. compensation) has been paid by the relatives of the killer. *Apuk* is therefore an obligation imposed upon the killer and his paternal relatives by the fear of indirect or direct punishment from supernatural powers. *Apuk* also prevents revenge.

The strength of mystical beliefs in commanding obedience to the law may also be seen in connection with the rules of evidence. Where a person who is accused of an offence denies it, if his denial is doubted, the court may ask him to take an oath before a *Banybith*. If, after the oath, he does not die or encounter mishap within a certain period, he is deemed to be innocent. A witness may also be asked to swear. The consequences of a false oath are also frightening. And where a person knows that he or she is bearing a false witness, he or she will refuse to swear, and this refusal will constitute an admission of the truth. The important thing about this belief is not really the truth behind it; it is important that the mind of the community is so prepared as to believe strongly that death or some severely disabling illness will be the consequence of a false oath. Except where the mind

---

[8] In his discussion of the subject, Capt Stubbs said: 'Failure to do this (i.e. to perform the purification rite) might lead to a patriarchal curse and expulsion from the clan.' Ref. File BGR/66–B–1 p.2.

of society is corrupted by foreign ideas (as is the tendency today), the oath compels one to state the truth, and the evidence or statement given under oath before a *Banybith* ought to be admissible in a court of law.

3.3 Public criticism

Public opinion or criticism also plays a very significant role in commanding obedience or allegiance to the law. Public criticism reduces the status of the offender or it makes him a laughing stock. The role of public criticism can be seen in the examples already given in the case of adultery. The public shuns the adulterer and the adulteress, and the latter feel themselves to be outcasts from society. This social attitude towards the offence deters potential offenders. In the old days, the dress of a woman who committed adultery used to be cut in a special way to indicate a mark of the offence so that any member of the society could see it and condemn it. This kind of social treatment is quite harmful to the moral prestige of the offender and makes the offence hated.

Songs generally designed to correct the conduct of society also contribute to obedience and allegiance to the law. Songs play the role of a free press in society. There are gifted men and women who carefully compose songs without referring to the name of any particular person, which are intended to promote high moral standards. Conversely, songs may condemn anything which tends to reduce the prestige or the moral standards of the people. Sometimes a song which imputes a certain kind of bad conduct to a particular person may be published. The advantage of such publications for the society is that every adult member must try to conduct himself or herself decently to avoid becoming the subject of condemnatory songs. In this way tendencies to commit crimes or offences are greatly diminished and allegiance to the law becomes established.

3.4 The fear of revenge

Although the fear of revenge has now been minimised because of the maintenance of public security, it has always served as an effective sanction. The fear of revenge is always collective. For example, where a man from tribal section 'A' causes the death of a member of tribal section 'B', all the members of tribe 'A' are collectively responsible for the offence. Any member of tribe 'B' may kill any member of tribe 'A' by way of revenge, unless compensation has been paid. And, unless the social equilibrium is so restored through the payment of the compensation, any relative of the victim is at any time expected to revenge by causing the death of the actual killer or his near agnatic relative or sometimes anybody from the killer's tribe or tribal section. Because of this vicarious or collective responsibility for the act of one person, the community feels bound to prevent, as far as possible, any member of it from unjustifiably causing the death of another person; and, if death is caused, compensation has to be paid within a reasonable time to prevent revenge.

The question which may be asked at this stage is: can these traditional sanctions survive the impact of modernisation or technological development? Some people express pessimism about their surivival. However, I am inclined to believe that although the strength of traditional beliefs is slowly weakening, the rules they established have already become part of the secular law.

Capt Stubbs seemed to be one of the people who expressed pessimism about the capabilty of traditional sanctions to survive the introduction of modern sanctions. He said: 'The improvement of public security (through the advent of modern government) has caused a *slump* in the stock of patriarchal curses.'[9] The inference from this statement is that he also believed that the fear of these 'curses' or the fear of religious punishments constituted a very important role in the observance of the law and the maintenance of discipline in society. Capt Stubbs lamented that the 'slump in the stock of patriarchal curses' resulted in the deterioration of tribal discipline which made the administration of the country difficult despite the introduction of modern sanctions or public security. In fact, his observation was correct and is a recognition of the relative strength of traditional beliefs over modern sanctions in maintaining discipline in society.

To some extent Capt Stubbs was right that 'patriarchal curses' or traditional beliefs were giving way to the newly introduced sanctions or the improvement in public security. However, I am of the belief that the 'slump' has not dealt a total or fatal blow to traditional beliefs, particularly religious beliefs and the sanctions associated with them. Through long usage, religious sanctions laid deep roots in society and much of them has become an integral part of our moral principles. Apart from modern sanctions which are imposed by the criminal law, moral principles have a great role to play in promoting observance of the law. Some people may not be aware that the moral principles they respect derive from religious beliefs or the fear of so-called patriarchal curses. These moral principles sometimes fill a gap where the criminal law has not declared certain acts as offences or where it has not provided penalties for certain acts which the community regards as anti-social. For example, *akeeth* or incest is not punishable by our

---

[9] File No. BGP/66/B–1.

penal code although it is anti-social. Despite the fact that the penal code does not provide a punishment for it, it is still regarded by the Dinka and other communities as immoral and to be avoided. This is so even in circumstances where one does not subscribe to the religious beliefs attached to it.

In conclusion, although it has been stated that the aim of African legal systems (of which the Dinka Law is a part) is the restoration of the social equilibrium destabilised by a wrongful act, this is in fact not the only objective. Another objective of African law is to deter people or prevent them from committing wrongful acts. This is very clear from the sanctions discussed above. In this respect, the difference between African Law and European Law is in the nature of sanctions imposed for the observance of the law on the one hand and, on the other, the existence of law enforcement agencies backed by facilities like prisons and cells necessary for custodial sentences.

CHAPTER THREE

The Family Law
(*'Lôônge-Kôôcē Ruāi'*)

1. *RUĀI* (MARRIAGE)

The Family Law (or personal law) refers to that part of the law which deals with the regulations of family relations or matters. At the heart of this law is *ruai* or the institution of marriage. *Ruai* or the institution of marriage is very important in that it is the root of the family and family relations. The family is a micro-society which expands to make a larger society and is ultimately the origin of a race or nation.

Marriage is defined by section 20 of the Re-statement of Bhar el Ghazal Region Customary Law Act, 1984, as:

> 'Union between one man or his successor and one or more women for their lives for the purpose of sexual cohabitation, procreation of the young and maintenance of the homestead, provided that such union may take place between one barren or childless woman and another or others for whom male consorts are provided; provided also that such union may take place between a deceased male person and one or more women through his successor.'

This definition contains many important features of Dinka marriage, such as:

1.1(a) *Union between one man and one or more women*
One of the main features of Dinka marriage is polygamy.[1] Dinka marriage is potentially polygamous. This means that while a marriage

---
[1] *Thieekē diar juec.*

subsists there is no any legal impediment in the way of the man (i.e. husband) to prevent his contracting another or other marriages. A temporary lack of wealth is the only impediment, for a man may be poor today and rich tomorrow, in which event he may be capable of taking on more wives.

As a matter of fact, polygamy is not a practice which concerns the Dinkas alone, it is a universal practice in most of Africa. There is much prestige in having more than one wife, and monogamous life may be the result of some kind of necessity.

'In general, monogamy is either a self-denying ordinance, in the sense that a man voluntarily renounces or abstains from polygamy, or it is dictated by inability to afford more than one wife. Where the traditional outlook still prevails, the possession of a number of wives is normally a mark of importance and success in life – for this, among other reasons, which the average African man would gladly achieve if he could. In other words, monogamy is, for the majority who are in fact monogamists, a matter of necessity rather than of choice.'[2]

We can even go further to state that polygamy does not only appeal to the average African man, it appeals also to the poor who may be clever to exploit other means to acquire more than one wife. Even to the highly-educated African man, Christian or non-Christian, polygamous life is an appealing prospect. The educated African man is not convinced that monogamy has anything to do with Christianity, except that he knows that it was adopted in Europe because of the economic conditions created by industrialization. An African man therefore does not believe that a monogamist is a better Christian than a polygamist.

However, the question which should now be asked is: is there a future for polygamy in Africa? At present, the availability of vast and free arable land together with strong family and social bonds helps to promote polygamous marriages. Today, a Dinka man with more wives is presumed to have enough land to look after them and to build a home for each of them. The fact that each wife has her own home at some distance from the home of a co-wife lessens the degree of tension which might be caused by rivalry over the husband. The degree of friction increases if co-wives live under the same roof.

But whether or not polygamous marriage can survive the pace of

---

[2] A. Philips, *Survey of African Marriage and Family*, Oxford University Press, 1953, pp.xi–xii.

modernisation is the crucial question at this stage. Modernisation or technological development may be accompanied by many unforeseeable events which may run counter to the norms of traditional society. It may create economic conditions which promote the spirit of individualism. For example, land is more likely to be scarce if the population increases through improvements in health care, better sanitation, a more balanced diet and so on. Secondly, as modernisation grows apace, the Government may claim land, which is almost free to-day, for development. If this continues on an ever increasing scale, there will be no more free land to sustain large families. Thirdly, if free land becomes scarce or non-available, the majority of people may resort to employment with the Government or private companies, and the wages or salaries may not be adequate to feed a large family. Fourthly, with modernisation, social relations would become weaker and weaker as family and social ties loosened under its impact. Lastly, as urbanisation increases, housing conditions will become problematic and render polygamous marriage financially undesirable.

1.1(b) *The scope of the union*

Another important feature of Dinka marriage is the scope of the marriage itself. For a Dinka and for other Africans, 'marriage', has a wider scope than is commonly understood. 'Marriage', as it is understood by the Dinka, is not only a union between a man and a woman or women, it is, in a wider sense, a union between the two families of the spouses. This extended part of the union is the most important aspect of Dinka and other African marriages.

This feature is a result of the strength of social bonds predominantly found in African communities and has been a matter of interest to many European writers. In the words of A. Philips,

'In seeking to identify the outstanding characteristics of African customary marriage, we may justifiably include the collective aspect of the marriage transactions and relationship. There is a considerable weight of authority for the statement that, from the viewpoint of the indigenous law and custom, a marriage is to be regarded primarily as an alliance between two kinship groups and only in a secondary aspect as a union between two individuals.'[3]

In their commentary on African marriages, A. R. Radcliffe-Brown and D. Ford wrote:

---

[3] A. Philips, *Survey of African Marriage and Family*, Oxford University Press, 1953, pp.xi–xii.

The Family Law

'New social relations are created not only between the husband and the wife, and between the husband and the wife's relatives on the one side and between the wife and the husband's relatives on the other, but also in a great many societies, between the relatives of the husband and those of the wife who, on the two sides, are interested in the marriage and in the children that are expected of it.'[4]

This collective aspect of the marriage union constitutes one of the fundamental differences between a Dinka or other African marriage on the one hand and an English marriage on the other. The concept of marriage in English Law was expressed in the famous case of *Hyde* v. *Hyde*,[5] as a 'union between a man and a woman for life'. A. R. Radcliffe-Brown also expressed the view that:

'We think of marriage as an event that concerns primarily the man and the woman who are forming a union and the State, which gives that union its legality and alone can dissolve it by divorce. The consent of the parents is, strictly, only required for minors.'

At this juncture I must state that the legality of a Dinka marriage does not lie with the State. Such conditions as the registration of marriages with the Registrar and the issue of marriage certificates either by the Registrar or the Church as visible evidence of the legality of marriages are very strange to the Dinka. In most, if not all, African marriages which are conducted according to customary laws, the legality of marriage rests entirely on the agreement between all the interested parties on both sides of the union, after fulfilling all the necessary requirements or conditions. But in England, a marriage acquires validity if it is registered by a person licensed by the State.

1.1(c) *Union for their lives*
'For their lives' refers to the lives of the married women and not the lives of the men. The phrase can mean that when a married woman dies (or married women, in the case of a polygamous marriage), the marriage union comes to an end. On the other hand, the death of the husband does not abrogate the marriage – see section 38 of the Re-statement of the Bhar el Ghazal Region Customary Law Act, 1984. However, this rule is not to be interpreted in absolute terms to

---

[4] *African System of Kinship and Marriages*, in *Readings in African Law*, Vol. II Frank Cass, London, 1970, p.89; and by Oxford University Press, 1950, pp.43–54.
[5] Law Report, London (1866) IP & D 130.

mean that the death of the wife automatically abrogates the marriage union. It does not, as will be shown later. The marriage union, as we have already noted, is wider; it includes the two families of the spouses, and so, the death of one principal member of this wider family does not necessarily bring an end to the union. Continuity of the union is the essential character of marriage and, except in some special circumstances, the marriage union continues even after the death of the wife.

The principle which allows the continuity of the union, established through marriage, after the death of one spouse or even of both spouses, is a feature of many African traditional legal systems. In support of this fact, A. Philips wrote:

'... the indigenous institution of marriage can only be understood if it is viewed as an integral part of the kinship system as a whole. It is here, for example, that we find the key to certain custom which, obviously, presupposes a conception of marriage as a transaction giving rise to reciprocal rights and obligations between two groups of kinsmen and *binding those groups together in a relationship which remains effective beyond the lifetime of the original individual spouses.* This principle of continuing relationship is closely connected with the institution of bride-price, and it finds expression, for example, in the *levirate* (or the somewhat difficult custom of "widow-inheritance"), under which a widow is expected to cohabit with one of her deceased husband's kinsmen and which imposes on the kinsmen of a barren or deceased wife an obligation to provide another woman to make good the deficiency or loss.'[6]

The last part of this quotation will be the subject of further discussion. The continuity of the marriage relationship after the death of a spouse, or of both spouses, has more significance, especially where there are children of the marriage. The children, as it were, stand between the two families, that is, they hold the two families together. The children, as will be seen later, constitute the main objective of a marriage union. The union is therefore deemed to have failed to achieve its main objective where it produced no child or children to create and maintain family ties with paternal and maternal relatives of the union. Therefore one of the few instances where the death of the wife may be treated as dissolution of the marriage union is where the marriage has failed to achieve its main objective, namely, the pro-

---

[6] *Readings in African Law*, Vol. II, Oxford University Press, 1950, p.187.

creation of the young. Even so the marriage can only be formally dissolved at the request of the husband. Such dissolution entitles the husband to recover the bridewealth cattle he provided for the marriage so that he may, if he wishes, marry another woman. If he is wealthy, that is, if he owns a lot of cattle, he may marry again without the desire to seek the dissolution of the first marriage. But, if he is of lowly means, he may get the first marriage dissolved by reason of the death of his wife and failure to produce an offspring, so that he may recover the bride-wealth of the marriage to enable him to marry again.

1.1(d) *Union between 'his successor and one or more women'*
A man may die while a bachelor or he may die while married. In the first case, his successor or somebody appointed by his family or relatives as a trustee to his affairs will be required to marry a woman for him. The marriage is actually conducted by the whole family, but the successor or the trustee is required to raise children with this woman for the deceased man. In the second case, where a man dies while still married, and his wife is still fertile, the successor or the trustee may continue the procreation of children with her for the dead man. The offspring of this union legally belong to the deceased man. The successor or the trustee merely discharges a social obligation.

In so far as marriages conducted in the names of deceased persons are concerned, the Dinka and the Nuer have a similar custom. In his *Manual of Nuer Law,*[7] Howell called these types of marriages 'Ghost Marriages'. He summarised the main characteristics of 'ghost marriages' as follows:

(i) It is the dead man to whose name the wife is married, who is considered the legal father of the children... while he is not the physiological father of the children, he is their legal father and it is from his name that they trace their descent.
(ii) The man who marries a wife to the name of his dead kinsman is father in all roles and in every respect the husband of the woman except in the strictly legal sense.
(iii) The physiological father fulfils all the domestic duties of husband and father. In this respect the characteristics are the same as in normal legal union, and it is only by inquiry that his true legal status can be discovered.

While the legal position among the Dinka is identical with the Nuer conception of marriages conducted for deceased persons, a few

---

[7] P. P. Howell, *Manual of Nuer Law*, Oxford University Press, 1954, p.74.

remarks need to be made here to qualify the extent of the responsibility of the man who undertakes the physiological operations. It is true that there are many instances where he really appears as the legal father until his legal status is discovered. But there are also many cases where the physiological father's role or his commitment to the deceased's wife may be limited, especially where the degree of the relationship between him and the deceased is somewhat distant. In such cases, the closest relatives of the deceased may take over the responsibility of fully caring for the woman and her children, while the physiological father merely discharges the duty of producing children with her. Sometimes, if the physiological father shows an inclination to take the woman as his legal wife or if his relationship with the deceased's wife proves to be very bad in that he does not look after her properly (i.e. where the closest relatives are not the ones charged with her welfare), the relatives of the deceased may agree to appoint someone else to undertake the physiological aspect of the marriage, or the woman may sometimes make the choice of another man among the deceased's family.

1.2 Why marry and produce children for the dead?

In the Dinka society, continuity of the lineage of the person is not only of primary importance, it is also sacred. It is sacred in the sense that it is in fulfilment of the Will of God that the lineage of a person, whether male or female, is not allowed to become extinct. This explains why marriages are conducted for deceased persons. It also explains why a barren or childless woman must 'marry' another woman to bear children for her. She, being the legal husband, can appoint a male consort to her 'wife' to undertake the physiological aspect of the procreation of children for her. In this respect, the woman becomes the legal 'father' of the children so produced.

In the case of a man who is impotent, a close relative of his, usually on the paternal side, is appointed to produce children for him. The appointed man is not supposed to usurp the legal rights of the woman's husband, nor is he supposed to enjoy the monopoly of the services the woman is required to render to her legal husband. This process of producing children for a deceased person (male or female) or an impotent man or a barren woman is called *Lo-hot*, which means 'entering someone's house'. The man who undertakes the sexual or physiological operation cannot be called the husband of the woman who merely bears children with him. He is only discharging the duties of a trustee, although such duties entitle him to some limited rights, apart from the rights which accrue to him normally as a relative of the deceased or of the husband of the woman.

1.3 Marriage objectives

Marriage has three main objectives to achieve: (a) sexual cohabitation, (b) procreation of the young (children) and (c) maintenance of the homestead (section 20 of the Re-statement of the Bhar el Ghazal Region Customary Law Act, 1984). We shall discuss these in turn.

1.3(a) *Sexual cohabitation*

Sexual cohabitation with any unmarried girl, or a woman married to another person, constitutes an offence. In the case of a married woman the offence is adultery, for which the adulterer pays seven cows in compensation. In the case of a girl, the offence is rape or *makē-piny* or *yuit* (see section 48 of the Re-statement of the Bhar el Ghazal Region Customary Law Act, 1984), if she does not consent to sexual intercourse; the accused is bound to compensate the girl and her relatives with five cows, apart from the penal sentence which the ordinary court may impose according to the State Penal Code. This compensation is technically known as *aruok*. If the girl becomes pregnant as a result of pre-marital sexual intercourse, which does not amount to rape, the accused may be required to marry her. If he refuses to marry her, he will be bound to pay one heifer as *awec* (i.e. appeasement or a form of 'compensation') to the relatives of the girl.

1.3(b) *Procreation of the young*

The second objective of marriage is the procreation of children. This objective is in fact the most important of the objectives of marriage. Society as a whole is concerned with the procreation of children. This is why polygamy is of great significance. There are several reasons why society puts a premium on the procreation of children. In the first place, children keep the lineage running perpetually. It is in fulfilment of the Will of God, the Creator of man. Secondly, the relationship or the union established between the two families in marriage would have no sound foundation without children issuing from the marriage. It is the offspring of the union who actually establish a blood link between the two families. The birth of children strengthens the marriage and makes it more meaningful, thereby making it very difficult for divorce to take place. Thirdly, in the old days, when there was no State Government to provide security for the people, it was the responsibility of the youth of each community or tribe to defend the land against enemies or invaders. In order to guarantee the defence of the land, it was important to have a large number of fighting men. This led to the emphasis on the need to have more children in a family. Fourthly, a large family enjoys great respect in society because it is associated with wealth, and a noble character is associated with a wealthy family. Consequently, a large family always attracts respect, honour and potential suitors who want to marry into it.

1.3(c) *Maintenance of the homestead*

The third reason for the importance of marriage is the maintenance of the homestead. In the distribution of labour in the family, female members are responsible for the management of the house while the adult male members are responsible for the management of livestock and heayy duties. A man must therefore marry in order to have a partner to maintain the house. This duty may not adequately be discharged by any woman other than one's wife. A wife also represents her husband in many respects when he is absent.

1.4 The requirements of marriage
1.4(a) *Consent (Gēm; Gam)*

In order to contract a valid marriage, there must be consent. It is provided by section 21(i) of the Code[8] that:

> 'The only consent which is material for the conclusion of a valid marriage is that of the parents, brothers and close paternal uncles in that order of importance.'

Such consent must be given by the relatives of the man as well as the relatives of the woman. The consent of the spouses must also be sought, although, in some cases, it may be ignored. In fact, each family together with its immediate relatives holds a council where every member expresses his or her opinion as to whether or not the marriage should take place. The majority view or that of the eldest male members of the family prevails. Sometimes a man and a woman may take each other as wife and husband without the consent of their parents. Such a union may be subject to ratification by the concerned relatives on both sides, if they agree. However, if it is rejected or not ratified, and the spouses insist on remaining as husband and wife, the marriage will hold only as a union between the two spouses. Legally, no rights as provided under sections 26 and 27 of the Code[9] will accrue. The husband will not be entitled to claim *akor* cattle provided by section 29, if his wife commits adultery with another person. In short, it will be a union between the man and the woman, which lacks

---

[8] Part II of The Restatement of the Bhar el Ghazal Region Customary Law Act, 1984.
[9] The Code of Dinka Customary Law, which is actually Part II of the Restatement of the Bhar el Ghazal Region Customary Law Act, 1984.

the most important legal consequences. It may be described as an irregular marriage since it lacks the essential legal requirements.

1.4(b) *Capacity in Marriage (Dīt)*[10]

It is a condition that no marriage should take place between two parties, unless they have reached maturity. Maturity is not determined by a particular age or rules of law. It is determined by certain physical features only; some of which have been enumerated under section 21(b) of the Code. For example, for a girl, the age of maturity is marked by the first period of menstruation, while for a boy, it is marked by certain physical or biological changes, such as vocal change, growth of hair in arm-pits or loin or by traditional marks designed to mark the end of boyhood.

1.4(c) *Bride-wealth (Hok-Thieek)*

By bride-wealth or *hok-thieek*, which is commonly but inaccurately called bride-price by foreign writers, is meant any number of cattle payable by the bridegroom (husband) and his relatives to the relatives of the bride (wife) as a consideration for the delivery of the said bride to him.

When consent is given to the marriage, the relatives on both sides meet to discuss the number of cattle to be paid as bride-wealth. Serious negotiations are always involved in fixing the number of cattle; there is no fixed number of cattle to be paid in all cases. The number is determined by several circumstances, for example, the amount of wealth the bridegroom and his relatives posssess, the character of the girl, the social status of the two families, the beauty of the girl, whether there are suitors competing over her and so forth.

As the Dinka are a cattle owning community, marriages among themselves and members of other cattle-owning communities are always conducted in cattle. Any marriage in which the bride-wealth is not paid in cattle is not treated as a perfect marriage in the eyes of the law. Where money or anything else is paid by a bridegroom or his relatives to the bride's parents or relatives during the engagement, it is not usually treated as part of bride-wealth; it is treated as a gift only.

However, with the mixture of many different communities these days, especially in the towns, inter-communal marriages are slowly beginning to take place. Dinka girls are being married by members of non-cattle owning communities. In many of these cases, the Dinka people (i.e. relatives of the woman) demand the bride-wealth to be paid in cattle. If the suitor has sufficient money, he is usually required

---

[10] Dit – A Dinka term for maturity.

to convert it into cattle with which to pay the bride-wealth; but where there are circumstances which make it practically impossible to obtain the cows and, at the same time, make it impossible to get back the girl or the woman so as to be married to a different man with cattle, the bride's relatives may accept money in lieu of cattle. But such cases are very rare indeed.

It is now necessary to determine the legal importance of bride-wealth. Some writers have attempted to explain the nature of bride-wealth, although their views are not uniform. For example, A. Philips stated that:

'There are more considerable difference of opinion as to the essential significance of the institution. Thus bride-price is variously interpreted as being primarily in the nature of compensation to the woman's family for the loss of one of its members (and that member a potential child bearer), as part of a transaction in which the dominant emphasis is on the formation of an alliance between the two kinship and/or groups; as a species of marriage insurance, designed to stabilize the marriage and/or give protection to the wife; as a symbol, or as a 'seal' marking the formal conclusion of the marriage contract.'[11]

A. R. Radcliffe-Brown also wrote that

'... The marriage payment can be regarded as an indemnity or compensation given by the bride-groom to the bride's kin for the loss of their daughter.... In societies in which the marriage payment is of considerable value it is commonly used to replace the daughter by obtaining a wife for some other member of the family, usually a brother of a woman who has been lost...'[12]

In fact, the significance of the institution of bride-wealth cannot be expected to have a single explanation. The points expressed by A. Philips do not differ much from what the Dinka believe to constitute the importance of the institution of bride-wealth. In the first place, the idea of compensation justifies the payment of bride-wealth. The concept of compensation rests on two grounds: (a) the girl or woman who is the subject of this payment has been brought up with immense care to make a good future housewife to somebody. Moreover, a

---

[11] *Readings in African Law,* Vol. II, Frank Cass, London, 1970, p.86 and also *Survey of African Marriage and Family*, Oxford University Press, 1955, pp.xi–xii.
[12] Ibid., p.86.

lot of expenses have been incurred in her upbringing and (b) the significance of this institution is that she must be married with cattle as her mother was previously married with cattle; that is, her relatives must be reimbursed for the expenses they incurred during the marriage of her mother.

Secondly, the institution of bride-wealth is significant for serving as a consideration for the services the girl or the woman will render to her husband and his relatives, and the children she will bear for her husband.

Thirdly, the payment of bride-wealth stabilizes the marriage since the bride's parents or relatives acquire economic benefits through such payment, and the husband and his relatives also obtain, apart from the girl or the woman, a reciprocal payment called '*arueth*', about which more shall be said later.

Fourthly, the institution of bride-wealth involves an element of prestige for the spouses as well as their relatives.

All these mutual benefits plus other benefits which are enumerated under sections 25 and 26 of the Re-statement of the Bhar El Ghazal Region Customary Law Act, 1984, create economic interests which must be protected by both the spouses and their relatives. The bride is usually committed to protect the economic interests acquired by her parents or relatives through her marriage. Unless she is a girl or woman of notorious conduct, she must feel morally bound to reciprocate the loving care and services rendered to her by her parents or relatives since childhood. For this reason she must try her best to avoid the breaking up of the marriage, unless there are compelling reasons against the continuity of the marriage relationship. The husband and his relatives are equally content with the marriage arrangement because of the reverse payment (*arueth*) they receive from the bride's parents or relatives as a consequence of the bride-wealth they pay to the bride's relatives.

1.4(d) *The final marriage ceremony*

Once the final agreement is reached over the quantity of cattle to be paid and there are no other impediments to the marriage, the agreed cattle are collected and delivered to the bride's relatives. Thereafter, preparations for the ceremony leading to her delivery to the husband follow.

1.5 Marriage as a social contract and not a commercial contract

The payment of bride-wealth has been the subject of mis-understanding by many foreigners who venture to study the Dinka Law. Such payment has been termed as 'bride-price' and regarded as the purchase price of a bride. These writers misleadingly equated Dinka or African marriages with commercial contracts. This is a grave mistake.

In commercial contracts, the only relationship between the parties is the economic interest. This economic interest comes to an end when the full price of the commodity is paid and the commodity is delivered to the buyer. Although a marriage contract also establishes economic interests, the main objective is the creation of permanent social rights and obligations. The rights and obligations arising from the marriage contract are summarised in sections 25 and 26 of the Code, and the reader may refer to the provisions of these sections.

A wife has both rights and obligations in the family of her husband. Certain duties which are imposed on the husband by reason of marriage constitute a denial of the idea that a man's wife is a commodity or a commercial article because bride-wealth has been paid to her relatives as a condition of her being delivered in marriage to him. The duties which are imposed on him by reason of marriage correspondingly constitute his wife's rights. The following are some of these duties.

Firstly, the husband is bound to maintain his wife. Secondly, he must provide suitable accommodation for her, together with sufficient agricultural land. Thirdly, the creation of a household is a joint responsibility of both the husband and his wife. Fourthly, where a husband has more than one wife, each wife with her children must have a share in the family cattle and other domestic animals. Fifthly, services or the procurement of food involving adventurous acts, for example, obtaining meat through hunting or getting fish from rivers or lakes, are duties which a man must perform for his wife and children. In fact, any heavy work is a duty which a man must discharge on behalf of his wife. It must also be stated that the woman is the mistress at home, that is, the administration of the marital home is almost her sole responsibility and she can organise her home without consulting her husband.

The above list does not exhaust the duties a man performs for his wife, which are numerous. Conversely, the rights a woman acquires by reason of marriage, essentially legalised by the payment of bride-wealth, are also numerous and cannot all be discussed here. I repeat that all the duties imposed on a man towards his wife or the rights a woman enjoys by reason of marriage are incompatible with the supposition that a woman becomes a commodity by the payment of 'bride-price'. She is not a property as has been wrongly understood by some of those pioneers of the Dinka or African law. She cannot be equated with an article one buys in a shop. She is a full member of her husband's family. A woman who has been married to a man without the payment of bride-wealth regards herself (as well as being regarded by others) as inferior. It also reflects badly on her relatives. Non-payment or payment of a few cows tends to indicate that she comes from a family of low status. On the other hand, failure to pay cattle tends to show that her husband is either a man of low means and, therefore, low status, or, if he has sufficient means, he is the type who neglects to discharge his social obligations.

In short, a Dinka or African marriage is mainly a social contract, although mutual economic interests are involved. It could be described as a purchase of continuous social relations. Many marriages have been conducted throughout history in order to bring about peace between warring communities. The husband is not entitled to mistreat his wife because he has paid cattle to her relatives. Their involvement with her welfare does not end with her marriage. In fact, the relatives of the married woman, after the conclusion of the marriage, are bound by law to make a reverse payment of cattle to her husband and relatives, as has already been mentioned. The rule is that, for every ten cows paid by her husband and his relatives to the relatives of the bride, the latter pay back three cows. The payment of bride-wealth cattle during the marriage may have reduced the husband and his relatives to poverty. *Arueth*, therefore, constitutes a restoration of some cattle to them so that they may continue to feed on milk. Further, the relatives of a married woman, despite the bride-wealth they have received, are always vigilant about her welfare. If her husband subjects her to continuous brutal treatment, her relatives may be entitled to call for divorce and return the bride-wealth property or cattle to the husband and his relatives. If the woman were like a commercial article, the seller would no longer be concerned with her condition after the completion of the contract of sale or purchase. The payment of bride-wealth should not, therefore, mislead people into believing that it is the price of a commercial article.

2. ADULTERY (*AKOR*)

Adultery or *Akor* is the commission of sexual intercourse between a man and a married woman. Adultery is a grave offence against marriage. All over Africa, adultery is recognised as both a criminal offence and a civil wrong which demands indemnification.[13] The customary law, however, is not so much concerned with the criminal aspect of the offence as with the civil. But since the act of adultery

---

[13] Dr Francis Deng, (1965) SLJR, p.538.

constitutes an infringement of the exclusive right of a man over the most sacred part of his wife, it is a grave provocation which is more likely to result in a breach of the peace, unless the law intervenes to repair the damage. The customery law does not, however, impose on the adulterer a penal sentence, such as imprisonment or fine. Instead it embodies a different kind of sanction.

The sanctions against adultery are partly legal and partly religious. Most of the religious aspects have already been discussed in Chapter two. The legal sanction, under the customary law is the payment of six cows and one bull by the adulterer to the aggrieved husband.[14]

Under the State Penal Code[15], the offence of adultery is committed by a man if he 'knows' or has 'reasons to believe' that the woman is married at the time of sexual intercourse between her and him. But, under section 27 of the Dinka Customary Law,

> 'every Dinka woman, who is not a girl, is presumed to be a married woman, and any man who commits sexual intercourse with such a woman does so at his risk.'

This rule is not a typical characteristic of the Dinka Law alone, it is commonly found in other African legal systems. For example, among the Sukuna tribe, liability of a man for adultery is absolute. It is the duty of the man to ascertain that the woman with whom he sleeps or whom he marries is eligible. Any statement which the woman may make to the man has no legal value, and the man cannot use it in his defence if accused of adultery, even if such statement was made before witnesses.[16]

> '...whatever the circumstances, the law always supports the husband against the adulterer. A man who takes a woman as his 'concubine' or invites her to follow him temporarily into his home must remember that he runs the risk of being charged with adultery. The native courts consider only the injury to the husband and take no cognizance of the possibility of ignorance on the part of the adulterer.'[17]

Among the Agar Dinka, during past years, a free woman (a free woman is she who has once been married, but has ceased to be

---

[14] S.28 of the Restatement of Bhar el Ghazal Region Customary Law Act, 1984.
[15] Sudan Penal Code, 1983, ss.432 and 433.
[16] *Maliyabwana* v. *Abdullah*, DC's Appeal No.41/42.
[17] Ibid.

married; she is not a married girl nor a married woman) used to wear certain beads *(tak)* on her head constantly. The wearing of the beads on the head served two purposes: it was an outward sign that she was a free woman and so anybody who wanted to go with her privately should not fear the risk of committing adultery; it also served as an advertisement to potential suitors that she was available for marriage.

But among the urban communities today, where there are women who engage in prostitution, this general presumption of marriage runs into difficulties. If a married woman in a town conducts herself in such a way as to create reasonable suspicion that she is one of the free women or prostitutes, it is likely that the presumption of her being married may be relaxed. This circumstance may be treated as exceptional to the general principle of absolute liability. But the presumption of marriage must really require a very strong evidence for rebuttal. The nature of the evidence must establish that the woman conducts herself in the manner which creates a reasonable belief among the local population that she is a prostitute. In other words, the evidence which is capable of rebutting this general presumption of marriage must not be of a subjective nature but objective. It must be capable of making a reasonable man in the locality entertain the belief that she is a free woman.

Under the State Penal Code, if a married woman denies her marriage at the time of sexual intercourse with another man and there are no other reasonable grounds to establish that she is a married woman, it is the woman alone who will be held responsible for committing adultery. Her liability is based on the ground that she knows that she is married. However, under the customary law, *mens rea*, or the state of mind of the offender at the time of sexual intercourse, is almost immaterial. It is, therefore, very risky to play with sex in the Dinka community. This wide scope of the offence is essential for its effective combat.

It is costly to risk the loss of six cows and one bull for a temporary enjoyment, which is also followed by public condemnation. But the payment of *akor* cattle to the aggrieved husband is made only for the first case of adultery. Where a married woman commits adultery for the second time or more, she will be regarded as a loose woman and therefore no cattle will be paid to her husband as damages.[18] At the same time, the law protects the society by removing the temptation on the part of a husband and his wife to make the act of adultery a continuous source of acquisition of wealth.

---

[18] Section 29 of The Restatement of the Bhar el Ghazal Region Customary Law Act 1984.

If a woman commits adultery for the second time or more, the adulterer may be imprisoned or fined by a court of law, according to the Sudan Penal Code. Alternatively, the husband is entitled to raise a divorce suit, if he feels sufficiently aggrieved, or if he believes that the woman will never amend her conduct. In the case of *Magot Kok* v. *Dorin DS/221/74*, the plaintiff, Magot Kok, sued the defendant for damages for committing adultery with his wife. During the trial it was established that she had also committed adultery with other people. The court stopped the claim for damages and advised the plaintiff to amend the petition to claim divorce if he wanted. The facts of this case did not show whether the plaintiff had, before suing the defendant, obtained *akor* cattle in a different case of adultery involving his wife. But it seemed he had not. It appears that the court felt that it was honourable for the plaintiff to abandon such a woman, rather than sue one of the many adulterers for damages.

But, in fact, the general rule is that where the husband elects to divorce his wife by reason of adultery, he is bound to sue the adulterer in order to obtain the *akor* cattle before the divorce suit is allowed by the court, while the marriage still remains valid.[19] It is the husband alone, or if he is dead, his successor or trustee who has a *locus standi* before a court of law in a suit where *akor* cattle are being claimed from the adulterer.[20]

In his discussion of what he termed *Widow Concubine* ('concubine' is a term I believe to have been used incorrectly here), P. P. Howell stated, inter alia, that:

'He (referring to the one he called widow-concubine) cannot compel her to live with him or claim compensation if she commits adultery. The compensation for adultery would concern her late husband as represented by his living brothers or legal heirs. He cannot divorce her or demand back her bride-wealth for there is no legal marriage between him and the widow, only between the widow and her late husband... The man's position is therefore, in theory, a precarious one. In fact most of these unions are arranged with the agreement of the dead man's legal representantives and thereby receive social recognition not only from the world at large but also from the dead man's family....'[21]

---

[19] Section 33 of The Restatement of the Bhar el Ghazal Customary Law Act 1984.
[20] Ibid., s.30.
[21] P. P. Howell, *Readings in African Law,* Vol. II, Frank Cass, London, 1970, p.143; also by Oxford University Press, 1950, pp.81–82.

There are a few comments to be made about this quotation. The Nuer and the Dinka have very much in common. Their way of life and geographical proximity have contributed greatly to a merging of cultures. Consequently, there is a great deal of similarity between their laws. Nevertheless, I would like to make some qualifications of one important point. In so doing we may still retain the use of the word 'concubine' although its use in this context is highly questionable. The status or the authority (we may even say the right) of the man who undertakes the sexual act with such a widow depends entirely on the degree of relationship between him and the deceased; on whether he was appointed by the deceased in order that he might exercise full care or the powers of an executor to continue to produce children with his widow; or whether he was only appointed by the deceased's representatives, with the limited authority to produce children only, or if they also assigned him additional responsibilities which are supposed to be discharged by the husband.

We would absolutely agree with Howell if the man's duties were only limited to the production of children while, at the same time, the degree of his relationship with the deceased was somewhat distant. In this situation it is true, as Howell said, that the deceased's brothers (or parents, if they are alive) or persons who are closer to the deceased himself than the 'man', will exercise other duties referred to above. But if he is, for example, a brother of the deceased or a paternal relative appointed by the deceased himself (as a trustee or executor), irrespective of the proximity of blood relationship, he is entitled to raise a suit in the case of adultery. Again, Howell is right in that the damages or compensation to be recovered will come in the name of the deceased.

Further, a 'concubine's' or widow's mate appointed by the testator's authority, or who by proximity of relationship, feels that he belongs to the deceased's family, can sue for the recovery of bride-wealth or divorce. But this statement must be qualified. A suit for the divorce of a widow must be the result of a joint action of the members of the deceased's family, together with the man who is responsible for the procreation of children (especially if he was appointed by the deceased with trustee's powers). In other words, there must be a collective or representative action in such a divorce case. If the 'man' is a distant relative who was appointed after the death of the deceased by his immediate relatives only to exercise the sexual functions and no more, his position may be said to be 'precarious' as Howell described. Again there is another remark which must be added here. The living relatives very much respect their dead kinsmen. For this reason, unless the living representatives of the deceased reasonably come to the conclusion that, by conduct, the woman has totally ceased to be the deceased's wife, for example, if she often leaves the family of the deceased and goes to look for non-relatives to have sex with and fails or refuses to take care of the deceased's children, she can be divorced. Her position is even more 'precarious' if she so conducts herself while she has no children with the deceased. But, in general, it is very difficult or rare to obtain a divorce against a widow.

We come now to the question of who can sue in a case of adultery where the husband is alive. According to Dr Francis Deng:

'In the case of adultery, the husband is normally the person entitled to sue. In a polygamous family, if the adultery is in relation to a young wife, and the man has a son, the son may bring the action in his father's name. It is, however, considered most undesirable for a person to sue in respect of his own mother's adultery. In fact such cases never seem to occur...'

Dr Deng went on to say that:

'The brother of the husband may recover for adultery in the name of the husband, and may take the compensation for himself. In such a case the husband has no further claim.'[22]

It is doubtful whether it has ever been part of the law that a son can raise a suit of adultery while his father is still alive and there is no indication that the father approves of the suit or that the son, by power of attorney, represents his father who, by reason of some

---

[23] (1965) SLJR 557.

Note: It is difficult for such cases to be pursued. But one case came before me in early 1982. I do not intend to disclose the names of the complainants, but they came from Gogrial after their return from the Anyanya war. The claimed *akor* cattle on the ground that their mother committed adultery with the respondent's father during the British rule and before these parties were even born. The case, according to them, was settled by Chief *Giir Thiik* and Chief *Mou Akeen* and others who are all dead. The case was also, according to them, tried either in the early thirties or forties. But the decree passed in favour of the representative of their father, who also died, was never executed. There were no documents to show that such a case was ever settled at all. The alleged witnesses and chiefs who allegedly tried the case were all dead. It was their mother who was alive but too weak even to walk. Their claim was dismissed in Gogrial and I also dismissed their appeal, partly because there was no evidence of such a case and partly because it was unconscionable for sons to raise an *akor* of their mother before a court. Such an act does not exist as a practice among the Dinka people. The right to sue for *akor* or damages in the case of adultery is legally vested in the husband whose wife has committed adultery or his legal representative.

infirmity, such as a physical disability, cannot appear in court. Further, it is also doubtful whether it has ever been part of the law that a husband's brother can sue for *akor* and take the cows for himself. Of course, we cannot deny the fact that these things can happen, especially in a society such as the Dinka where the family property or rights are communally shared or owned. But this is not the law at present.

The legal position, as it exists now, is expressed by section 30 of the Re-statement of the Bhar El Ghazal Region Customary Law Act, 1984 as follows:

'The husband or his successor, if he is dead, is the only competent party to sue in the case of adultery.'

It is now very clear that in the case of adultery the law vests the right to sue for damages in the husband, and if he is dead, the next qualified person is his successor. The parents or brothers or other close relatives of the husband may be co-plaintiffs. But the first plaintiff is the husband or his successor. Many reasons were advanced by the Chiefs and Elders during the Wanh-alel Conference in May 1975 in justifying this rule.

It was argued that the family and other kinsmen have an obligation to a member of their kinsgroup to secure him in marriage with a girl. But it is not their duty to break up such a marriage. They accumulate wealth for a long time to enable this person to get married. Once this duty is discharged, there are others also waiting in the queue to get married. If the person who has been married already gets divorced he will no longer have priority in the queue. Consequently, if anybody in the kinsgroup is allowed to raise a suit in respect of a man's wife and such suit results in the termination of the marriage, the duty will revert to his relatives and he will have to be placed in a position of priority, since he was not the cause of the divorce of his wife. Giving the right to every kinsman, apart from the husband, to raise a divorce suit would lead to instability in the family.

The second reason is that the first person to be gravely provoked by an act of adultery is the husband. If he tolerates the wrong done by his wife, no-one else should take it upon himself to raise a suit. After all, the damages for adultery go to the husband and, if he waives his right, it should not be taken up by anyone else. The third reason is that, if the husband feels comfortable with his wife, despite the wrong she has done, nobody else is entitled to stir up trouble between the couple by raising a suit of adultery.

However, the relatives of the husband may play a role behind the scene by pressurising him to lead them in raising a suit either for adultery or for divorce. This happens in circumstances where the husband's kinsmen feel convinced that the woman is not worthy to remain a wife. But the husband must equally be satisfied of this to raise the suit.

We now come to the question of the paternity of the child who is the product of adultery. The general rule, as provided by section 32 of the Bhar el Ghazal Region Customary Law Act, 1984, is that:

> 'The child who is the product of sexual intercourse between a married woman and another man belongs to the legal father. But, if the legal father elects to divorce his wife and disowns the child, his wife's relatives will be entitled to have the child.'

Dr Francis Deng cited two cases[23] on the issue from the work of Howell. These are two Nuer cases which resulted in anomalous decisions. Although I mentioned before that the customary laws of the two communities are similar, the *ratio decidendi* established by the decisions in those two cases are alien to the Dinka Law. It is also doubtful if they really reflect or represent the Nuer Law. The principle which these cases established is that, where a man commits adultery with a married woman, the adulterer is bound to pay six cows to the legal husband as compensation, provided that the act of adultery has not caused pregnancy to the woman. Conversely, if the woman gets pregnant and produces a child as a consequence of adultery, the said child belongs to the legal father and this factor mitigates the amount of damages to be paid by the adulterer to the aggrieved husband by reducing the number of cows from six to one.

An unconfirmed explanation given to Howell which was said to be the justification for the rule is the gain of a child by the legal father or the woman's father who presumably needs more children. This factor, therefore, mitigates the gravity of the wrong which has to be expressed in a reduction of the amount of damages. According to Dr Deng, Howell's view on this point was that:

> 'the return payment was a way of avoiding confession over the legal paternity of the child, since the cattle otherwise have a flavour of a legitimization[24] fee by the biological father. It is argued that unless

---

[23] *Deng Kac* v. *Nyuon Makuac* and *Not Pet* v. *Gac Nyol* in (1965) SLJR 541.

[24] 'Legitimization' of children is a term of doubtful use. Legitimacy and illegitimacy are unknown terms in Dinka Law. They are alien terms which are also strange to the Nuer Law. The legal notions attached to these terms in the legal systems where they are used do not exist in our legal systems.

the cattle are returned, the adulterer might claim the child. This is particularly so, should the marriage be subsequently dissolved.'

In Dinka Law, the payment of damages is never based on the fact that the adulterer has failed to produce a child with the woman with whom he committed the wrong. It is a compensation which must be paid irrespective of whether or not there is a child from the act of adultery. According to section 34 of the Bhar el Ghazal Region Customary Law Act, 1984, if the marriage is subsequently dissolved and the husband recovers the bride-wealth cattle which had been paid, *akor* cattle or compensation for the adultery goes to the relatives of the divorced woman. The adulterer, who is regarded as a thief, does not come into the picture. The wife's relatives would, however, not be eligible for these cows if the divorce were to be granted before the adulterer was sued, because they would have no *locus standi* in the case. But, if the husband claims the 'bride-wealth' cattle from his in-laws as a consequence of the divorce, the court may allow him to retain the *akor* cattle in place of some of his original cattle by way of a set-off.

Where adultery is committed by a married woman with a relative of her husband, the husband has no right to divorce her. The grant of divorce normally entitles the husband to recover bride-wealth cattle he had paid to her relatives. Such a recovery would constitute a loss of property on the part of her relatives. But the law does not allow innocent people to suffer loss, when this kind of offence is committed by a relative of the husband.[25] He must bear the full consequence of the conduct of his relative.

The payment of *akor* cattle to the complainant depends on whether the adulterer made a contribution to the bride-wealth at the time when the woman was married. If he contributed a cow or cows to the marriage, he would not be bound to pay *akor* or damages. He would only pay *awec* (i.e. appeasement) in the form of a heifer, provided the payment did not necessarily absolve the adulterer of a penal sentence. But such a contribution mitigates the gravity of the sentence. However, if the adulterer relative never made a contribution, he would be bound to pay the *akor* cattle in full.

Dr Francis Deng seems to support this point with a different argument that blood relationship is a mitigating factor in the amount of indignation the act of adultery produces in the husband and the

---

[25] Section 30 of the Restatement of the Bhar el Ghazal Region Customary Law Act, 1984.

amount of damages the adulterer will be required to pay. The reason he put forward to justify this view is that

> 'the adulterer in such a case would be regarded as interfering with what is their joint interest in the wife. On these grounds, it has been argued that the husband should be less indignant the closer the relationship.'[26]

Because of the strength of social or kinship ties among the Dinka or among African communities in general, it is possible that tortious acts committed by kinsmen may be tolerated or the degree of reaction against a wrong committed by a relative may be less vigorous, in spite of the degree of bitterness it must have caused. To this extent Dr Francis Deng may be right.

As was said before, a man has an absolute right over the sacred parts of his wife. In the Dinka concept, a married woman may be described as the 'wife' of all the relatives of her husband in so far as her services are concerned. She may be required to do anything for any relative of her husband, but her private body is never a subject of joint ownership. There are a few exceptions where a man may be permitted to have sex with the wife of his kinsman, for instance, if the husband is impotent. Even this is not always possible if the husband refuses it. But the main reason why a relative may be permitted to have sex with the wife of his kinsman is the procreation of children which, as previously stated, is the prime objective of marriage.

Frankly speaking, sex cannot be shared. Blood relationship is not a licence for anyone to have sex with a kinsman's wife and expect a less vigorous reaction. The legal position on the subject now (as far as the Dinka of Bhar el Ghazal are concerned) is provided by s.31 of the Re-statement of Bhar el Ghazal Customary Law Act, 1984, as follows:

> 'When a woman has committed adultery with a relative who had contributed a cow or cows during her marriage as part of the bride-wealth, the relative who has committed the offence is only bound to pay a cow to the husband or his successor or trustee (i.e. if the husband is dead) as *awec*; but, if such a relative had never paid any cow or some cows as contribution to bride-wealth, he is bound to pay six cows and one bull as *akor* (or *aruok*) damages or compensation to the husband or his successor.'[27]

---

[26] (1965) SLJR 545.
[27] The word *awec* appears in the section as *awac* (damages) but it was a clerical error and should have been *awec* (i.e. appeasement).

As is evident from this section of the law, it is not the blood relationship in itself that serves as a mitigating factor. It is the contribution one makes to the bride-wealth which constitutes a mitigating factor. Some people even argue that if contribution towards the bride-wealth serves as a mitigating factor in the act of adultery, married women will always become the victims of this wrong from all those who help the husband during the marriage. Of course, this is an extreme view. In practice it is not common ground for the commission of adultery. No such case has been recorded of a man contributing cows towards a marriage in order to commit adultery; nor is the sanction against him likely to be any less severe.

It may also be added that such a person is still liable for a penal sentence under the Sudan Penal Code. Even the person who has paid full compensation (*akor*) to the aggrieved party is not absolved from a penal sentence by the Sudan Criminal Code.

However, I do not intend, by this argument, to reject the whole of Dr Deng's conclusions. There is an element of truth in his emphasis upon the closeness of the relationship between husband and adulterer. This point will hold good if, for example, a man goes with his brother's wife or his father's wife. It is a wrong against the whole family which includes the accused. The aggrieved husband, if he is seriously provoked and does not want to forgive his brother or son, may relieve himself by taking a penal action against him. But if he resorts to an action in customary law, he may not expect much, if any, benefit since the property, out of which he would expect the damages to be paid to him, is their common or family property. But if the wrong doer is, for example, the son of a paternal uncle (i.e. son of one's father's brother), the law is in favour of the aggrieved party, provided the son or his father never made a contribution towards the bride-wealth (s.31 of the Restatement of the Bhar Ghazal Region Customary Law Act, 1984). However, it is possible that recourse to the legal processes may be waived if the elders intervene to make an appeasement or if relations between the families are very cordial.

3. DIVORCE *(PUOKĒ-RUĀI)*

Introduction
Some European writers have doubted the correctness of the use of the term 'divorce' in connection with the termination of African marriages.

> '...the term 'dissolution of marriage' is preferred, because it decreases the likelihood of confusion between Western legal

notions of divorce and the African customary machinery for terminating marriage.[28]

Despite this remark, the authors of this volume still retained the use of the word 'divorce' in favour of the word 'dissolution' because they felt that the word 'dissolution' was too wide for the limited aspects of the subject which they had selected for discussion. Like these authors, I do appreciate the difference between the Western notions of 'divorce' and the African concept of 'termination of marriage'.

The wide scope of the African marriage, I believe, is one of the contributing factors to the difference in the notions attached to the use of the word 'divorce' in all aspects of the termination of a marriage. For example, in the African concept, there is nothing wrong in using the word 'divorce' in the circumstance where a marriage is terminated by reason of the death of one spouse. As marriage is a union between two families, it must, in most cases, remain continuous after the death of one spouse. In exceptional cases, if the living spouse, jointly with his or her relatives, wants the marriage to be brought to an end, they may go to the court and state the reasons why the union should not continue to exist. If the court agrees (or if both sets of relatives agree out of court) it will allow the 'divorce'. To the European, whose concept of marriage is a union only between the spouses for life to the exclusion of others, the term 'dissolution of marriage' by reason of death must be the appropriate one and not 'divorce'.

Apart from this difference of notions on the termination of marriage, there are other differences also. English Law has had a long historical development in the field of matrimonial suits, dating back to the period of the Ecclesiastical Courts. Through its long historical development, English Law has acquired characteristic features which are not found in African legal systems. In fact, the difference in ideas on 'divorce' is one of the consequences of this historical development. In the field of matrimonial suits, various types of judicial reliefs have been developed. Each type of relief is determined by the nature of the ground or act upon which recourse is being had to the court. Some time back recourse was even had to Parliament, for example, in the case of a *divorce vinculo matrimonii*. Further, a divorce *a mensa et thoro* which did not, at the time of the Ecclesiastical Courts, dissolve marriage nor allow the parties to re-marry, was granted on the grounds of adultery, cruelty, or unnatural acts. The Matrimonial Causes Act, 1857–1923 gave authority to the Courts to pass a decree for *divorce vinculo matrimonii* (which, previously, could only be obtained by

---

[28] *Readings in African Law*, Vol. II, Frank Cass, London, 1970, p.209.

petitioning Parliament by means of a Private Bill, because of the difficulties of granting divorce in the Ecclesiastical Courts) on grounds of adultery in a husband's petition and adultery coupled with such aggravated enormity as incest, bigamy, rape, bestiality, sodomy, cruelty and so forth.[29] It also became possible through the Act[30] for the Courts to pass a decree for separation where it could instead pass a decree for *a divorce a mensa et thoro*. Further, the Courts had the authority to pronounce a decree of nullity of marriage on grounds of affinity, consanguinity, mental incapacity, impotence, impurberty and so forth.

Another characteristic feature of English Law unknown to the African traditional system, which again makes the concept attached to 'divorce' by Westerners different, is the procedure of granting decrees for divorce tentatively, subject to confirmation or being declared absolute at certain periods. For example, every decree for divorce or for nullity of marriage shall, in the first instance, be a *decree nisi*[31] not to be absolute until after the expiration of certain number of months (Judicature Consolidation Act, 1925), reduced to 3 months under the Matrimonial Causes Act, 1957. By section 40(4) of the Matrimonial Causes Act, 1957[32] 'A certificate...that the decree has been made *absolute*[33] shall be prepared and filed by the Registrar. The

---

[29] *Rayden on Divorce,* 7th ed., Butterworths, London, 1942, p.7.

[30] Section 7 of the Matrimonial Causes Act, 1857. *Note:* this section was repealed by the Judicature (Consolidation) Act, 1925. Refer also to sections 14(1) and (2) the Matrimonial Causes Act, 1950.

[31] *Decree Nisi:* 'A decree, order, rule, declaration, or other adjudication of a court is said to be made 'nisi', when it is not to take effect unless the person affected by it fails to show cause against it, within a certain time, that is, unless he appears before the court and gives some reasons why it should not take effect. The petitioner in divorce or nullity proceedings may normally apply for a decree nisi to be made absolute after three months from the granting of the decree nisi, otherwise the respondent may do so.' – *Osborn's Concise Law Dictionary,* 6th edition, by John Burke, p.231.

[32] Every decree for divorce or for nullity of marriage is, in the first instance, a decree nisi not to be made absolute until after the expiration of 3 months from the pronouncing thereof, unless the Court shall fix a shorter time, – section 12, Matrimonial Causes Act, 1957.

Note: 'Up to the passing of the Matrimonial Causes Act, 1937 application for *decree nisi* to be made absolute could be made only by the spouse in whose favour the decree nisi had been made – section 9(b) of that Act amended section 183 of the Judicature (Consolidation) Act, 1925 (now section 12(3) of the Matrimonial Causes Act, 1957)...' – *Rayden on Divorce,* 7th ed., 1942, p.727.

[33] *Decree Absolute:* complete and unconditional, a rule or order which is complete and becomes of full effect at once. Ref. *Osborn's Concise Law Dictionary,* 7th ed., Roger and Bird, Sweet and Maxwell, 1980, p.3.

certificate shall be authenticated by fixing thereto the Seal of the Registry.'

To pursue the differences in notions attached to 'divorce' by Westerners and Africans, we may at this stage refer to *Osborn's Concise Law Dictionary*, 7th edition, page 112, where it refers to 'divorce' as a 'dissolution of marriage'. This was the meaning attached to divorce before the Matrimonial Causes Act, 1857, in the jurisdiction of the Ecclesiastical Courts. The Dictionary goes on to say that *divorce a mensa et thoro* was from *bed and board*, now represented by a *judicial separation* and *divorce a vinculo matrimonii*, from the bond of marriage, is now represented by a *decree of nullity*.

From this explanation it becomes clear that the word 'divorce' in English Law was one time wider in scope and so its meaning could be expressed by the use of the wider term 'dissolution of marriage'. But, through historical evolution, some of the components of divorce are now expressed in different technical terms. For example, as stated above, one of its components – *divorce a mensa et thoro* – is now represented by *decree for separation*, while the other component – *decree a vinculo matrimonii* – is being represented by a *decree for nullity*. It may be said that the separation of the other components of the term 'divorce' has narrowed the grounds for which it can be granted; and so it may be stated that the meaning of the word 'divorce' is now narrower than it was before.

The corresponding term to 'divorce' is *puokē-ruāi* or *dakē-ruāi* in Dinka. *Puokē-ruāi* has a wider scope which justifies the use of the word 'dissolution of marriage' to correspond with it in nearly, if not, all cases. The Dinka Law has not created many heads of relief in matrimonial suits as is the case in English Law, a fact which is responsible for the narrowing of the scope of the word 'divorce'.

Further, divorce or *puokē-ruāi*, as understood in Dinka Law, does not involve the stages or the procedural requirements of English Law. A divorce or *puokē-ruāi*, once granted or decreed, is absolute or final, although this does not rule out the possibility that the parties may in future agree to re-marry each other. Also, Dinka Law does not embody other reliefs, such as a *decree for separation*, which has the same effect and force as a decree for *divorce a mensa et thoro*;[34] nor does Dinka Law embody the difference between a 'decree for divorce' and a 'decree for nullity'. Any decree which brings a marriage to an end carries one terminology only, and that is *puokē-ruāi*.

However, in the light of Western concepts of 'divorce', which are unknown to Dinka Law, we will concentrate on the use of the word

---

[34] Section 14(1), Matrimonial Causes Act, 1950.

puokē-ruāi (or *dakē-ruāi* in discussing the subject of 'divorce' here.[35] The word *puokē-ruāi* will fit the circumstances where the use of 'divorce' or 'dissolution' may be appropriately employed. *Puokē-ruāi* refers to absolute termination of marriage, irrespective of the grounds for which it is granted.[36] For example, it would fit the circumstances where English Law would pass a decree for nullity. The use of Dinka terminology minimises the ambiguity or misunderstanding which has been discussed above. However, I do not intend to dismiss totally the use of the word 'divorce', but where it appears it should be understood in the wider sense attached to the word *puokē-ruāi*, which stands for all cases where the marriage is absolutely terminated irrespective of the grounds for it.

3.1 Puokē-ruāi (Divorce) reverses the marriage objectives

Puokē-ruāi is an institution which tends to undermine the very existence of society.[37]

Marriage, as an institution, is intended to lay down a sound, permanent and cordial relationship between the spouses and between their respective relatives. Many social and economic interests which arise from it have been clearly spelt out in the Restatement of Bhar el Ghazal Region Customary Law Act, 1984. Because of these mutual interests which develop between the two sides of the marriage, *puokē-ruāi* becomes a source of lamentation to those who hold the marriage very dearly, or those whose interests are adversely affected by it.

3.2 Puokē-ruāi must take place in Court

In order to lay down a sound foundation for the preservation of the sacred institution of marriage, the authority to grant divorce is vested in a court of law. That is, as a gernal rule,[38] *puokē-ruāi* must always be granted by a court, with or without the agreement of all or more parties to the marriage. This means that *puokē-ruāi* cannot take place outside the courts through the mutual agreement of the spouses, or the spouses together with their relatives or through a

---

[35] Of course, the use of the words 'divorce' and 'dissolution' has been employed in previous parts of this Chapter. But in the discussion of the subject of 'divorce', and in view of European notions of the word, we intend to concentrate on Dinka terminology here.

[36] Unlike English Law where the nature of matrimonial relief is determined by the grounds for it.

[37] While the marriage (*ruai*) lays down a foundation for the society, *puokē-ruai* erodes that very foundation. It may therefore be described as anti-social.

[38] Section 36 of the Restatement of Bhar el Ghazal Customary Law Act, 1984.

unilateral decision of one of the spouses.[39] But, it does not, strictly speaking, mean that any divorce or dissolution of marriage outside the court is invalid. It does not even involve penalty when *puokē ruāi* takes place out of court, and the court cannot bring together the parties who have decided to reject each other. The court's power is limited and, therefore, cannot absolutely guarantee or compel the parties to maintain marital harmony at home.

In many instances the parties may be unable to settle their rights or claims where divorce takes place out of court and they may want to have recourse to the court for adjustment of their claims. The court's response, however, will be negative, since the parties have in the first place decided to divorce themselves out of court. This is one weapon the court has to use to enforce this general rule. It may, therefore, be stated that where divorce takes place out of court, the court will not lend its support to any party who makes a claim arising out of the marriage, unless the court has affirmed *puokē-ruāi*. The affirmation of *puokē-ruāi* which takes place out of court must rest on reasonable grounds.

3.3 Reasons why divorce must take place in court

The first basis for the general rule that *puokē-ruāi* must take place in court is to make the break-down of marriage difficult. Moreover, hardships likely to affect the children of a marriage as a consequence of divorce may be prevented by the court. It is a rule which is based on policy not on equity. As a matter of policy, the society is determined to protect the sacred institution of marriage and to prevent social hardships that may accompany *puokē-ruāi*.

In the case of *Maguek Atony* v. *Marial Dorin and others*[40] the appellant married the first respondent's sister. It was a case of what has become known by anthropologists as a 'ghost marriage'. The marriage was made for the appellant's elder brother who died a bachelor. The appellant had five children with the first respondent's sister but he treated the woman very badly. There were frequent quarrels and beatings. He neglected her. For many years the woman lived with her brother and depended on him for food. Although the woman was prepared for *puokē-ruāi*, her brother refused to consent to it and many attempts were made at reconciliation.

Her brother's refusal was merely based on the social hardships that might befall the children. When the ill-treatment became an indefinite

---

[39] Section 40 of the Restatement of Bhar el Ghazal Region Customary Law Act, 1984.
[40] Aliamtooc Regional Court, CS/351/77.

practice, the first respondent jointly with his sister petitioned the court for divorce. The court of first instance granted the divorce but there was no order made for the recovery of the bride-wealth cattle by the appellant, since the number of cattle claimed by both sides of the marriage was equal. The children were given to the appellant. When the appellant found that he was losing more through divorce, he submitted an appeal to a higher court for the restoration of the marriage relationship and promised to amend his conduct. But, although the appellate court was prepared to confirm the decision of the lower court, it decided to reverse the decree in the interest of the five children. The interests of these children were not economic but social in the sense that a child must have a father who is also the legal father or the trustee of his father, otherwise his social status will be in jeopardy.[41]

The second reason why it is important to grant divorce in court is for the purpose of publicity. The public who attend the court as audience later pass the word to those who did not attend it. Those who hear of the declaration of divorce by a court take judicial notice of the fact that divorce has been granted and the woman has become free. Any member of the public who therefore takes her after the declaration of divorce is free from the risk of committing *akor* or adultery since 'every Dinka woman, who is not a girl, is presumed to be a married woman, and any man who commits sexual intercourse with such a woman does so at his risk.'[42]

Puokē-ruāi takes effect as soon as the court declares it. But when it takes place out of court, it is often difficult to tell whether it takes effect as soon as the parties agree or after the husband has recovered the bride-wealth cattle from her relatives. It is this uncertainty, combined with the other reasons already stated, which necessitates the making of the general rule that divorce must be declared by a court of law so that the time it takes effect becomes definite. Sometimes divorce declared out of court seems to take effect immediatly when the parties agree, but there are times when it appears to take effect only after the return of the bride-wealth cattle. There are in fact two conflicting views here.

The first view is that *puokē-ruāi* takes place when the bride-wealth has been returned. In the case of *Adut Puouwak* v. *Tiera*

---

[41] Apart from the lack of necessary maternal care when a father redeems his children from his divorced wife's relatives by paying *aruok*, the children also suffer from public criticism as the offspring of bad parents who failed to maintain a harmonious union. The parents' bad character reflects on the children.

[42] Section 25 of the Restatement of Bhar el Ghazal Customary Law Act, 1984.

Macar, Maker Macol, CS/377/71, which was decided in Rumbek, Adut, the plaintiff had married the sister of the first defendant. Relations broke down between the two families and the woman separated from the husband and went to live with her relatives. Her parents informed the husband that they were prepared to return his cows and that they were going to marry her to someone else. The husband accepted it. But the woman was given in marriage to the second defendant while the plaintiff's cattle had not been returned. The plaintiff went to court to raise a case of adultery against Maker Macol and against Tiera Macar for abetting the act of adultery.

The court held that the divorce did not take effect before the cattle were returned to the plaintiff and that the act of adultery was committed when Maker Macol took the woman as his wife. Maker Macol was ordered to pay five cows to the plaintiff as damages while Tiera Macar, the abettor, was punished. However, the court directed that if they wanted divorce to take effect, they had to return the bride-wealth cattle first to the plaintiff and that they had to do this in court.

In one case in Aweil district, a woman deserted her husband from the rural area and went to live in the town for many years. The link between her and the husband was cut and she married somebody in the town and had seven children with him. Her relatives, who were still retaining the cattle of the first husband, seemed to have acquiesced in the second marriage, since they were paying frequent visits to the new home and accepted some cattle from the new husband.

The first husband went to court to raise the question of adultery against the second 'husband', claiming that the woman was still his wife since her relatives had not returned his cattle. Her relatives, who were jointly the defendants in the case, contended that the plaintiff's silence for many years was evidence that divorce had taken place and that, if he had claimed his cattle, they would have been returned. But the court came to the conclusion that, despite the plaintiff's silence for many years, the first marriage remained valid as long as the cattle had not been returned. Silence did not amount to divorce. If the parents of the woman wanted the divorce to take effect, they ought to have given back the cattle of their own volition. The second defendant was ordered to pay damages in cattle and to restore the wife with all her children to the plaintiff who was the legal husband. This was an extreme decision which was very harsh to the second 'husband'. But it conforms with the rule that a Dinka woman, who is not a girl, is presumed to be a married woman and anybody who commits sexual intercourse with her does so at his risk.

The second view is where the court holds that *puokē-ruāi* takes effect although the bride-wealth has not been returned to the husband.

The Family Law

But cases where the acts of both spouses appear to constitute a dissolution of the marriage present intricate problems. The above case is one example. Other examples are provided by two conflicting decisions made by the Main Courts in Rumbek.

In the case of *Macuny Malok* v. *Sol. Amiro CS/462/71*, the plaintiff married the daughter of the defendant before the Anyanya war[43] in the Southern Sudan. When the war intensified in the sixties, the plaintiff had a quarrel with his wife and she was taken to her father. No *puokē-ruāi* took place, although there was a separation. The plaintiff joined the war. Some years later she was given in marriage to someone else. When peace was established, the plaintiff returned home and sought to reclaim his wife. The court held that divorce had taken place. The fact that the man separated from his wife and later left to stay away for many years without any indication that he still retained the link with his wife was the evidence of an intention to abandon the woman for good.

However, in a similar case, the court decided to the contrary. This is the case of *John Gum* v. *Martin Makuek Abol CS/574/72*. John Gum, the plaintiff, before joining the war, took his wife to her parents and left her there but there was no evidence of any dispute. He joined the war and remained there for many years. Defendant Martin later married the woman while her relatives still retained the plaintiff's cattle. When the war was over, the plaintiff returned and sued the defendant for damages for committing adultery with his wife. The defendant's argument was that the plaintiff had deserted his wife and that constituted a dissolution of the marriage. But the court held that the marriage remained valid as long as the plaintiff's cattle were in the possession of her relatives. The defendant was ordered to return the woman to the plaintiff and to pay damages in addition.

These two decisions may be reconciled on the ground that in the former case the conduct of the plaintiff showed that he intended to dissolve the marriage when he took his wife to her parents after a dispute and this intention was confirmed by his conduct afterwards. But in the latter case, the plaintiff merely took his wife to her parents to give her proper care during his absence and there was no proof that he intended to divorce her.

A third reason, which may be regarded as a by-product of granting *puokē-ruāi* in court, is that it affords the public an opportunity to judge who, of the two contesting parties (husband and wife), is to blame for the misconduct, or to acquaint themselves with the reasons

---

[43] The seventeen year war between the Southern and Northern Sudan which ended on 3rd March, 1972.

for the grant of divorce. The innocent or less guilty party has more opportunities open to him or her to get married again to another person without much difficulty. The party proved to be troublesome may find it difficult to enter a subsequent marriage after being divorced in public. A guilty woman would have fewer chances of a second marriage than a man. A divorcee is described as *adeer-jōōk* (meaning she is 'carrying' a nasty character on her head and that such a character is more likely to be extended to her new home if she is subsequently married). But the society will forgive her conduct and absolve her from this description if she proves her innocence before the court during divorce proceedings. The same attitude prevails among the Tswana. They have a saying, which goes like this: 'Seize the breast of a widow, that of a divorced woman is unsuitable'. She is regarded as a loose woman who cannot be expected to maintain her new home.

3.4 Whether *Puokē-ruāi* may be obtained at ease.

A litigant must give very sound grounds why he or she must obtain divorce. It is not true, as some Western writers tend to imply, that African marriages can be abrogated with ease or without any grounds.

In Volume II of *Readings in African Law*, page 209, it is stated that:

'it is not clear whether there are grounds for divorce in customary law. Many writers have inclined to this view...'

However, the editors of this volume went on to say:

'But there is good reason for doubting its validity – particularly if any analogy with recognised grounds of divorce in English Law is suggested.'

The opinion of these writers may either be contemptuous of African customary law or a hyperbole. The statement may be true to some extent with respect to certain tribes or communities in Africa, but it is not true of all. An extract from the work of H. Cory refers to the Sukuna tribe as an example of the ease with which certain tribes can obtain divorce.[44] He cited a case showing that once upon a time a man from the Sukuna tribe was tired of living with his wife, took her to her father, left her there and claimed the recovery of bride-wealth cattle he had paid. Further, he stated that if the father-in-law was not happy with his son-in-law, he would send for his daughter and return

---

[44] *Readings in African Law*, Vol. II, Frank Cass, London, 1970, p.209.

the bride-wealth. Assuming that there were no other undisclosed reasonable grounds for such cases of divorce, it cannot be taken for granted that this is true of every customary law in Africa. I quite agree with the editors of this volume in stating that:

> '... it is worth noting that, in most traditional African societies, divorce was very rare. In some societies divorce was unknown, in others it was recognised, but subject to procedural intricacies which involved not only the parties, but also their parents and other members of their immediate kin groups. It is certainly untrue to say of all the customary laws that divorce is obtained at the will of either of the parties.'[45]

A Dinka court or a court applying Dinka Law, after careful consideration of all the issues for which the divorce is demanded, may either grant it or refuse it. In the case of *Bona Mou Ngot* v. *Alek Nyang Dhieu PC/BGP/CS/8/74*, Bona Mou Ngot, the plaintiff, petitioned the Province Court, Wau, to divorce the defendant, Alek Nyang Dhieu. The cause of action was based upon the fact that the defendant insulted the children of the plaintiff. It is not clear from the decree whether these were the children of the plaintiff by another wife or his children with the defendant. The nature of the insult was gravely provocative. She said that 'any child of Bona Ngot would not be satisfied even if the oil pours down his or her anus' *(acie mith leu bik kueth te cok mōk ya kuĕrpiny ne ke thāār)*. It means that these children are exceptionally greedy. None of them is ever satisfied even if the stomach cannot hold the amount of food (rich food full of fat or oil) he or she has eaten and the oil pours down from the anus because there is no space in the stomach. In a way it is an innuendo. It means that even the father and his kinsmen are as exceptionally greedy as these children.

The court, however, refused to grant divorce but ordered Gabriel Nyang Dhieu, the brother of the woman, who was a co-defendant, to pay two heifers to the plaintiff as *awec* (appeasement).

As previously stated, divorce cannot easily be allowed since it adversely affects the social and economic interests of both parties. The elders, among the people, make all necessary effort to resist it. They can only allow the parties concerned to go to court when the reasons for demanding divorce are very strong or when they fail to convince the parties to change their minds. Even where the divorce suit has been raised, the court has the last opportunity to persuade the

---

Readings in African Law, Vol. II, Frank Cass, London, 1970, p.209.

parties to reconcile, or it may exercise its discretionary power to reject the suit on the grounds illustrated by the case of *Maguek Atony* v. *Marial Dorin and others*, already cited above.

3.5 Grounds for divorce (Puokē-ruāi)

We may now proceed to discuss the grounds for divorce. The reasons for which a court may grant divorce may be summarised under three main headings. The first heading is where the marriage has totally failed to achieve its fundamental objectives. The most important objective of marriage, as has been stated before, is the procreation of children. It is the children who maintain the link between the two families who are related by marriage. It is also the children who perpetuate the genealogy of the people. But, the barrenness of a woman, the impotence of a man, or death of children through *akeeth* or incest and so forth may not result in a grant of divorce. Because of the reasons stated above, alternatives may be found to save the marriage. A man can remain with his wife despite her barrenness and still marry another woman, if he has sufficient means to do so. Further, the case of impotence may be settled by finding a relative of the husband for his wife to produce children with for him. The problem always arises if the husband refuses to accept another man to replace him for the purpose of procreation. In this case the woman would be compelled either to have sex secretly with a relative of her husband or seek divorce.

In the case of *Thokmer and others* v. *Malual Cindut CS/452/72*, the daughter of the first plaintiff was married to the defendant, who later proved to be impotent. As a result, his wife and her father went to court to petition for divorce. When the court was satisfied that attempts by the wife to adopt the practice of *lo-hōt* were resisted by her husband, divorce was granted and the defendant was allowed to recover the bride-wealth cattle. The defendant appealed to the Main Court but failed. The decision of the lower court was confirmed.[46]

The second important heading where divorce may be granted is where the marriage has irretrievably broken down, that is where attempts to reactivate it have totally failed, for example, where misconduct of the wife has become so gross that neither her husband nor his relatives have the confidence to maintain the slightest hope that she will improve her conduct, or when she is so inefficient or so lazy or

---

[46] In the case of *akeeth*, purification rites may be conducted after her confessing the identity of male relatives who went with her and so divorce may not be granted. But, if she conceals other male relatives or all of them, the husband will be entitled to divorce.

troublesome that she is unable to maintain the homestead. On the other hand, where the husband neglects his wife or becomes so cruel that the life of his wife or the safety of her body is gravely endangered, divorce may eminently be granted.[47]

The third major reason which may justify divorce is a serious deterioration of the relation between the close relatives of the spouses. Of course, the wife and the husband will also be involved in such a conflict. Break-down of relations between the relatives of the spouses is important in cases of divorce, because the Dinka marriage, as previously mentioned, is wide in scope. It includes the relatives of both sides as parties. Deterioration of relations may be brought about by disputes over cattle, or if the wife's relatives encourage or support her in causing trouble for him and his relatives, or when the wife is generally mistreated by the husband and his relatives. It may also be caused by any grave acts of misconduct committed by one or more relatives on the one side of the marriage against one or more relatives on the other side, or where a woman's relative commits sexual intercourse with her.

For example, in the case of *Manyiel Cindut and others* v. *Marial Manok and others, CS/450/71*, the first plaintiff Manyiel Cindut had married the sister of the first defendant, Marial Manok. Manyiel had many other wives. The first defendant comitted adultery with one of these wives. Although this offence was exceptionally grave in that it was committed by a brother-in-law, and thus angered all the parties to the marriage on the plaintiff's side, the elders on both sides met to solve the matter without going to court as this would be likely to have an adverse effect on the marriage between Manyiel and the sister of the first defendant. After a few years, the same defendant repeated the offence. Manyiel was joined by all the relatives on his side and decided to take more drastic measures this time, since the defendant had no respect for the marriage relations between the two families. Manyiel Cindut, the plaintiff, decided to go to court in order to break up the marriage relationship between him and the defendant's sister in the first place, and then to prosecute the defendant himself. However, the court refused to grant divorce, for the sake of the children of the marriage. The second reason why the court turned down the request for divorce was so that the defendant's sister should not suffer the consequences of her brother's act when she was innocent. The court ordered the defendant to pay cattle to Manyiel as *awec* and warned him to refrain from such conduct.

---

[47] Refer to *Maguek Atony* v *Marial Dorin and others* (supra).

3.6 The legal consequences of Puokē-ruāi

'It will already be evident that since marriage and divorce are essentially matters of concern to a wider family group and not just the spouses, the break-down of marriage involves important personal and proprietary consequences. These occur particularly in regard to the custody of children... doubtless because they are the most important aspects of the subject...'[48]

These effects of *puokē-ruāi* (or *dakē-ruāi*) are enumerated under section 41 of the Re-statement of Bhar el Ghazal Region Customary Law Act, 1984, as follows:

(i) relieving the spouses of their marital relationship;
(ii) freedom of the woman to marry another man;
(iii) recovery of bride-wealth cattle or property and offspring and all other rights due to the husband from his wife's relatives;
(iv) recovery of *arueth* (reverse payment) and all other rights due to the relatives of the divorced woman from the husband and his relatives;
(v) right of the husband to take the children, provided that he pays *aruok* cattle to the relatives of his divorced wife.

Most of these effects do not require discussion. Besides, they have already been mentioned in the discussion of other subjects above. We do not therefore need to discuss all the effects of *puokē-ruāi* here. We will only select two issues for discussion because of their significance and because they are inter-related. They are: (1) the recovery of bride-wealth and (2) the right to take the children. These are the areas in which there is much judicial contest.

'In the case of divorce, the trouble is usually about the custody of the children or the return of cattle, in a sense two aspects of the same matter... The important thing to bear in mind is that no arrangement can be made with regard to the children without reference to the question of *Thakha* (bride-wealth) and vice versa'.[49]

The two problems which may face a court applying the Venda Law

---

[48] *Readings in African Law*, Vol. II, Frank Cass, London, 1970, p.243.
[49] J. J. Van Warmelo, W. M. D. Bhophi, *Venda Law* in *Readings in African Law*, Vol. II, Frank Cass, London, 1970, p.243.

equally face a court which applies the Dinka Law. There is a similarity in the general principles; differences exist only in details.[50]

Among the Dinka, the general rule is that, in the event of *puokē-ruāi*, the husband, and his kinsmen who contributed cows to the marriage, are entitled to recover the cattle they had paid as bride-wealth (equally, of course, the bride's relatives are entitled to recover the *arueth* cattle they had paid to the husband and his kinsmen plus other rights which may be due to them). The second general rule is that the father (husband who has just been divorced) is entitled or has the right to have all the children of the marriage which has just been terminated. But the right to take the children is qualified by another rule which stipulates that the father of the children is entitled to take them when *puokē-ruāi* has been declared, provided that he has paid *aruok* cattle to the relatives of the divorced woman. This means that the father's right to take the children after *puokē-ruāi* lies in abeyance if he has not paid *aruok* cattle, which is five cows for each child, or ten cows if the father failed or delayed to pay the *aruok* cattle to the children's maternal uncles until they became mature. In section 10 of the General Explanations and Definitions of the legal terms (in the Code of Dinka Law – Part II of the Act)[51], it is stated that:

> '... when divorce or dissolution of marriage has taken place between a man and a woman, the relatives of the woman whose marriage has been dissolved have the *power* to retain or take the children into their custody. If the father intends to obtain his child or children, he shall pay to the ... woman's relatives a specific number of cows (i.e. 5) for each child.... This payment of cattle for the redemption of children by the father is called *Aruok*.'

We need to explain the significance in the choice of the words 'right' and 'power' in connection with the children after *puokē-ruāi*. These words fall within the category of legal concepts which are always difficult to define correctly or to distinguish from each other. Over centuries jurists have devoted a great deal of attention to the study of these concepts and have made many attempts to determine what each concept really means and how it can be distinguished from other

---

[50] 'The children always belong to the father but the amount of bride-wealth which has to be returned is reduced by five head of cattle for each living child and two head of cattle for each child which has died.' (H. Cory on *Sukuna Law*). This rule is the same as the Dinka rule which entitles the father to have the children and the maternal uncles to receive *aruok* cattle. But the difference is in the payment of *aruok* cattle for the dead children. Dinka Law does not consider the dead children.

[51] Part II of the Restatement of Bhar el Ghazel Region Customary Law Act, 1984.

similar concepts. Despite all these attempts there is no consensus of opinion yet. In practice, however, the practitioner must use each concept in a given situation to convey a specific intention or serve a specific purpose and leave the jurisprudential analysis of the concept in question to the jurists to determine what it actually means or should mean. Practitioners may often benefit from the juristic analysis except where the theory or analysis does not accord with practice or reality. We will therefore seek the assistance of juristic opinion on the distinction drawn between 'right' and 'power'.

> 'On the face of it, the distinction is obvious: a right is always a sign that some other person is required to conform to a pattern of conduct, a power is the *ability* to produce a certain result.'[52]

This distinction requires an illustration to make it clearer. The *right*, for example, to make a will can be dissected into a privilege to make a will (there is another privilege to make a will), *rights* against other people not to be prevented from making one, and *powers* in the sense of ability to alter the legal conditions of persons specified in the will.

Two jurists, Hohfell and Dr G. L. Williams (among others) tried to express these concepts in other ways. For example, where there is a right vested in someone, there is a corresponding duty imposed on another: that is, 'right' is correlative of 'duty'. At the same time, 'power' is correlative of 'liability'. Another alternative expression is that where there is a 'right' vested in one person, the opposite of this is 'no right'. These are some of the attempts made by the jurists to explain what 'power' or 'right' means. Still it is not easy for the layman to grasp these distinctions.

Another authority defines 'power' as

> 'The ability conferred on a person by law to determine, by his own will directed to that end, the legal relations of himself or others (Salmond). A power is the converse of disability. It differs from a right in that there are no accompanying duties. Powers are public, i.e., when vested by the state in its agent or employee or private when conferred by one person on another . . .'[53]

Further, the same authority defines 'right' as

---

[52] R. W. M. Dias, *Jurisprudence,* 2nd ed., Butterworths, London, 1964, p.237.
[53] *Osborn's Concise Law Dictionary,* 6th edition, by John Burke, p.258.

'An interest recognised and protected by the law, respect for which is a duty, and disregard of which is a wrong (Salmond)... A right involves (1) a person invested with the right, or entitled; (2) a person or persons on whom that right imposes a correlative duty or obligation; (3) an act or forbearance which is the subject matter of the right...'

It is essential to devote time and space to the discussion of these two concepts to enable one to ascertain what it means to say that 'the father has a *right* to have the children and the maternal uncles have the *power* to retain the control over the children when *puokē-ruāi* takes place.' How can these two terms be reconciled? How can the father exercise his right over the children when the maternal uncles have the power to prevent him from taking the children? May it also be said that the use of the term 'power' in the Act is wrong and that it is correct to say that what is vested in the maternal uncles is a right, and consequently, this logically leads to the conclusion that both parties have concurrent rights over the children?

In the juristic analysis, if the father is vested with the right to have the children, it alternatively means that 'duty', which is a jural correlative of right, is vested in the maternal uncles. Likewise, the vesting of 'right' in the father means 'no right' is vested in the maternal uncles, who are under *duty* or obligation (without any conditions) to deliver the children to their father. If they (i.e. the maternal uncles) fail or neglect or refuse to hand over the children to their father, they commit a wrong for which some legal action may be taken against them. In other words, the father can claim and obtain his children even if he has not paid *aruok*. Further, if we still pursue the line of the juristic argument, where a right is vested in 'A' there is no power vested in 'B' who is supposed, by reason of the same right vested in 'A', to be under a duty. Again if, as it is provided in the Act, the maternal uncles have the power to retain the children if they do not receive *aruok* cattle, it conversely means that the father is under a disability. This further means that the father who is under a disability cannot be expected to claim rights over the children, that is, he cannot be under a disability while at the same time he has a right against the person vested with the power over the same subject matter.

These concepts can be reconciled. It is a fact that the father has a right to have the children according to the law. At the same time the maternal uncles of the children have a right to receive *aruok* cattle for each child when divorce takes place, before the children are taken by their father. Even if the children are already given to the father, their right of *aruok* cattle can be pursued and the sanction they can employ for the enforcement of their right is the taking of control over the children. It may be stated that there are *concurrent interests connected with* the children. But there are no *concurrent rights over* the children. There are concurrent rights which can constitute different causes of action. The existence of these concurrent rights means that there are jural correlative duties imposed on each side. The father has a right over the children but this right, as was mentioned before, lies in abeyance till he discharges the duty which he owes to the children's maternal uncles. At the same time, if the father has discharged his duty by paying the required number of *aruok* cattle, his right ceases to remain in abeyance and it automatically raises a correlative duty on the children's maternal uncles to deliver the children to him.

To express it another way, the father has a right over his children and the maternal uncles do not have a right to them but a right to obtain *aruok* cattle in relation to the children. In other words, these rights do not directly conflict. One is a right of the father over children. The other is a right of the maternal uncles over the *aruok* cattle in relation to the children. The law only gives the maternal uncles a power which they can use as a sanction to compel the children's father to pay *aruok*. Hence, if the father fails to discharge his duty, the maternal uncles are entitled to exercise the 'power' to take the custody of the children. The exercise of this power correlatively puts the father under a liability or, in the opposite term, in a disability, and this prevents him from exercising his right to take the children. The liability or the disability is lifted if the father fully discharges his duty which correlates with the right of the children's maternal uncles.

In conclusion, the use of the terms 'right' of the father over the children and 'power' of the maternal uncles to take custody of the children is correct. Their usage does not diminish the interests of both sides at the time of divorce. To state it more definitively the father has a right over the children while the maternal uncles have a right to obtain *aruok* cattle from the father. In order to guarantee that the father pays *aruok* cattle, the maternal uncles are, by law, vested with the 'power', which puts the father in a disability that prevents him from exercising his right. In other words, the vesting of this power in the maternal uncles puts their duty which jurally correlates with the father's right to the children, in abeyance.

The analysis of these concepts may be illustrated by the case of *Angelina Gabriel* v. *Cyrillo Malou, PC/BGP/CS/12/76*. The Province Court, Wau, ordered divorce at the suit of the plaintiff. In the same suit the Court (which was applying the customary law) held that Cyrillo Malou was entitled to the custody of his daughter (i.e. a child of this marriage). But his right to take the child was not to be exercised till he had paid the *aruok* cattle. Meanwhile, the child was delivered to the mother. It was implicit from this decision that if the father, Cyrillo Malou, thereafter intended to exercise his right to recover the child, he had to pay *aruok* cattle. If he failed to pay *aruok* cattle he would lose his right to the child and the right to that child would be vested in the maternal uncles. In such a situation the interest of the maternal uncles becomes a right and no longer a power over the child.

This case clarifies what appears to be a confusion or a misunderstanding over the use of the concepts, namely, the 'right' of the father over the children and the 'power' of the maternal uncles over them. The power of the maternal uncles, as the case illustrates, is a sanction or a veto which compels the children's father to pay *aruok* cattle. The power disables the father from obtaining the children. However, the right of the maternal uncles relates to the *aruok* cattle and not to the children. The claim of *aruok* cattle and the claim of children, whether in exercise of right or power, can be subjects of different causes of action; hence there are no concurrent rights over the children.

3.7 The relation between the bride-wealth and the father's right to children

Let us now consider the relation between the payment of bride-wealth cattle and the right of the father to the children.

The payment of bride-wealth signifies that marriage has been legally concluded. The question of paternity over the children does not arise. The children of the union belong to their father since the inception of marriage. But while the bride-wealth has not been paid the marriage is vitiated or legally tainted. In such circumstances, the option lies with the maternal uncles. They have the liberty to take the woman and her children at any time. Their interest over the children in this case is not merely a power but a right. The father has no legal right over the children since he has not married their mother. 'Marriage' in this context is where formal agreement has been made by the relatives of the spouses and bride-wealth has been paid[54]. It is essentially the bride-wealth which legalises paternity over the children. But it must not be understood, as some writers tend to establish, that the bride-wealth legitimises the children. The term 'legitimation' or 'legitimization' in the context of other legal systems has legal notions which accompany it, and these are not part of our law.

The difference between the non-payment of bride-wealth and the

---

[54] The full payment of the agreed number or amount, except the part for which payment has been deferred, if any.

non-payment of *aruok* cattle after the grant of divorce of a marriage where bride-wealth has been paid is that in the former case, the father has no right over his children (as well as over the wife) from the inception of marriage. In the latter case, he has the paternity rights over his children from their birth. However, the exercise of his right over the children is rendered inoperative by the veto power of the maternal uncles when he recovers the whole bride-wealth and neglects to pay the *aruok*. In the case of a father who has not paid bride-wealth, the maternal uncles may choose to take the woman and her children and refuse to accept the offer of *aruok* cattle, or they may take the woman and allow the father to pay the *aruok* cattle if he intends to redeem the children. If this is done, then, the father will then enjoy the paternity right for the first time.

Sometimes the union may break down between the spouses before the woman's relatives start to exert their claims. In most cases the man separates from the woman and retains the children although he never married their mother. If this happens the maternal uncles of the children can claim them. The court will award them the children since the father has no rightful claim. If he offers to pay the *aruok* and this is accepted by the maternal uncles, he will be allowed to take the children, but only after the cattle have been received. Thus, in the case of *Mabor Adhel and Buoi Ajak* v. *Amon Mon, CS/4/76*, the defendant, Amon Mon, and Madam Atem Makoi, a relative of the plaintiffs, took each other as husband and wife, but no bride-wealth was paid and there was no involvement of the relatives of the couple in the union. The spouses brought forth a child (a female). After a few years the union was repudiated by the spouses alone, but the defendant retained the child.

In this respect, the plaintiffs raised a civil suit against the defendant claiming *aruok* cattle. Alternatively, they entreated the court to deliver the child to them if the defendant was unable to pay the *aruok*. The court held that:

(a) since the defendent did not pay the bride-wealth, he never had any right of paternity over the child but the right was vested in the maternal uncles;
(b) alternatively, since the maternal uncles were willing to receive *aruok* the defendant was ordered to pay. Meanwhile, the maternal uncles were entitled to take the child until they received the cattle.

It has been stated before that the relatives of the woman have the option of breaking up the vitiated union and taking her and the children with them. Sometimes there may be social impediments which prevent her relatives from taking her together with the children. In such a situation, her relatives will abstain from interfering with their union but press for the payment of bride-wealth cattle. But while the man and woman still remain as husband and wife, and the maternal uncles of the children are unable to get bride-wealth because the children's father has no cattle to pay, the maternal uncles may suspend their right to claim cattle as bride-wealth[55] or *aruok*. If there are daughters or a daughter among the children, they will wait till she or they become mature and marry. If bride-wealth is paid in their marriage, the maternal uncles can exercise the right which had been suspended until that time. They will have two claims to raise simultaneously; first, they can claim a sufficient number of cattle equivalent to the number they would have obtained in the form of bride-wealth; second, they can claim a limited number of cows as a share which constitutes the entitlement of the maternal uncles in the marriage of their sister's daughter. When these claims are satisfied, the problems are solved.

3.8 All claims must always be settled in a divorce suit
When divorce is granted for a marriage in which the bride-wealth has been paid and of which there are children, there will be claims and counter-claims. In a Dinka court, it is always the practice to declare *puokē ruāi* and to adjust all other rights or claims and counter-claims arising out of the marriage, or as consequences of divorce, in a single suit. This saves time and avoids the inconvenience that might be caused by raising several suits. It is also economical since it is only the divorce fee which will be paid.

3.9 Procedure
Where a divorce suit is raised by either spouse, the court will first determine, after hearing all the necessary evidence, whether to declare divorce or not. If it decides to grant divorce, the first issue or cause of action is disposed of; the court will then move to the next issue which will be regarded as a second cause of action. This is the claim for the bride-wealth paid (i.e. the original cows and their offspring).

A great deal of evidence is always required to determine the number of cows which are alive and in possession of the in-laws or in possession of third parties to whom they had been transferred by the in-laws through various transactions. Those which died naturally through no

---

[55] While the woman's relatives suspend their right to the bride-wealth, they expressly or implicity extend recognition to the validity of the marriage.

fault of the in-laws or of third parties to whom they had been transferred will also be determined and excluded. These cows will be discounted from the claim except those which died through negligence or fault of somebody or those which were slaughtered. The husband and his kinsmen will be entitled to all the living cattle with their offspring, whether they are in the possession of the in-laws or in the possession of third parties.

In the latter case, the question of tracing (which will be discussed later in Chapter 4) will be involved. Where the cows cannot be traced for certain reasons or where a cow dies through negligence or fault of somebody, the husband and his kinsmen will be entitled to *damages*;[56] when the question of bride-wealth is disposed of, the court will move to a third issue, which is the question of a counter-claim raised by the relatives of the woman. Apart from other rights, the counter-claim always consists of two headings, namely (i) the recovery of the *arueth* cattle (with their offspring), which requires evidence as in the case of the claim for bride-wealth; and (ii) the recovery of *aruok* cattle for every child of the marriage which has just been brought to an end. But where the issue of *aruok* is not brought up as a counter-claim during the divorce, it may be the subject of a subsequent cause of action raised by the maternal uncles against the father of the children. After all, *puokē ruāi* and its various legal consequences, though they are usually disposed of in one suit, can be subjects of different causes of action. Further, there is no absolute uniformity in holding that the father takes his children only when he has fully paid the *aruok* cattle. He may be allowed by the court to have his children before he pays the *aruok* cattle; but this does not, of course, abrogate the right of the maternal uncles to sue for *aruok* after that or alternatively entreat the court to be allowed to exercise their power to take the children.

In the case of *Buol Yuol* v. *Irneo Dut, PC/BGP/CS/76*, a divorce suit was instituted before the Province Court of Bhar el Ghazal in 1976. The court passed a decree for divorce but did not order the payment of *aruok* cattle to the relatives of the divorced woman. Later, a relative of the woman (note: their relationship is not indicated) raised a civil suit before the same court for *aruok* cattle (since the issue of the return of the bride-wealth was not raised, the raising of *aruok* suit implies that bride-wealth cattle had been returned already). The court held that:

---

[56] If the husband or any of his kinsmen has any other claim apart from bride-wealth, it can be disposed of at the same time.

(a) The defendant was obliged to pay four cows and one bull as *aruok* (or the equivalent value of these cows in money assessed to be Ls.140.000 m/ms).
(b) alternatively, if the defendant failed to pay *aruok* cattle to the maternal uncles, the only child of the marriage, by the name of Dominic Irneo, must be delivered to the plaintiff.

When the number of *aruok* cattle and the *arueth* cattle which are proved are added together they are balanced against the number of bride-wealth cattle which have been proved and a set-off is made. The first point in the proceedings will be the order for delivery of the children to their father. After all this, the proceedings for *puoké ruāi* or divorce are deemed to have come to an end. What follows thereafter is the execution of these orders.

4. THE CUSTODY OF CHILDREN AND MAINTENANCE ORDERS

Among the legal consequences of *puoké ruāi* we find that, in many legal systems, the problems of the custody and maintenance of the children as well as their mother (before she is subsequently married) pose serious considerations for the courts. Some legal systems, for example, the patrilineal system, fix a period after which the father is entitled to take over the children from their mother. This imposes an obligation on the father to maintain his child or children while in the custody of their mother. Some legal systems also require that a man must maintain his divorced wife till she is subsequently married by another man, or until she is able to live independently through her own income.

Before we consider whether these legal consequences of divorce are phenomena of the Dinka Law, it is necessary to make a survey of some other legal systems. We will start with the English Legal System.

In an English court, the issue of the custody of the children is of prior consideration, even before a decree for divorce or separation or nullity of marriage is passed. An English court is entitled to make interim orders while the petition for divorce pends before it. For example, section 26(1) of the Matrimonial Causes Act, 1950, provides that:

'In any suit for judicial separation or for nullity or dissolution of marriage, the court may, at any time after the petition has been served and before its final decree, make interim orders with respect to the custody, maintenance and education of the children... and in suit for restitution of conjugal rights the court has power to make similar orders with respect to children of the petitioner and respondent.'[57]

Such orders as referred to above may be made to remain valid until the child reaches the age of 21. But at the age of 16 the child is free to leave his father's home and the latter can do nothing about it. The emphasis upon these orders is directed towards the welfare of the child and, for this reason, the custody of the child before attaining the age of 21 goes to the spouse who will fulfil these conditions.

'The court has to make orders for the custody, maintenance and education of children up to the age of 21 years, though it is not usual to make an order for custody of a child who has reached 16 years... if a child of 16 is minded to leave its father's home, the father cannot reclaim it by *habeas corpus*, or otherwise... the paramount consideration of the court in exercising its discretion is not punishment of a guilty spouse, but the children's welfare, against which a father's common law right to their custody does not prevail.'[58]

Section 1 of the Guardianship of Infants Act, 1925 still stresses the welfare of the child as being more important than the claim of either spouse. The section provides that:

'where in any proceeedings before any court (whether or not a court within the meaning of the Guardianship of Infants Act, 1886) the custody or upbringing of an infant is in question, the court in deciding that question, shall regard the welfare of the infant as the first and paramount consideration and shall not take into consideration whether from any other point of view the claim of the father, or any right at common law possessed by the father, in respect of such custody or upbringing is superior to that of the mother or the claim of the mother is superior to that of the father.'

The English Law does not only make provisions for children's maintenance but it also provides for wives who are divorced or where separation or nullity of marriage is being decreed. Section 19(2) of the Matrimonial Causes Act, 1950, states that:

---

[57] *Rayden on Divorce*, 7th edition, Butterworths, London, 1942, p.387.
[58] Ibid., p.534.

'On any decree for divorce or nullity of marriage the court may... order the husband to secure, to its satisfaction, to the wife such gross or such annual sum of money for any term not exceeding her life, as it shall deem reasonable, having regard to her fortune (if any), to the ability of the husband and to the conduct of the parties.'

In some other legal systems, though the right of the father to have the children is recognised, a certain specified period may pass before the father is allowed to exercise his right to take the children from their mother. Islamic Law contains provisions relating to the ages for which the children must remain in the mother's care before they are taken by the father. But it should not be understood that Islamic Law is a uniform system with uniform provisions. There are various sects or schools of thought which have developed different rules over certain specific aspects of the family law. Modern reforms in different Islamic countries have led to the development of rules differing from the traditional principles. With regard to the custody of children, Syria, for example, has made a provision in its family law which has similar effects to those envisaged by the English Law. Article 145 of the Syrian Law of Personal Status provides:

'If a wife becomes disobedient and her children are more than five years of age, the *Gadi* may place them with whichever of the spouses he sees fit, provided that he has regard to the welfare of the children in the light of the circumstances of the case.'[59]

In the Sudan, the Judicial Circular No. 34 (1933) which is derived from the Hanafi school of thought, regulates the custody of children. It provides that:

'a daughter (after divorce between the parents) remains in her mother's custody till she reaches 9 years and a boy till he reaches 7 years. But if their welfare cannot be guaranteed in the mother's care, the father takes them soon after they are weaned. Further, if the divorced wife is subsequently married by another man, the father takes his children immediately.'

Sharia Law gives greater attention to children's welfare.

In so far as the question of custody and maintenance of the children as well as maintenance of the wife or wives is concerned, there is a

---

[59] Norman Anderson, *The Law Reform in the Muslim World*, first published in (1960) SLJR under the title: *The Modernization of Islamic Law in Sudan*, p.68.

marked difference between African legal systems and other legal systems, such as the English or Western systems. Sharia Law too is markedly different from African legal systems on these matters.

Western societies have become more cosmopolitan and have thereby lost the characteristics of the original societies. Where family and kinship ties remain very strong, most, if not all, of the African communities prefer to give primacy to the maintenance of strong family or social bonds over economic interests. Through centuries of economic and technological development, Europeans have almost lost sight of the importance of social bonds. They pay more attention to economic interests and consequently human relations have become less significant, and the family, in the Western sense, has become smaller and smaller. Because of this fundamental break-down of social or family bonds in Western societies, more social and economic hardships would befall children and divorced wives, unless the law intervened to provide remedies.

Although there is no complete uniformity of legal rules among African societies, it has to be stated, in general terms, that the question of the custody of the children and their maintenance as well as the maintenance of the wife are not serious considerations for the courts. In some societies they do not even arise; in others, the maintenance of the children is the issue that may arise.

African societies differ from Western societies as far as social relations are conserned.[60] Because of the strength of social and family ties among African societies, the concern about the welfare of a child, which demands legal protection in Western societies, does not arise at all. The general rule (in almost all African legal systems, including Dinka Law) is that as soon as the court declares divorce, the father, provided he has fulfilled the obligation of paying *aruok* cattle, is entitled to take all his children at once. There is no provision that the children remain in the custody of their mother till they reach a certain age. The exception is in the case of a suckling.

In fact, a few writers have devoted some attention to the discussion of these two issues in African law. Perhaps it is the insignificance of these issues in African societies which deters many writers from discussing them at length. J. J. Van Warmelo and W. M. D. Plophi on *Venda Law* are among the few writers who paid some attention to this subject. They wrote:

'If a divorced woman has too small children to be taken from her,

---

[60] Owing to the ever increasing economic domination of the daily lives of people in the West (or where people have lost the characteristic features of their original society), the strength of social or family relations is correspondingly diminished.

not all *thakha* (bride-wealth) is returned. For every child that stays with the mother the *thakha* is reduced by one cow that is termed the 'beast' of the child; provided he has fulfilled the obligation of paying *aruok* cattle, he is entitled to take all his children at once. There is no provision that the children remain in the custody of their mother till they reach a certain age. The exception is in the case of a suckling child. There is no doubt that the children will always be well-taken care of by their father. If they are very young or very small there are members of his family who will take the necessary care of them. The question of the maintenance of a divorced wife by her former husband does not also arise because she immediately becomes a member of her family till she is subsequently married. It would even be an insult to her and to her family if she continues to be maintained by her former husband.'[61]

Here, there is a slight difference, especially in details, between Venda Law and Dinka Law. In the case of the custody of children, Venda Law stresses the father's right to retain his children after divorce. One of the reasons given is '... The fear that after all another man's children cannot be kept, and for this reason even if all the *thakha* has been repaid it is now common for the father to retain custody...' But in Dinka Law as in Sukuna Law,[62] 'An infant in arms remains with the mother until it is weaned and no maintenance can be demanded by the maternal family when the father comes to fetch his child.' However, there is a similarity between Venda Law and Dinka Law in that the two laws do not make provisions for the maintenance of divorced wives. The maintenance of a divorced wife is the responsibility of her relatives and not her husband and his relatives.

We may conclude the discussion of these issues with the following statement: the nature or the strength of family or social relations with the distinctive features or characteristics of African societies, does not allow any significance to be given to the question of maintenance and custody of children after divorce, because their welfare is never in dispute.

5. DISTRIBUTION OF FAMILY PROPERTY AFTER DIVORCE

The distribution of family property as a consequence of divorce is a subject of minor importance in African societies. For this reason it has

---

[61] *Readings in African Law*, Vol. II, Frank Cass, London, 1970, p.253.
[62] H. Cory on *Sukuna and Custom*, in *Readings in African Law*, Vol. II, Frank Cass, London, 1970, p.254. The legal position of Sukuna Law is exactly the same as Dinka Law.

not attracted the attention of many writers on African legal systems. Among the Dinka, the nature of property which concerns the law consists of (i) bride-wealth property; (ii) *Arueth* (reverse payment); (iii) *Aruok-cattle* (cattle for the redemption of children) and some other collateral benefits which may have passed between the two sides of the marriage; for example, *dan wēr-piu* (i.e. a heifer paid by bride-relatives to her husband before he can eat at his in-laws' hospitality), and so forth. Once the court has disposed of these rights, its work is completed.

But some African legal systems have a few provisions for the distribution of family property between a divorced couple. According to H. Cory, on the Sukuna Custom,

> 'A wife must be allowed to retain possession of her private property, that is property she brought with her from her father's house, inherited property, clothing, gifts from her husband and gifts from the members of her own and her husband's family; then property acquired by the wife through her skill.[63]

According to Venda Law:

'When a man and his wife are divorced, the property in their household is divided according to whether it is to stay or to be taken away by its respective owner. Everything belonging to the husband is put into his own category, no matter what class of goods or property it belongs to, because it remains his property in all circumstances. The wife has no claim even to the smallest part thereof. The wife's property (i.e. what is ordinarily considered to be hers when married) falls into four categories:

1. what she was given by her husband and relatives;
2. what she acquired by her own efforts, but belongs to her husband nevertheless;
3. what she was given by her own relatives and
4. what she acquired by her efforts and belongs to her entirely.[64]

As far as the Dinka are concerned, the most important movable property consists of livestock. Livestock is always under the dominion of the husband or a product of his effort. But there are a few instances where a married woman acquires livestock through her own indepen-

---

[63] *Readings in African Law*, Vol. II, Frank Cass, London, 1970, p.254.
[64] J. J. Warmelo and W. M. D. Plophi, on *Venda Law*, in *Readings in African Law*, Vol. II, Frank Cass, London, 1970, p.256.

dent efforts. If this can be definitely proved, she will be entitled to take it when she is divorced. She can be allowed to take her ornaments and some utensils, if she wants. But these types of property, namely, the utensils and ornaments do not really call for litigation. These are domestic arrangements which can be settled at home (or out of court) because they are regarded as subjects of minor importance. But certain ornaments, for example, *guēn-jāng* (previously referred to) and *tung-akôôn* (carved elephant tusk) must be taken by the husband unless the wife brought them from her relatives into the marriage. There is no legal dispute or claim which a woman can raise over the ownership of the family home. If the divorced wife brought anything from her relatives or got it through other sources which are not connected with her husband she may also take it with her.

6. JURISDICTION AND CHOICE OF LAW IN DIVORCE CASES OR DISPUTES ARISING OUT OF MIXED MARRIAGES

The preceding pages dealt with marriages and the divorce law as administered among parties whose personal law is the Dinka Customary Law.

Where all the parties to a marriage dispute or divorce case are the Dinka of Bhar el Ghazal Region, the question of jurisdiction or choice of law does not arise. The problem arises where the parties have different customs or personal laws.[65] The question is whether a Dinka court has the power to assume jurisdiction and to apply *lex fori* (Dinka Customary Law) where one party to divorce proceedings has a different personal law. The problem requires discussion under separate headings.

6.1 Cases arising out of marriage or divorce between the Dinka and members of other tribes

Professor C. d'Oliver Farran, author of *The Matrimonial Laws of the Sudan*, who is the only writer on the subject of marriage and divorce in Southern Sudan, suggests that the law which governs marriage where the spouses have different personal laws is the personal law of the husband. But if the parties have chosen a legal system to govern the marriage at the time of the marriage agreement, that law should apply. He also suggests the splitting up of the different aspects of

---

[65] Custom or customary law and personal law are synonymously used, see footnote to page 8 for the relationship between custom, personal law and church law.

marriage into those to be governed by the personal law of the husband and those to be governed by the personal law of the wife.

Of course, these suggestions are inspired by his knowledge of private international law, and the importation of these rules to regulate mixed marriages between indigenous Sudanese is inconceivable. The rules of private international conflict of laws which govern the question of marriage and divorce are unknown to any tribal community in the Southern Sudan and their importation cannot be accepted.

Marriage and divorce in customary law are governed by a single legal system which is indicated by the stated intention of the parties at the time of the marriage agreement. The terms of the marriage contract are always formulated by the relatives of the girl or the woman according to their customary law. Before the re-division of the Southern Sudan, many Dinka officials in Juba married Bari girls. Such marriages were always conducted according to Bari customary law. The application of the personal law of the woman to govern the marriage or its consequences and divorce cases does not apply only in the cases of the Bari women or girls, but is true of many, if not all, the tribes in the Southern Sudan. This fact is also confirmed by section 83(2) and (3) of the Re-statement of Bhar el Ghazal Region Customary Law Act, 1984, Part 3 (i.e. the Code of Luo Customary Law). It is also supported by section 7(b) of the same Act (i.e. the Code of Dinka Customary Law). It may therefore be stated as a general rule that according to the customary laws in Southern Sudan, it is the personal law of the woman or girl which governs marriage, its consequences and the divorce. Perhaps there is an exception to this rule, but this is not yet apparent.

If the bridegroom and his relatives do not accept the terms offered by the girl's relatives according to their customary law, they are free to withdraw from the marriage negotiations. But as it is the man who proposes to marry a girl or a woman, he cannot dictate the terms of the marriage according to his personal law to her relatives. He must either submit to the application of the personal law of the girl or withdraw. When divorce takes place, it is the same law which governs the marriage and its consequences that governs the divorce, that is, it is the same law which determines the rights accruing from the marriage that can properly determine the rights claimed by the parties at the time of divorce.

Where the husband seeks divorce before his own court, he is usually referred to the court which applies the personal law of his wife. During the Wanh-alel Conference, which resulted in the codification of the Dinka Customary Law in 1975, the Dinka chiefs and the chiefs from other tribes emphasised that this was the correct procedure. This practice has been adopted by many Chiefs' Courts under my jurisdiction in Wau, Rumbek and other places. Sometimes the local courts may commit irregularities. A court may assume jurisdiction and apply the personal law of the husband instead of the personal law of the wife in a divorce case, but this is not, of course the accepted practice. Sometimes the court in the husband's tribal area may assume jurisdiction in a divorce case, but will apply the personal law of the wife. Sometimes a husband may seek a grant of divorce in the court of his tribal area if he thinks that this may be more advantageous to him. But, unless the relatives of his wife submit to the jurisdiction of this court, they are entitled to refuse and can, with the backing of their own court, resist the execution of any decree that might be passed. This compels the husband to seek divorce in the tribal court of his wife or a court which has common jurisdiction. In short, it is the personal law of the wife which governs the marriage and divorce. It is also the court of her tribal area which has jurisdiction in divorce cases. But as stated before, the husband's tribal court may assume the jurisdiction, provided it applies the personal law of the woman.

6.2 Divorce cases or disputes arising out of marriages among the Dinka Christians

Marriages among the Dinka Christians as well as among the Christian members of other tribes in the Southern Sudan seem to take a dual nature. The marriage is first conducted according to custom and, after it has been brought into existence in the eyes of the customary law, the parties celebrate in church. During the celebration in the church, the couple undertake certain commitments or promises according to the Christian faith. In marriages of this nature, the question which arises is: what law must govern the marriage, its consequences and divorce? Secondly, which court has the jurisdiction when a dispute arises out of this marriage, or when one of the parties calls for divorce? The Chiefs' Courts always assume the jurisdiction in such cases and apply the customary law. The question is whether these courts rightly assume jurisdiction and whether the application of customary law in these cases is correct. According to Professor Farran, the Chiefs' Court has no jurisdiction in such cases.[66] He argues that jurisdiction belongs to the former Civil High Court (presently the Province Court), and the law applicable is the English Common Law

---

[66] C. d'Olivier Farren, *Matrimonial Laws of the Sudan*, Butterworths, London, 1963, pp.258-271.

if the parties are Roman Catholic, or a mixture of English Law and the non-Mohamedan Marriage Act, 1926. In support of his argument, he cites judicial authorities from Rhodesia (now Zimbabwe) and other parts of Africa, especially the decisions of judges from South Africa who were explicitly contemptuous of the customary laws of the African people. He also cited two judicial decisions in the Sudan which were made by English judges.

The two judicial decisions are in *Bamboulis*[67] and *Farida Fuad Sameer*.[68] The parties in both cases were non-Sudanese domiciled in the Sudan. These judicial decisions do not at all cover the cases of divorce between indigenous Sudanese Christians who have their own tribal customary law. The decision in *Bamboulis* v. *Bamboulis* has been heavily criticised in subsequent cases. Its authority has always been rejected by the Court of Appeal. The case of *Farida Fuad Sameer*, on which Professor Farren relies, did not decide that jurisdiction in cases of divorce between Sudanese Christians belonged to the former Civil High Court. The problem before the Court was whether jurisdiction belonged to the Sharia Court or the Civil Court because one party was a Muslim convert although he was a Christian at the time of the marriage. The Court held that the Sharia Court had no jurisdiction and that this belonged to the Civil Court. These cases in fact do not support the view advocated by Professor Farran. Also, the foreign judicial decisions he cited, apart from being biased, have no authority in the Sudan. Some of these decisions were based on the supposition that a Christian who marries in the Church is civilised, but if he sues his wife for divorce before a tribal court which applies the customary law, he reverts to primitivity. These judges must be taken to have been acting under the influence of racial hatred and prejudice. Therefore, it is a gross mistake to cite these cases as authorities which should govern cases of divorce in Southern Sudan.

Further, section 4 of the Non-Mohamedan Marriage Act, 1926 specifically shows that its provisions do not extend to marriages conducted according to the customary law. Also against Farran's view are the judicial warrants which have been issued, from time to time, by the Chief Justice of the Sudan, giving the Chiefs' Courts jurisdiction in such cases. Besides the judicial warrants, a recent decision of the Court of Appeal rejected the view put forward by Farren. This decision is found in the case of *Gibril Barbare* v. *Reen Abdel Massih Khalil (1966) SLJR 53*. Both parties in the case were Sudanese. The appellant was a Dinka. They were Christians and were married in

---

[67] (1954) Cases in the Court of Appeal and High Court, p.76.
[68] (1957) SLJR 21.

Church. The respondents sued the appellant on the issue of maintenance of the children. The case was tried by a Province Judge. The Court awarded an amount of money to the (plaintiffs) respondents for the maintenance of the children. The defendant (appellant) appealed to the Court of Appeal for revision. The Province Judge did not state the law on which he based his decision. Relying on the decision in *Bamboulis* v. *Bamboulis*,[69] the appellant's advocate demanded the application of the English Law. In rejecting this argument, the Court of Appeal held that:

'If it was rightly or wrongly ruled in *Bamboulis* v *Bamboulis*, that was a case of divorce between non-Sudanese domiciled in the Sudan where the court enunciated the rule that divorce is not one of the consequences of marriage but a relief from these consequences. We cannot apply it in a case of this (a) between Sudanese to whom their personal law (which is their custom) must apply and (b) of maintenance which is one of the consequences of marriage.'

The case was referred back to the Province Court with a directive to determine the appropriate customary law applicable to the dispute.

It is clear from this decision that the appropriate law to govern divorce cases or other disputes arising out of marriages between Sudanese Christians is the customary law, and not the English Law or a mixture of English Law and the Non-Mohamedan Marriage Act 1926. There is nothing to prevent a Chiefs' Court from assuming the jurisdiction in these cases. Major Wylds, once a District Commissioner of Yambio district, who rightly supported the assumption of jurisdiction by Chiefs' Courts and the application of customary law in divorce cases between Christians married in Church, was unjustly criticised by Farran in very severe terms.

6.3 Divorce cases in marriages between non-Muslim Dinka girls or women and Muslim men

The most controversial problem of conflict of laws is presented by cases of divorce or marriage between non-Muslim Dinka girls or women and Muslim men. The conflict cannot be solved merely by converting the girl or woman to Islam, because she does not have independent authority to give consent in her marriage to the exclusion of her parents, brothers, sisters and uncles or cousins. Her consent is part of the general consent of the whole family and other close

---

[69] (1957) SLJR 21.

relatives. Even where the Muslim man pays the bride-wealth and satisfies all other necessary conditions required by custom at the time of the marriage contract, any attempt on the part of the girl to enter subsequently into the Islamic form of marriage cannot be recognised by the customary law. Although this marriage is valid in the eyes of Sharia Law, Dinka Law will insist on the validity of the original form but deny that of the subsequent form entered into according to Islam.[70] The rights which are claimed by the relatives of the woman at the time of divorce are as important as those achieved through the marriage and for this reason, the Dinka parties will insist on the application of the customary law to govern the marriage throughout and to apply also at the time of divorce. The law which governs the marriage also governs the divorce. On the other hand, the Muslim would prefer the marriage to be conducted in a form acceptable to Islam, otherwise no legal benefits will accrue from it. For example, the children, who are deemed to be illegitimate, will be deprived of the right of inheritance, unless the woman is a Muslim or a Kittabiya.[71]

Islamic Law does not embody any rules of conflict for the solution of these problems. Dinka Law requires the personal law of the woman to govern the marriage and the divorce. Sharia Law, on the other hand, requires the marriage, its consequences and the divorce to be governed by it, provided the acceptable Islamic form was entered into.[72] The State law does not, however, afford any help either. The position is that the judges of the lower courts of the State, which are always confronted with this kind of issue, often act according to their allegiance to a particular legal system. It is unfortunate that appeals from these types of cases have not yet been decided by the Court of Appeal or the Supreme Court. This would have provided a test for senior judges of these courts as to whether to prefer one legal system to the exclusion of the other, according to their allegiance to the said system, in the absence of rules of conflict on the issue. The rules of private international conflict of laws cannot, however, serve any

---

[70] It has already been mentioned that it has been provided by section 7(a) of the Restatement of Bhar el Ghazal Region Customary Law Act, 1984, that the law applies to persons who take Dinka girls or women in marriage.

[71] Similarly, no legal rights accrue according to Dinka Law, if a girl or woman enters into an Islamic form of marriage without the consent of her parents, unless it is ratified by them.

[72] Sharia judges have never hesitated to assume jurisdiction and to apply Islamic Law even in the circumstances where one party to the marriage is a non-Muslim. Under S.38 of the former Civil Justice Ordinance, 1929, the Sharia Court had no jurisdiction in such a case, unless the parties consented, in writing, to the jurisdiction of the Sharia Court.

useful purpose here, since it is less likely that they will be accepted by the proponents of these legal systems.

The cases which frequently appear before the lower courts are those in which disputes arise out of marriages between Muslim men and non-Muslim women (who are usually illiterate), and where the Islamic form is used without the consent of the woman's relatives.[73] Such marriages have been regarded by Muslims as valid in the eyes of Islamic Law, but the Dinka do not treat them as valid according to customary law.

Where a dispute arises out of such a marriage and the woman's relatives come afterwards to claim bride-wealth so that they may thereafter affirm the union as a legal marriage, they are regarded as strangers to the Islamic marriage by the Muslim man. If they go to the Sharia Court to claim their rights or alternatively raise a claim to take the woman and her children, and their rights are denied, they will be turned down on the grounds that they have no *locaus standi* before this type of court. If they choose to go to a civil court, the Muslim man will refuse to submit to the jurisdiction of the court. The case of *Joseph Athian Deng and his sister Maria Deng* is one of the cases which illustrates this point. Maria Deng was married by a Muslim policeman from the Northern Sudan without the consent of her relatives. Maria Deng, who is illiterate, was made to sign a document with her thumb. Her parents learned afterwards that she was married and Joseph Athian, her brother, came on behalf of other relatives to make a claim for bride-wealth as a pre-condition for the affirmation of the marriage. At this time, Maria Deng had been 'divorced' by her husband before the Sharia Court, which at the same time passed an order for the delivery of the children to their father. As it was unknown to Sharia Law, no order was passed by the judge for the payment of *aruok* cattle for the children as required by Dinka Law. Consequently, Maria refused to deliver the children to their father as ordered.

When her brother, Joseph Athian, arrived, he raised a claim for the payment of *aruok* cattle before the Sharia Court but he was turned down, since he was not a party to the *Gasima* or written document of the Islamic form of marriage. He tried to pursue his case through the civil court. The civil court admitted the case but the Muslim party

---

[73] In the majority of these cases, the woman being married does not understand the contents of the written contractual document and their legal consequences. Sometimes the Islamic form of marriage is entered into despite the fact that the woman being married has not been converted to Islam. The case of Maria Deng is an example. She was a Christian.

refused to submit to the jurisdiction of this court. The Sharia judge, however, protested by writing to the Grand Kadi with a copy to the Chief Justice, on the grounds that the civil court had no jurisdiction to entertain the case since the marriage was conducted according to Islamic Law, despite the fact that the woman was not in fact converted to Islam. Even if the Sharia Court had jurisdiction, there was no question of *res judicate* as was alleged by the Sharia judge, because the issue raised in the civil court was an entirely different cause of action. But since the Muslim party could not legally be compelled to appear before the civil court, the matter had to be referred to the Chief Justice and the Grand Kadi at their request. However, as there is no law on the point, the Chief Justice had to refer the matter to a special committee for study and to make recommendations, which it was thought might lead to a form of legislation or the making of a judicial circular directing how the conflicts on such cases should be resolved. Some other cases related to the question of jurisdiction and the conflict of laws were subsequently referred to the Chief Justice and were again referred to the same committee for study. But the committee never produced anything to remedy the gap; or if it made recommendations at all, they have never influenced any form of legislation on the promulgation of a judicial circular in this field.

The conflict between the rules of Customary Law and Sharia Law has been felt since the time of the Anglo-Egyptian administration. In 1954, the District Commissioners of Western Nuer (Bentiu) and of Yirol, one of the Dinka districts in the former Bhar el Ghazal Province, who were confronted with this conflict of laws and jurisdicition over the cases of divorce and custody of children, had to consult McDowell, J., the then justice of the High Court for the Southern Circuit, for directives. One of the cases at Yirol was between a Dinka non-Muslim woman and a Muslim driver. It was a case of divorce and custody of children before a Chiefs' Court. The Muslim first submitted to the jurisdiction of this court. The court granted divorce and postponed the delivery of the children to the Muslim driver, since they were very young. All the parties felt satisfied with the judgement. But the next day, the Muslim party, acting on the advice of his friends in the market, returned to the court and argued that, according to the Dinka Customary Law, he would be entitled to get the custody of the children at once, since he had paid *aruok*. The court could not go back on their previous decision. The man, joined by Hassan El Rehah, the head of the Muslim community in the market, petitioned the District Commissioner, Mr Withers. They abandoned their argument based on the Dinka Customary Law. They maintained that it was an Islamic marriage and that they were not bound by the decision of the Chiefs'

The Family Law

Court based on the Customary Law. Relying on section 38 of the previous Civil Justice Ordinance 1929, Mr Withers held that they were bound by the decision of the Chiefs' Court since they had submitted to it before. But they threatened to go to Sharia Kadi. Mr Withers referred the matter to McDowell, J., in Juba for directives. McDowell, J., directed that:

> 'If the girl was a professing Moslem when she went through a Moslem form of marriage, with a Moslem man, then the marriage, divorce, and rights to the children are governed by Sharia Law. As the parties consented to their case being heard by the Town Court, the Court had jurisdiction (s.38 CJO). The man cannot now turn round and say that he does not like the jurisdiction of the Town Court and therefore does not recognise its jurisdiction. If at a later date the man applies for the custody of the children that is another matter; he can then apply before the Sharia Kadi but until that happens the decision of the Town Court stands.'

As cases of jurisdiction and conflict of laws over divorce increased, McDowell, J., circulated a note directing how they ought to be disposed of by the District Commissioners. The note directed as follows:

1. If at any stage of the relationship between a Nuer/Dinka[74] girl and a Mohamedan (she being over the age of consent and if a minor her parent, or guardian with full knowledge consenting) a form, no matter how brief, of marriage according to Mohamedan religion is gone through, all the subsequent transactions or consequences are liable to be interpreted according to the Sharia Law.
2. But if the Nuer/Dinka wish the consequences of marriage to be governed by customary law and to retain jurisdiction of the Chiefs' Court, no Mohamedan form of marriage shall be entered into.

According to Professor Farran[75] a Muslim man, who has acquired domicile in the Sudan, may marry a pagan woman according to the customs. This marriage is irregular according to Islam, until the

---

[74] This directive did not necessarily apply to the Nuer and the Dinka cases only. It was by nature of general application all over the South where marriages were conducted with Muslim men.
[75] *The Matrimonial Laws of the Sudan*, (1957) SLJR, p.196.

woman is converted to Islam, in which case the marriage is retrospectively transformed into an Islamic form and is solely governed by the Sharia Law. But if the woman remains a pagan, the marriage is solely governed by the customary law. The essential points from McDowell, J's directive and Professor Farran's views can be summarised as follows: Firstly, where a Muslim man marries a non-Muslim girl according to the customary law, the Chiefs' Court has jurisdiction and the customary law governs the consequences of the marriage and divorce. Secondly, the marriage is retrospectively transformed into Islamic, if the woman is subsequently converted to Islam at any stage of the relationship. According to McDowell, J., the consent of the girl, if she is of the age of consent, to the Islamic form of marriage is material. But if she is under the age of consent, her parent or guardian's consent becomes necessary. Thirdly, if the parent or guardian of the girl insists on retaining authority over her, no form of Islamic marriage shall be entered into and the jurisdiction of the Chiefs' Court will prevail. Customary law will govern the marriage and the divorce. Finally, according to Farran, if the woman, and not the man, is a Muslim, the Sharia Court will have no jurisdiction. The jurisdiction belongs to the Chiefs' Court and the customary law will apply. This view is inspired by his knowledge of private international law, but it does not prevail in the customary law of any tribe which Professor Farran had in mind.

It is worth mentioning that attempts made by McDowell, J., and Professor Farran to find a compromise between the two legal systems whereby Muslims and non-Muslims can solve legal disputes arising out of marriages and cases of divorce, cannot pass without appreciation. However, there would be many shortcomings still prevailing even if the Sudanese courts were today following their views. For example, if a marriage which has been originally conducted according to the customary law is retrospectively transformed into an Islamic form by a subsequent conversion of the woman, problems are created unless the subsequent introduction of the Islamic form receives the consent of all the legitimate parties to the marriage on the side of the girl. Such marriage is not valid, according to the Dinka custom, although it is valid according to Islam. The *Gasima*, which is the contractual document or evidence of an Islamic form of marriage, will only contain the names of the man and the woman as parties. The witnesses to the marriage contract must be Muslims. This form deprives the relatives of the woman of their rights as they are the legitimate parties to the marriage, according to their personal law. If they claim any rights arising out of the marriage, the Sharia Court will not give them audience. They may alternatively demand divorce if a dispute arises, and consequently claim the children if the *aruok* cattle are not paid to them, but still they will not be able to succeed in the Sharia Court. If they go to a Civil or Chiefs' Court, the Muslim party will refuse to submit to its jurisdiction. The case of *Joseph Athian Deng and his sister Maria Deng*, already referred to above, illustrates these difficulties.

If the man and his wife, who are not the only legitimate parties to the marriage, according to Dinka Law, are allowed by Islamic Law to introduce a new form of marriage which fundamentally alters the terms of the previous agreement, it means that a fresh marriage contract, which abrogates the previous agreement, has been introduced. What is the justification for allowing one party to introduce a form which fundamentally alters the terms of the previous agreement in his favour? The consent of the woman to the subsequent introduction of an Islamic form of marriage, which prejudices the rights of her relatives, does not validate such marriage, according to the customary law. Since her consent alone is not sufficient for the conclusion of a valid marriage, she cannot alone enter into a subsequent form of marriage, which will adversely affect the rights of her relatives at the time of divorce, or when any dispute arises out of the marriage. But the subsequent introduction of the Islamic form of marriage might be recognised by Dinka Law, if it were consented to by all the legitimate parties on the woman's side,[76] provided that such consent was preceded by a full explanation of all the terms and their legal consequences, and was properly understood by them. In this case it would be understood that the parties on both sides had agreed to make a fresh contract or to vary the terms of the previous contract. We would fully agree with McDowell, J., if he were to extend the consent for the subsequent introduction of the Islamic form of marriage to the relatives of the girl or the woman, whether or not she had reached the age of consent, since their consent is essential to the validity of marriage in Dinka Law.

As the situation now stands, it requires the State to intervene to find a fair solution. The directives which McDowell, J., issued to guide the District Commissioners only functioned at the time of British rule in the Sudan but were soon forgotten after Independence.

---

[76] The consent of her relatives to the subsequent introduction of the Islamic form of marriage may be construed as waiving their rightful claims where a dispute later arises. However, there is no equity in favouring one legal system to have the opportunity of being introduced at a later stage, to rescind or substantially alter an agreement already made by all interested parties on the side of both spouses, according to a particular legal system, unless all those parties to the previous agreement consent to the subsequent change.

Although Wilson Aryamba, J., previously a Judge of the Supreme Court stationed in Juba, circulated the directive of McDowell, J., to the judges in the Southern Sudan some years ago, its contents seem to appeal only to non-Muslim judges. Wilson Aryamba, J., hinted at the necessity for legislation in this area. I also believe that harmony can be ensured by making a fairly balanced legislation in this area. The legislation should embody the following rules:

(a) Where all the interested parties on both sides desire to contract a mixed marriage, they must, at the time of the agreement, make a choice of the legal system which shall govern the marriage, divorce and custody of the children and so forth, provided that this choice of law shall only be valid when it is preceded by a fully understood explanation of all the legal consequences involved by these interested parties;

(b) the choice of law and the explanation of the legal consequences, referred to in the preceding paragraph, shall be made before a Civil or Chiefs' Court where the bride is a non-Muslim or before a Sharia Court or Kadi where a bride is a Mohamedan.

(c) Where a couple, irrespective of any form of marriage, have taken each other as husband and wife, without the consent of their relatives, who are supposed to be the legitimate parties to such marriage, the marriage, the divorce and the custody of the children shall be governed by the personal law of the woman. This is the position supported by the Dinka and the Luo Codes[77] as well as by many other customary laws in Southern Sudan.

Although the Sharia Law is immutable and does not admit of being supplemented or modified by legislation, social requirements or communal inter-dependence necessitate introduction of some reforms.[78] While the Muslims are a part of the whole human society

---

[77] This rule would not be unfair to Muslims since the interests to be produced by it are reciprocal. For example, it would serve the interest of the Islamic Law if the woman or girl is a Muslim; on the other hand, if the woman or girl is a non-Muslim, the rule would serve the interests provided by her customary law.

[78] 'There are many problems that await solution, as regards Islamic and Customary Law. Some are problems of reforms of some of the rules of these laws, reforms necessitated by the changed circumstances as regards our ideas of modern man, human rights and equality of the sexes, which may not be adequately reflected in these legal systems,' (Ref: Natale O. Akolawin, *Islamic and Customary Law in Sudan Legal System* in *Sudan In Africa* (1985) 2nd ed., Khartoum University Press, p.299.

some adjustments in the law become inevitable. Introduction of reforms in Islamic Law in order to suit social and modern development has already taken place in several Arab states. Sudan ought to follow the example of the other progressive Arab states on this point, especially in view of its large indigenous African non-Muslim population.

CHAPTER FOUR

Some Aspects of The Law of Property

Introduction
Property is the subject of a vast amount of litigation before the Dinka courts, because it is essential to the life of man. It is the subject of numerous economic and social transactions which are daily conducted by men and women.

However, despite the importance of property to the lives of men in society, the Dinka language lacks a single appropriate word or legal expression which exactly corresponds, at all times, with this English term. 'Law of property' may be said to correspond with *long de kedē*, meaning 'law of thing'. *Kedē* stands for property or thing. But it is still better to express it in plural terms as *lôông ke kāng*, meaning 'laws of things'. In this sense *kedē* means 'the thing' and this is one meaning which is conveyed by the word 'property' in English Law.[1]

In English Law 'property' may also be used to mean *ownership*.[2] But *kedē* does not convey the meaning of 'ownership'. The Dinka Law (or language) shifts to the use of another word which conveys the notion of ownership. The word *adôôc* stands for property with the sense of ownership embodied in it. But there is still a difference between *adôôc* and 'property' in the sense of ownership. *Adôôc* essentially conveys the sense of property which is being owned or under the ownership of someone, or it may mean 'property' or 'thing' which is capable of ownership.

However, despite the lack of a single word or legal expression which exactly corresponds, at all times, with 'property', the idea of

---
[1] Crossley Vaines *On Personal Property*, 4th ed., Butterworths, London, 1967, p.3.
[2] Ibid.

property does exist and may be conveyed through the usage of various expressions.

Property in English Law has been the subject of numerous classifications. Some classifications are provided by nature, for example, movable property and immovable property. An animal or a stick is a movable property while the land or a thing attached to it, such as a tree, is an immovable property. Some classifications are legal, for example, real property and personal property; or the distinct classes of real property, such as corporeal and incorporeal hereditaments.[3]

But these classifications do not mean much, as far as the Dinka Law is concerned. What matters in the law is whether a wrongful act has been committed with respect to the property owned or legally possessed by another person and, if so, the next issue is the nature of the remedy to be awarded to the aggrieved party. The class to which the property under dispute belongs is immaterial.

In this Chapter, the discussion on the subject will be divided into three parts, namely:

1. The transfer of title to property and the tracing of property;
2. The intestate and testimentary succession; and
3. The land law.

Owing to the peculiarity of the nature of the individual's rights over 'land', it is more appropriate to discuss the subject of land (as property) in a separate part. There is some uncertainty as to whether an individual or a private person enjoys the ownership or possessory rights over the land he occupies. The subject of land law will therefore be discussed as Part 3 of this Chapter.

However, in Part 1, the discussion does not cover all aspects of the law of property, but is centred on a few problems relating to the following, which are the subjects of much litigation, namely:

1.1 the transfer of title to property;
1.2 the tracing of the original property which is the subject of dispute or wrongful transfer; and
1.3 the rights of innocent third parties.

The analysis of the subjects selected in Part 1 of this Chapter requires some references to be made to the English Law of Personal Property, because of the universality of the principle involved in both

---

[3] Hereditament means the property which used to pass to heirs on intestacy before 1926.

legal systems. Although Dinka Law has not yet developed more sophisticated principles or concepts in its branches of the law of personal property, is has made much progress in the rules which relate to the transfer of title to personal property. These rules are in fact a replica of the maxim: '*Nemo dat quod non habet*', which means:

> 'No one can give a better title than his own; he can give possession, but not a title which is not vested in him'.[4]

Perhaps this is the most important principle in the law of personal property.

Two cases are selected for the illustration of this maxim. One is an English case and the other is a Dinka case. The two illustrations show the universality of the maxim or principle.

The case of *Hollins* v. *Foweller (1875), L.R.7H. L.757*, is usually regarded as a classic illustration of this maxim. The facts of the case are as follows:

> A Liverpool broker, Hollins, purchased cotton from another broker, Barley, who had obtained it from Foweller, the owner, without title in circumstances of fraud. Hollins purchased the cotton in good faith and delivered it to the manufacturer, but when sued in conversion by Foweller he was held liable. Blackburn, J., stated the philosophy behind the law as follows:

> 'When a loss has happened through the roguery of an insolvent it must always fall on some innocent party and that must be hardship...'

The converse of this rule is that: '...even an innocent interference with the property of another gives rise to an action for conversion.' The case of *Hollins* v. *Foweller* still illustrates this converse rule.

The Dinka case selected to illustrate the general maxim referred to above is the case between one Marial and others.

Sometime before 1977, a certain Marial and others, who were reputed cattle thieves, left Rumbek area and went to the Nuer land, south of Bentiu. They stole a number of cattle and brought them to their land. When they arrived, they began to distribute the stolen cattle among themselves. One of the thieves complained against their leader for lack of parity in the distribution of the stolen property. He

---

[4] Crossley Vaines; *On Personal Property*, 4th ed., Butterworths, London, 1967, p.153.

sued the leader in order to obtain a cow so as to maintain parity. The chiefs' court, which applied the customary law, rejected the claim on the ground that none of them had acquired a good title to any of the stolen cattle. It was held that the title was still vested in the owner who was unknown at the time of the trial of the case. It was further maintained that if the true owner came and proved his title, the cows would be taken from the thieves and restored to him. The thieves had only acquired possession.

The plaintiff felt dissatisfied with the court's decision and appealed to the district judge, who upheld the appeal for unstated grounds. The respondent appealed to the Province Court. The decision of the court of first instance was confirmed while the decision of the district judge was reversed.

Although these thieves were able to acquire possession, they did not, according to the customary law, acquire a valid title; consequently, none of them could pass on any better title than he had. The district judge might have overlooked this rule, apart from the fact that a court of justice could not possibly spend its time administering 'justice' among thieves with respect to stolen property.

The principle or the maxim which is under consideration involves the doctrine of 'tracing' of property, which might have been the subject of wrongful transfer. But differences exist here between tracing in English Law and tracing in Dinka Law; the difference between the two legal systems basically rests on the fact that, unlike the Dinka Law, the English Law mainly deals with the problem of tracing in 'currency', which is the main property that exists as a medium of exchange, and, consequently, it is the subject of more disputes, where the issue of tracing arises for consideration. 'It should be said at the onset that although the operation we shall discuss is described as "tracing", what is actually involved has nothing to do with the identification of individual coins or notes.'[5]

The rules of tracing as they exist in English Law may be summarised as follows:

(i) In certain circumstances, a right to trace money exists both at law and in equity, although owing to the wide scope of the equitable remedy, the common law right is now of academic interest.
(ii) At law, a limited right to trace was allowed as between principal and agent...
(iii) The legal right to sue fails at the point at which the money

---
[5] Re Diplock's Estate, *Diplock* v. *Wintle (1948)2 All E.R. 318, 347.*

ceases primarily to be identifiable, e.g., where the agent pays it into an account at a bank where it is mixed with his own or another's money.

(iv) Equity, given a fiduciary relationship between the owner and the recipient, permits tracing into a mixed fund, and even if the money passes into the hands of an innocent volunteer. Within the limits mentioned below, the difficulty of identification is no bar....[6]

According to the well known phrase of Atkin, L. J., 'the common law halts at the banker's door, but equity lifts the latch, walks in and examines the books.'

Although equity goes farther than the common law in the tracing of property, this process would not, in Dinka Law, be regarded as tracing of property. The concept of tracing, in Dinka Law, presupposes the existence of an identifiable material which constitutes the subject of tracing, for example, cattle or other domestic animals or some property other than animals. In cases where property, such as currency or money, cannot be identified after mixture with other money or where an identifiable property has perished or has ceased to exist, or exists but is impossible to find, tracing will not be called at issue in making a claim; but any payment made to the claimant is treated as compensation, that is, payment of some different property in lieu of the original property. In Dinka Law, tracing relates to the recovery of the original property but not its substitute or equivalent.

The second difference between tracing in English Law and Dinka Law is that, in English Law, 'there is no right of tracing as against purchaser for value without notice. Where money has come into the hands of innocent third parties, the equitable right of tracing is exercisable against such persons only if they are volunteers and, if the money has been paid into a mixed fund, the right is exercisable only where some means of identification in disentanglement from the fund remains.'[7]

In Dinka Law the innocent third party buys the property at his risk. Whether the innocent party acquires the property for value without notice of the fact that the seller or the one who transferred the property to him had no title, this does not save him. There are exceptions which will be explained later when the details are discussed. But these exceptions in fact have different considerations or are made on different grounds.

---

[6] Re Diplock's Estate, *Diplock* v. *Wintle (1948) 2 All E.R. 318, 347.*
[7] Ibid.

The details as to the transfer of title, tracing of property and rights of innocent third parties, will now be discussed.

1. PERSONAL PROPERTY

1.1 The transfer of title or ownership of property

It has been indicated before that the Dinka Law embodies a general principle which corresponds with the general maxim: *'Nemodat quod non habet'*. Further, it will be evident that the transfer of title and the tracing of property are so much inter-related that there is no particular section of the Act (i.e., The Re-statement of the Bhar el Ghazal Customary Law Act, 1984) which purely deals with the *transfer of title* without an element of tracing. But, in all the sections which relate to the tracing of property, it is obvious that the question of the transfer of title is embodied, for there cannot be any right of tracing without having the title. This may be seen in section 63 of the Act, which provides that:

> 'The owner (of property) is entitled to trace his property into the hands of anyone who has acquired possession in good faith or bad faith from anyone who has no title to it.'

From the heading of this section it is obvious that the title cannot be transferred by a non-owner. The provisions of this section may be re-worded without altering the meaning, as follows: 'No one can pass a better title than his own.'

From this legal provision, it is very clear that it is the 'ownership' and not 'possession' which qualifies one to transfer a good title to another person. Of course, the section is silent about the question of possession but it is implicit that 'possession' which is not coupled with 'ownership' cannot give rise to a right to transfer of title. This point is confirmed by all other sections which deal with the transfer of title and the right to tracing. For example, ss. 56 and 57 of the Act emphasise the question of ownership. Section 56 makes it clear that

> 'the true owner is not deprived of his title when possession of such property has been transferred through (i) theft, (ii) robbery, (iii) breach of trust, (iv) deceit or fraud, and (v) any other wrongful means.'

Although the thief (or any of the rogues described by any term under this section) has acquired *corpus* and has *animus possidendi*, yet, he is not entitled by law to pass a good title to another person.

The Dinka Law does not allow 'possession' to enable one to pass the title because, not only would it adversely affect the owner's rights, but thieves would benefit. The owner is absolutely protected against the acts of non-owners whether they are thieves or not. Further, the rights of the original owner are superior to the rights of the innocent third party who might have acquired the property for a valuable consideration and without being aware of the lack of title on the part of the seller or transferor. All the third party can do is to sue the rogue to recover the price.

In the case of *Chief Majak Malok Akot* v. *Nyadiyiel and others*[8], Nyadiyiel, with some friends, stole a bull from Majak's cattle camp at a place called Alau. They brought it to Rumbek town and sold it in an open market to a man of Chief Yiegi Dongrin. The buyer had no knowledge that it was stolen property. Chief Majak Malok Akot identified his property in the possession of the buyer. He brought the buyer to the legal authorities and there the identities of the thieves were disclosed. They were apprehended and ultimately convicted. The court, at the same time, passed the following orders: (a) that the stolen bull be delivered by the buyer to the original owner, Majak Malok Akot, because the title was still vested in him. The fact that the buyer had obtained possession of the bull in good faith for value from the thieves did not deprive the true owner of his title; (b) that the innocent buyer had the right to recover from the thieves a sum of money equal to the amount which he had paid to them as the cost price.

In another case,[9] the sale took place outside the market while the buyer had knowledge of the fact that the property was stolen. The case was first tried by a criminal court and it made the same ruling as in the case of Majak Malok Akot, that where a person buys property, whether in or outside the market, with or without the knowledge that it was stolen by the seller (or sellers), the title to such property remains vested in the owner. The buyer later sued the thief to recover the value he had paid. The facts of the case were as follows:

'The plaintiff bought a bull from the defendants outside the market for Ls.23.000 m/ms. The bull was stolen from a third party and the plaintiff bought it in the knowledge that it was stolen property. The third party identified his bull in the possession of the plaintiff and accused him. The plaintiff (accused) was convicted under section 353 of the Sudan Penal Code for receiving stolen

---

[8] Cr/App/217/70.
[9] *Majok Akok* v. *Dut Cuot Ager and Riak Ager*, CS/172/70.

property and was sentenced to two months imprisonment, and the bull was returned to the true owner. After serving the sentence, he sued the defendants so as to recover the money he had paid to them for the purchase of the bull. He succeeded. It was held by the Main Court, presided over by Chief Arôl Kacuol, that he could recover the sum of Ls.23.000 m/ms which he paid.'

If the case of Majak Malok Akot had been tried according to the English Law, it would have been held that the title passed to the buyer since the sale took place in market overt; but that the title reverted to the original owner following the conviction of the thieves.[10] This exception is aimed at encouraging the public to sell goods in market overt so as to minimise cases of purchase or sale of stolen property.

But Dinka Law differs here from English Law. Sale in market overt does not deprive the owner of his title. However, the other root-cause of the existence, in English Law, of this exception is that commercial business has become a vital part of livelihood and needs protection. On the other hand, this is not so much the case with the Dinka community. Commercial business has not yet reached the scale where it would be necessary to protect innocent purchasers by law. Secondly, Dinka Law cannot incorporate such an exception, because it would encourage thieves to take risks or calculate their chances of selling other people's property in open markets. Once a person has identified his property, he must take it because he still retains the title, unless he has voluntarily given it up.

Further, in Dinka Law, the recovery of the stolen property by the owner from the third party or the innocent buyer does not depend on the conviction of the thief. The recovery is based on the fact that the owner has never lost his title. This, as mentioned, before, is one of the areas where English Law differs from Dinka Law. In English Law,

'The property in stolen goods sold in market overt revests in the person from whom they were stolen upon the thief being

---

[10] Section 22 of the Sale of Goods Act, 1893. See also s.3(1) of the Sudanese Act: *Recovery of Lost and Stolen Property Act, 1924*, which provides (a) 'Where a thief or a dishonest receiver had been prosecuted to conviction, the true owner could recover his property and an innocent purchaser could be compensated out of a fine on the convicted person and, (b) 'Where there had been no conviction of a thief or dishonest receiver, the true owner had to refund to an innocent purchaser, from whom he recovered his property, the price paid by that purchaser, if the purchase had been made in open market.'

prosecuted to conviction. This rule was instituted to encourage the prosecution of thieves...."[11]

Section 24(1) of the Sale of Goods Act, 1893, also provides that

'Where goods have been stolen and the offender is prosecuted to conviction, the property in goods so stolen revests in the person who was the owner of the goods or his personal representative....'

In Dinka Law, the conviction of the thief is not a prior condition to the recovery of the title by the owner. A Dinka person may not seek the conviction of the thief if he gets back his title.

Another difference between English Law and Dinka Law is that in the latter there is no exception to the general rule which enables a person who has legal possession to pass title to a third person. The case of *Col. Mathet* v. *Mathiang Yang* was brought for settlement before the Kuei Regional Court (in Rumbek district) in 1977. Mathiang Yang obtained a loan of Ls.50.000 m/ms from Col. Mathet and promised that he would refund the loan at a future date by giving a cow to the latter (i.e. the creditor). But Mathiang (the debtor) secured the loan by depositing a cow with the creditor. After a long delay in discharging the loan, the creditor disposed of the cow to a third party who received it for value and in good faith. The debtor (and his son-in-law), without refunding the loan, went and obtained the cow from the third party (in circumstances where the taking could be equated with theft). The debtor, after taking the cow, delivered it as *arueth* to his son-in-law. The creditor (on his behalf and on behalf of the third party) sued the debtor and his son-in-law for the return of the cow. It was held by Kuei Regional Court that the debtor had the ownership which he had passed to his son-in-law. The right of the creditor was to raise a suit to claim the refund of his debt; but the creditor, though he had legal possession, could not transfer good title to a third person.

The creditor's legal possession, coupled with his claim for the refund of the debt, had put him in a position similar to that of the unpaid seller which, in English Law, could enable him to pass a good title to a third party.[12]

It might be said that the decision of the court was unfair. The conduct of the debtor in delaying the refund of the loan was bad. Further, even if the delay did not allow the creditor to appropriate the

---

[11] Crossley Vaines, *On Personal Property*, 4th ed., Butterworths, London, 1967, p.167.
[12] Section 48 of the Sale of Goods Act, 1893.

property and then pass good title to another, it was wrong for the debtor to take away the cow from him and deliver it to his son-in-law, leaving the debt to remain unsecured.

The *ratio decidendi* of this case can be stated as follows:

(a) that an owner of property may pass a good title to another person even though there is a charge levied against that property; or, conversely

(b) that a non-owner who enjoys legal possession of a property which, for example, he holds as security for a debt, cannot, under any circumstances, pass a good title to another.

It must be stated, therefore, that possession of any nature does not necessarily enable one to pass a good title to anyone else.

1.2 The right of the original owner to trace his property into the hands of others

The right of tracing prevails in the following cases, namely:

(a) Where the original transaction for which the owner transferred the property to another person has been abrogated or has ceased to exist. The commonest example is where property has been transferred in performing a marriage. If such a marriage has ceased to exist or divorce (*puokē-ruai*) has been declared, the original owner is entitled to trace his cattle or property to the hands of anyone who has acquired the title or possession through subsequent marriages or other transactions. The general rule which governs this point is provided by section 53 of the Re-statement of Bhar el Ghazal Customary Law Act, 1984, as follows:

> 'When divorce or dissolution of marriage has taken place, the husband is entitled to trace his cattle into the hands of anyone who has acquired possession or title to them from his in-laws through subsequent marriages, provided that he shall only be entitled to recover damages from in-laws for any cattle delivered by them to the third parties through sale or discharge of certain obligations,[13] while the marriage was still valid.'

The same property may pass through many hands due to subsequent marriages or other legal transactions. Where the original marriage breaks down, the title reverts to the original owner; and, consequently, the right of tracing arises.

---

[13] For example, when the in-laws passed it to the third party as *apuk* or compensation for injury inflicted or death caused to somebody.

In the case of *Moses Abaker* v. *Issa Makuac, RMRY/Civ.App/24/77*, (a case of marriage conducted according to Dinka Customary Law), the marriage had been conducted between the spouses and their relatives. Bride-wealth was paid in money. The money paid for the bride-wealth was distributed among the relatives of the woman, according to the customary law. Afterwards, divorce took place between the two families and the husband claimed the recovery of the bride-wealth. It was held that the declaration of divorce resulted in the reversion of title to the bride-wealth money to the husband. The third parties who took a share in the bride-wealth were ordered to re-pay the money to the original owner – the husband.[14] But, in the Dinka conception of tracing of property, this refund does not constitute the act of tracing. Essentially, tracing means the recovery of the original property and not its value or substitute. In this particular case, it can be said that the title to the bride-wealth property reverted to the original owner and that he could claim from any third party any sum of money equivalent to what he had paid. This does not mean, of course, the restoration of the actual original currency.

Further, title to property may be passed by a donor or a giver to a donee or a recipient; but where the gift is revoked, the title to the gift property reverts to the donor or the giver of the property. Section 59 of the Act provides that:

'Title to property may be transferred by way of gift or donation provided that the donor (or the giver) has better title against anyone else at the time of the transfer to the donee.'

While section 59 regulates the transfer of title by way of gift, section 60 of the Act entitles the donor or the giver to recover the property if the gift is revoked. It provides as follows:

'The title to any property which has been transferred to another by way of gift or donation reverts to the original owner (donor or giver) when revocation of the gift is effected.'

Tracing of property by the original owner includes the offspring or its produce.[15] The case between *Marial Reec and Manhom Gol on the*

---

[14] The rights legally acquired by third parties are adversely affected, provided the relationship between the first or original parties has been terminated. It is not always necessary to join the third parties as defendants in the suit.
[15] Section 55 of the Re-statement of Bhar el Ghazal Region Customary Law Act, 1984.

one hand, and Meen Makerlil, on the other RMRY/Civ/App/34/77 illustrates this point. The wife of Meen Makerlil and the sister of Manhom Gol were friends. As a token of friendship, Meen Makerlil and his wife gave property (a cow) to Manhom Gol and his sister. Manhom Gol married the daughter of Marial Reec (the appellant). Some of the offspring of the cow in question were transferred to Marial Reec as part of bride-wealth and other offspring remained with Manhom Gol. Later, the wife of Meen Makerlil died and he decided to terminate the marriage. He also revoked the gift because Manhom Gol did not, on a reciprocal basis, pay him a cow as a gift of friendship. He went to Kuei Regional Court to sue Manhom Gol to return the gift cow with its offspring and to trace the other cows which had passed, through marriage, to Marial Reec.

It was held that since the gift was revoked, the title to the original cow together with its offspring reverted to Meen Makerlil, the giver. It was further held that Meen Makerlil was entitled to trace his cows, that is, the offspring of the original cow, into the hands of Marial Reec, who, in good faith, acquired them through the marriage of his daughter.

Those cows in the possession of Manhom were collected in execution of that decree, but Marial Reec appealed to the district court. He argued that Meen Makerlil was not entitled to trace the cows (gift cows) into his hands but was entitled to recover damages from Manhom Gol. The appeal was upheld by the district court, in accordance with Rule 61 (of the then Local Order – now section 60 of the Re-statement of Bhar el Ghazal Customary Law Act, 1984), which provides that:

> 'Where revocation of gift takes place, the donor (or the giver) is not entitled to trace the property given or donated into the hand of anyone who has lawfully or in good faith acquired possession or title to it before the revocation of the gift is effected, but he is only entitled to recover damages from the donee or the receiver of the gift.'

Although the title reverts to the giver or donor on revocation of the gift or donation, according to section 60 of the Act, section 61 does not permit the right of tracing to be exercised against a third party, provided the third party acquired the property in good faith. This implies that if the third party acquired it in bad faith, the original owner is entitled to recover it. This is one of the areas where 'good faith' protects the third party against the exercise of the right of tracing by the original owner.

The above decision was based on tracing property in circumstances where the title to the property had been legally passed to another person but had reverted to the original owner, due to the abrogation of the original transaction. In those cases, the transfer of property was made by the original owner of it or by the person who had legally acquired the title.

(b) We now come to the case of tracing where property has been wrongfully transferred, for example, by a thief or by a person who may have the legal possession but without the title, that is, a transfer by a non-owner.

While section 56 of the Act emphasises the retention of title to property by the original owner, where the acquisition of its possession or the physical transfer of such property has been made in a circumstance which constitutes one of the following: theft, robbery, breach of trust, deceit or fraud, or through any other wrongful means, section 57 of the Act confers upon such owner a right to trace the title to his property which has been the subject of transfer in one of those instances.

In the case of *Mabur Abiel* v. *Makur Dhuol RMRY/Civ. App/7/77*, the dispute between the parties was over a stolen cow. The cow was stolen by Makur Dhuol (the respondent) from Mabur Abiel (the appellant). The respondent alleged that he found the cow and regarded it as lost property, but he could not prove this point as he had no witnesses; nevertheless, he succeeded before the Regional Court. Mabur Abiel lodged an appeal to the district judge against the decision of the court of first instance. His argument was as follows: (a) that, the respondent stole his cow; (b) that, his cow had offspring while in possession of the respondent; (c) that, some of these offspring had been transferred by the respondent to a third party called Maker Manyiel; (d) that, since he still retained the title to the stolen cow and its offspring, he was entitled to recover those cows in the possession of the respondents and to trace the rest of the cows into the hands of the third party (whom he had in fact joined as co-defendant – consequently a co-respondent) and (e) that he was entitled to recover damages from the respondent for the offspring of his original stolen cow, which died naturally in his possession and for those which died naturally in the possession of third parties who acquired them from him.

As the evidence from the records of the court of first instance was very scanty, a hearing was ordered. The appellant produced eleven witnesses who were unanimous in supporting his case; but the respondent failed to produce a single witness and even he himself declined to appear in court on the day of the hearing. The district judge proceeded with the hearing. In passing the judgement, he reversed the decision of the court of first instance on the ground that the appellant had proved his title to the cow in dispute. It was also established that it was a stolen cow. Its offspring, some of which had died and some of which had been transferred to the third party, Maker Manyiel, were also disclosed by the witnesses and the court passed a judgement in favour of the applicant, in this respect.

In his decision, the district judge first invoked the provisions of section 56 of the Local Order (now s.56 of the Re-statement of Bhar el Ghazal Region Customary Law Act, 1984), because the respondent's act was exactly covered by the provisions of that section. It was, accordingly, held that the appellant did not lose his title to the stolen cow.

The consequence was that the court had to resort to the provisions of section 57 of the Local Order which permits the original owner to trace his property which has been acquired, or acquired and transferred to a third party, in one of the circumstances described under section 56 of the Local Order. The appellant was therefore entitled to recover the cows which were alive and still in the possession of the respondents. Secondly, he was allowed to recover from the third party, Maker Manyiel, the offspring of the stolen cow which were alive and in the hands of the said third party. Thirdly, in applying the provisions of section 58 of the Local Order (now section 58 of the Act), it was held that the appellant was entitled to recover damages for any offspring of the stolen cow which died naturally in his possession or in the possession of any of the third parties who had acquired them from him (i.e., from the thief – respondent).

It can be observed from the provisions of section 58 of the Act that good faith only protects the third party in the case of the recovery of damages for a stolen property which has ceased to exist or has perished. The original owner is entitled to claim damages from the thief and not from the third party, unless the thief is not traceable.[16] But good faith does not protect a person when the property of the original owner exists or is identifiable in the hands of a third party. For example, a finder of lost property may sell it or transfer it to a third party who receives it without the knowledge of the fact that it is a foundling; nevertheless the true owner will be entitled to trace it into the hands of the third party.[17] A dictum in the case of *Mageer Makoi v. Yang Majok RMRY/Civ.App/5/77*, illustrates this rule.

---

[16] This condition is not embodied in section 58 of the Act.
[17] Section 62 of the Restatement of Bhar el Ghazal Region Customary Law Act, 1984.

In 1954, Yang Majok (the respondent) and one Cadar Majok had their cattle in one camp. Some time later, they moved to a new cattle camp, where Marier Makoi, the appellant's brother, was camping with his cattle. Some days later, a certain Mangeth Dhong brought policemen to drive away the respondent's cattle (these cattle were in the possession of Cadar Majok) from the camp. After this, the appellant's brother also moved away to encamp in a new place. During their movement, the appellant's brother, Marier Makoi, found a bull on the tract, where the people from the Atuot tribe were passing with their cattle. Marier Makoi kept the foundling for himself. Later on, somebody slaughtered the said bull and gave a cow to Marier in place of the bull. This cow (*Yom* in colour) had offspring while in Marier's possession. Marier and his brother, Mageer Makoi (the appellant) shared the offspring of the original cow. It was obvious that Mageer Makoi did not receive these cows in good faith.

In 1977, the respondent Yang Majok sued the appellant, claiming the 'yom' cow with its offspring on the ground that they were his. As far as the claim against the appellant, Mageer Makoi, was concerned, it was the exercise of a right to trace the offspring of a foundling into the hands of a third party. The court of first instance held that the respondent was entitled to trace his cows into the hands of the appellant, Mageer Makoi.

On appeal against this decision, it was held that the respondent was entitled to trace his cattle into the hands of the third party whether he acquired them in good faith or bad faith. But the case failed on other grounds and so the appeal of Mageer Makoi was allowed.

1.3 Exceptions to the right of tracing

The right of the owner to trace his property is not absolute in all cases. There are a number of exceptions to it. But in circumstances where the right to trace property cannot be exercised, the owner (or original owner) is entitled to recover damages. These exceptions may be categorised as follows:

(a) where it is practically impossible to recover the original property; and
(b) where the law refuses to allow the right of tracing to be exercised against third parties.

1.3(a) *Impossibility of recovering the original property*
Tracing stops where the original property has perished or has ceased

to exist. However, in such circumstances, the original owner is entitled to recover damages. In the case of *Maker Mabor v. Daniel Marial Buot PC/BGP/CS/34/75* (see facts below), it was held by the court that 'the husband (or any of his kinsmen), at the event of divorce, is entitled to recover damages from his in-laws for any cow or a bull which the latter had slaughtered while the marriage was still valid.'

But the right to recover damages also has its exceptions. For example, in cases of marriage with bride-wealth cattle, if a cow paid as part of bride-wealth dies naturally while the marriage still subsists, the original owner (the husband or his kinsman) is not entitled to recover damages for that cow,[18] because the death of the original cow is an act of God or nature.

But where property or a cow, which is part of bride-wealth, is transferred by a second party to a third party in discharge of a debt or through sale or in discharge of a certain obligation (other than marriage), such as payment to a third party by way of compensation, and if the said cow dies in the possession of the third party, the husband or his kinsman is entitled to recover damages, not from the third party but from the in-laws, who made the transfer to the third party.[19] Although the death of the original cow is an act of God or nature, the original owner is entitled to recover damages. The philosophy behind such payment of damages for a dead cow is that the second party (the in-laws, in this case) who transferred it to the third party benefited from the original property – the benefit being the discharge of the obligation.

In the case where the property or the cow has been transferred by the second party to a third party in settlement of marriage, it will be the subject of tracing, unless the property or the cow has perished or died in the hands of a third party. In this case, the original owner is entitled to recover damages from the second party. The same rules also apply if property paid as *arueth* by the in-laws to the husband or his kinsmen perishes or dies. It must also be noted here that payment of damages, as a consequence of the impossibility of recovering the original cow, is not only confined to cases of marriage. The question of marriage constitutes the commonest example. If a person, by committing a breach of trust, transfers livestock property to a third party and it dies there, or a thief steals property or livestock and transfers it to a third party in whose hands it perishes or dies, the

---

[18] Section 54 of the Restatement of Bhar el Ghazal Region Customary Law Act, 1984.

[19] Section 58 of the Restatement of Bhar el Ghazal Region Customary Law Act, 1984.

original owner can only claim damages from the thief,[20] because there is nothing to trace since the original property does not exist. Further, it must be noted that the questions of transfer of title and the tracing of the original property by the original owner are not confined to livestock. They are applicable to property in general.

1.3(b) *Circumstances where the law stops the right of tracing*
There are circumstances where the law prevents the original owner from exercising his right of tracing. Some of the instances where the law stops the tracing of property are mentioned in section 54 of the Re-statement of Bhar el Ghazal Region Customary Law Act, 1984, and these are cases of transfer of property to third parties through (i) sale, (ii) debt, (iii) and other obligations (these obligations exclude transfer through subsequent marriages). The example of 'other obligations' in (iii) above, is where the transfer has been made in discharge of tortious liability, for example, payment as *apuk* (compensation) for homicide or personal injury and so forth.

The rule which forbids tracing with respect to property sold can be illustrated by the case of *Maker Mabor* v. *Daniel Marial Buot PC/BGP/CS/34/75*. The facts of this case were as follows:

> Malē Marial Noi married Pec Buot in 1950 with cattle which included two cows and one bull, subjects of the dispute in this case. Relations deteriorated and divorce took place in 1959. Malē, despite divorce, did not claim his cows (which had by then increased in number). He died in 1973. After his death, his representative, the plaintiff, raised a suit for the recovery of the bride-wealth cattle.

The judicial contest was between Maker Mabor (representative of Malē) and Daniel Marial Buot, who represented his father, Buot, and his sister, Pec. The case was contested in so far as the number of cattle claimed was concerned. But, for the purpose of the principle under consideration, we will refer only to the issue of one cow and one bull. The cow, – 'bil', was sold by the defendant's father while the marriage was still subsisting. This fact was admitted by the defendant. While the marriage was still valid, a bull was also sold by one of the defendant's relatives. This relative paid a cow to the defendant's father in replacement of the said bull. This fact was also admitted by the defendant. The court held:

---

[20] Section 58 of the Restatement of Bhar al Ghazal Region Customary Law Act 1984.

(i) that the defendant was bound to pay another cow as damages in place of the cow 'bil', which had been sold. It is to be noted also that the court could not order that 'bil' be traced from the buyer, because transfer by sale is one of the exceptions to the principle of tracing;

(ii) that the heifer, which was paid as damages for the slaughtered bull, be delivered to the plaintiff.

The ratio decidendi of this case may be stated as follows: that where divorce takes place, the husband is entitled to recover the bride-wealth cattle but is not entitled to trace any cow (or property) which had been transferred to a third party through sale by his in-laws during the subsistence of marriage; however, he is only entitled to recover damages (that is, a different cow) in place of the original cow or property which had been sold.

In cases of transfer of property through sale and discharge of a debt, the law forbids the right of tracing, as a policy of preventing the re-opening of settled obligations. A person who has acquired property through purchase or in the discharge of a debt owed to him must have confidence that he has acquired a good title to the property. There would be no security of property if the title which a person legally acquired in such transactions were to be re-claimed or disturbed by the original owner. This policy is also aimed at promoting transactions of an economic nature. But this is so only in as far as the sale or the payment of property in discharge of a debt is made by a person who has the ownership of or title to the property. If the property was sold by a thief, or if a person steals property and transfers it to a third party in discharge of a debt, the original owner will be entitled to trace it, even if the sale was in the open market. This has been discussed before.

The last point where the law stops the tracing of the original property is in the case of gift.[21] The reasons which justify the refusal to trace property in this instance are not very clear. But it seems that since a giver or donor voluntarily transfers property or makes a free gift, the interest of the recipient or donee who obtained the property gratis should be balanced with the interest of the third party who might have acquired it from the donee for value. Any inconvenience caused by the revocation of the gift should not be allowed to affect the third party as long as the property has ceased to exist.

---

[21] Section 61 of the Restatement of Bhar el Ghazal Region Customary Law Act, 1984.
Note: perhaps the list of such exceptions is not exhausted.

1.4 The rights of innocent parties

This subject has been indirectly covered during the discussion of (i) the transfer of title to property and (ii) the right of the owner to trace his property. At this stage, only certain parts of this subject will be emphasised. The protection of the rights of innocent parties may be divided into the following categories:

(a) cases where an innocent person obtained the property from the owner; and
(b) cases where the innocent party received the property from a non-owner.

1.4(a) *Where the property is obtained from the owner*

The commonest examples here are the instances where a person receives property through (i) marriage, (ii) sale, in discharge of a debt, or any other obligation. This list is not of course exhausted.

1.4(a) (i) Acquisition of property through marriage

Property may be transferred by the owner, 'A', through marriage to 'B' in a subsequent marriage. 'B' may pass the same property to 'C'; then 'C' to 'D' and so on. If the original marriage between 'A' and 'B' is terminated, all the series of subsequent marriages through which the property of 'A' (the original owner) has passed will be affected since, by the dissolution of the first marrige, the title to the property in question reverts to 'A' (section 53 of the Restatement of Bhar el Ghazal Region Customary Law Act 1984). 'A's' claim will penetrate or pass through all the subsequent marriages up to the last person who is in possession of the original property which 'A' had passed to 'B'.

There is a phrase, which intermediary parties usually use, when the original owner ('A' in this example) is exercising his right of tracing. It goes: *Yin aca pat*. This phrase needs a little explanation. The intermediary party says to the owner: 'Your property or cow came into my possession, but I passed it to another person in a subsequent marriage. I have opened the door for you. You go to my in-laws to lodge your claim against them.' Every intermediary party may be deemed to have actually or constructively made this statement till the original owner reaches the last person, who still retains the property. In this example, 'A' may go up to 'D'. The court will order 'D' to return the original cow or property to 'A'. However, the court will not ignore the rights of all the intermediary parties who are so affected. 'D' will be reimbursed by 'C', and 'C' by 'B'. 'B' will not go forward, because the marital relationship between him and 'A' has broken down. Any mutual claims between 'A' and 'B' will be adjusted by the same court.

The rule which entitles innocent parties to be reimbursed by the next intermediary party is not embodied in the Re-statement of Bhar el Ghazal Region Customary Law Act, 1984.[22] If the original owner does not insist on obtaining what he calls *nhiem-cie* (i.e., his original property; literally, *nhiem* is 'hair', *nhiem-cie* therefore means 'my original hair'), all this inconvenience caused by tracing will not take place. 'A', in our example, will try to prove the number of his original cows with their offspring in the possession of 'C', 'D' and so forth; then 'B' who is directly obliged to refund 'A' will pay 'A' the equivalent number. So 'C' and 'D' will remain undisturbed.

Again, the original owner, 'A' (as in this example) is entitled to recover damages for property or cattle which perished or died after their transfer by 'B' to the third party (through marriage, sale, discharge of debt or any other obligation). In such cases, it is not the innocent party (e.g., 'C' or 'D' in our case) who will pay damages to 'A', the original owner, but it is the second party 'B' who will be bound to pay damages to 'A'. Again, this is another protection afforded by the law to third parties or innocent persons.[23]

1.4(a) (ii) Acquisition of property through sale, discharge of debt or any other obligation

'Any other obligation' here may mean liability to pay damages or compensation for a tortious act done to somebody, for example, where injury or death has been caused to another or damage to the property of another has been caused and so forth. All these cases are covered by sections 53 and 54 of the Re-statement of Bhar el Ghazal Region Customary Law Act, 1984. The general rule is that the original owner is not entitled to trace his property or claim damages from an innocent party who acquired the property through any of the instances or transactions referred to above, if the original transaction or relationship has been abrogated. The rights of the original owner are directed against the second party (who has the direct relationship with him). The law protects the discharge of obligations of this nature, except in the circumstances which appear below.

1.4(b) *Where the innocent party obtains property from a non-owner*
The following are examples of the instances where an innocent party may obtain property from a non-owner: (i) through the action of a rogue, and (ii) through the action of a finder.

---

[22] It is already mentioned that the Act does not embody all the rules. But there are many decided cases which illustrate this rule.
[23] Section 54 of the Restatement of Bhar el Ghazal Customary Law Act, 1984.

1.4(b) (i) Acquisition of property through a rogue

By the word 'rogue', we have in mind the person whose act falls into one of the 'wrongs' prescribed by section 56 of the Re-statement of Bhar el Ghazal Region Customary Law Act, 1984.

Where an innocent person acquires property directly from a rogue, or through a person who acquired it from a rogue, the owner (according to section 56 of the Act) does not lose his title; and so, by section 57, he is entitled to trace his property into the hands of anyone, whether the latter received the property in good faith or not. The rights of the innocent person cannot compete with or override the claims of the original owner. In other words, where the interest of the true or original owner competes with the interest of an innocent third party, the former's interests prevail.

The only protection afforded by law to the innocent third party is provided by section 58 of the Act. This section requires the true owner (or the original owner) to recover damages from the rogue, if the property has perished or has ceased to exist in the hand of the innocent party. Damages will not be recovered from the latter (i.e., the innocent party). The last line of section 58 seems to be ambiguous. It says:

> '... the true owner is entitled to recover damages against the person who made the wrongful transfer or acquisition of possession from him.'

The ambiguity is posed by the phrase 'or acquisition of possession from him.' One explanation may be that *him* refers to the true owner. The second explanation may be that 'him' refers to the rogue. If it refers to the rogue, then the innocent third party is not protected against the recovery of damages. If the former explanation is the correct one, then it is the rogue alone, and not the innocent third party, who is bound to pay damages to the owner.

However, having taken part in the Conference which restated the rules, and having taken part in their drafting and passage as an Act, I am confident that the word 'him' was not intended to refer to the rogue, but refers to the true owner. This being the correct meaning, the innocent third party is exempted from the claim of damages by the original or true owner. But there is one instance where the innocent third party will be bound to pay damages, and this is when the rogue cannot be found. This rule is not embodied in the Act, but it is of common application in the courts when it is impossible to find the rogue or where the rogue has no material means to pay damages for the property which he stole and passed to the third party.

1.4(b) (ii) Acquisition of property through a finder or by one who acquires it from a finder.

The case of finder, though he is not in law the owner of the foundling, has to be treated separately, notwithstanding the fact that the position of the innocent third party is the same as in the case where the acquisition of property came through a rogue. A rogue acquires the *corpus* through wrongful means or through dishonest conduct, then he asserts *animus possidendi*. On the other hand, a finder obtains the *corpus* with honest conduct. After having obtained the *corpus*, he may either continue to maintain his honest conduct, in which case he may keep the property and look for the owner or he may keep it till the owner finds it in his possession; or he may acquire dishonest conduct by asserting *animus possidendi*. Sometimes the existence of *animus possidendi* may not be a result of dishonest conduct but a consequence of the fact that reasonable attempts have been made over a very long time (sometimes many years) to find the true owner but to no avail.

All these circumstances require a very cautious approach on the part of the court. If the conduct of the finder was dishonest, the innocent third parties will not be absolved. The general rule is provided by section 62 of the Act, as follows:

> 'The true owner is entitled to trace his property into the hands of anyone who has acquired possession whether in good faith or bad faith through the finder.'

This is in fact a general rule which does not cover the whole law about foundlings. It does not cover all aspects of the finding of property. For example, if the finder has kept the property honestly and with care, sometimes it may reproduce. If the owner afterwards appears to identify it, he can pay a reward to the finder of his own accord or the court may order him to do so. By keeping it well, the finder deserves a reward. Consequently, if, during this long non-availability of the true owner, the finder passes the property or its produce to a third party, if the honesty of his conduct is established, the third party may not be seriously affected by the claim of the original owner. The offspring or the produce that has passed to the third party may be regarded as the reward of the finder for his services. The original cow or property with some of its offspring or produce will be returned to the finder. Again, the difference between a finder and a rogue is that if the finder maintains his honest conduct and waits for the true owner, but the cow or the property unfortunately dies or disappears or perishes through circumstances beyond the finder's control, the true owner will not be entitled to claim damages. But in such circumstances a rogue will be bound to pay damages.

2. INTESTATE AND TESTAMENTARY SUCCESSION

Introduction

Succession is one of the modes by which the transfer and acquisition of property may be conducted. Owing to the extensive involvement of family concerns in the issues of succession, it has been treated, under the Act,[24] as part of the subject of Family Law. But, since it mainly relates to the transfer and acquisition of ownership of property, I have decided it would be more appropriate to deal with it in the chapter concerning the Law of Property.

Upon the death of a person who owns some property (usually referred to as his estate), such property may pass to others in one of two ways, namely, by intestate or by testamentary succession. The estate or the property of the deceased is said to pass by intestate succession in circumstances where death takes place when he (or sometimes she) has not made a will for the distribution of his estate. On the other hand, testate or testamentary succession occurs where the deceased made a will before his death.

The Dinka have technical words which, to some extent, correspond with 'intestate or testate succession'. However, these Dinka terms sometimes have wider scope than their equivalent technical words in English. '*Bēēr*' (e.g. *bēēr kāng*) is a Dinka word which may correspond with intestate succession or inheritance. It may also correspond with testamentary succession. But the word may change its shape according to the context, as is the case with many Dinka words.

As I said before, '*bēēr*' has a wide scope. It may describe the status of a person whose parents are dead, for example, '*abar*' ('*abar*' comes from the same root as '*bēēr*'). It may also indicate the right to succession or the person who is entitled to succession: For example, '*raan ci bār-kāng*' (i.e. legal heir or person who has been entrusted with the deceased's estate). '*Raan ci bār-kāng*' may not necessarily be the legal heir; he may be a trustee. Another technical term is *ciēn*. *Ciēn* (or *acieen*) has another meaning which is entirely different from the subject under discussion. It means 'curse'. But *ciēn* in the sense of succession relates to testate or testamentary succession; it does not include intestate succession.

---

[24] Sections 51 and 52 of the Re-statement of Bhar el Ghazal Customary Law Act, 1984.

Some Aspects of The Law of Property

2.1 Who are the legal heirs?
The legal heirs are defined by section 51 of the Re-statement of Bahr el Ghazal Customary Law Act, 1984 (Act No.1), as follows:

> 'Where a person who owns property dies intestate, the following persons shall be his heirs:
>
> (a) Wife (or wives) and children.
> (b) Parents or brothers, if there are no wife (or wives) and children.'

This section deals with the situation where the members of the inner family (i.e. wife, husband, children, parents and brothers) are alive or some of them are alive.

Section 52 of the Act deals with the situation where the relatives of the inner family (i.e. legal heirs) are not alive. It provides for the vesting of the estate in trustees, who are defined in order of priority. I prefer to use the word 'trustee' in place of 'administrator' or 'executor' of the deceased's estate. In Dinka Law, the functions of the holder of the estate conform with the functions of a trustee. The concepts of 'administration' or 'execution' are alien to the Dinka Law. A testator, just before his death, may appoint a person to take charge of his property, but this person plays the role of a trustee.

Section 52 provides as follows:

> 'Where a person who dies intestate has no wife, children, parents or brothers, his paternal uncle, if no maternal uncle, shall hold the possession of the property as trustee. He shall use this property in marrying a woman for the deceased and transfer any balance of the property to the deceased's newly married woman, who shall also hold it as a trustee for her children.' (See 2.4 for order of priorities).

2.2 The main principles to be observed in dealing with the deceased's estate
In dealing with the question of succession or in administering the estate of a deceased person, there are four main related principles to be observed, and these are:

2.2(a) *One must have a family*
Every person, especially if male, must have a family of his own so that his lineage remains continuous. Consequently, if he dies while he has no wife and children, it is the duty of his living kinsmen to raise a

family for him, using his estate or part of it.¹ Such relatives will also make their own contributions, apart from the estate.

2.2(b) *Property as a source of power for raising a family*
The next principle to observe is that property is the source of power or the means by which a family has to be raised; further, when the family has been so raised, it must have the property in order to maintain self-sufficiency. A family which lives under hardship, through lack of food, maintains a very low status in society, and such a low status has many social and economic repercussions.

2.2(c) *Communal ownership of family property*
The third principle is that property is jointly or communally owned by the family members. There are exceptional circumstances: where the family has grown large (i.e., if some men within the family marry), some members will separate to maintain responsibility for newly-raised families. Even where the family has grown large and has broken up into small units, each unit will communally own its property. Further, there will still be a loose union maintained between the small units under the umbrella of the original family and they will use their property in discharging major obligations (i.e., marriage or compensation for causing the death of a person).

2.2(d) *The estate must remain within the family*
The fourth principle, which is very important indeed in cases of succession, is that *the estate of the deceased must generally remain within the family*.

All the four principles establish two main objectives which have already been mentioned and I repeat them specifically here. They are:

1. the property must remain within the family so that the family can maintain self-sufficiency in food;
2. the property must remain to raise a family or families for the deceased or any other members of the family.

2.3 The consequences of the above principles
The principles which have been stated above have the following consequences.

---

[25] It is not, however, necessary that he should have an estate so that a family can be raised for him. The living relatives have a duty to use their own property for raising his family.

2.3(a) *Limitation imposed upon the testator's freedom of bequest*

A testator may intend to exercise his liberty by making a gift or bequest to somebody out of his property or make a bequest out of the estate to a person of his choice who is not a legal heir. But he does not have that absolute freedom (although, to a limited extent, he can make a bequest) to dispose of the whole or substantial part of the family property. The law protects the family, by preventing the head of the family from disposing of the whole or substantial part of the estate to persons outside the family. After all, the property is not his alone, it is a family property. Although he might have brought more property into the family, other members have also made their contribution. The family property does not only consist of the contributions of the living members, but it also consists of part of the property inherited from those members of the family who have died. Hence, the family property is not only the property of the living ones (including the testator himself), but the ownership of it includes the dead. 'The African conception of family may be expressed as consisting of large number of people, many of whom are dead, a few of whom are living, and countless numbers of whom are yet to be born.'[26]

Such limitations on the owner of property or the head of the family are universal in Africa. 'Any person who possesses something may, upon seeing death approaching, direct that such and such a thing be left to a certain person. But he should not bequeath to a non-relative anything of value, such as a beast.'[27]

But these limitations do not, of course, deprive a person, upon seeing his death approaching, of his right or power to dispose of some part of the property in the discharge of outstanding social obligations and debts. These are the obligations which are, in fact, imposed upon the family property and whether he dies before discharging them or not, the living members will thereafter be bound to discharge them.

2.3(b) *Duty imposed upon the trustee of the deceased's estate*

There is a prime duty imposed upon a trustee by the above principles and the Act.

The trustee must use the property to raise a family for the deceased who died without a family. The reasons for this duty have been made clear already, and so it is not necessary to repeat them here. I would like to add that the trustee's duties are terminated only after he has

---

[26] K. A. Busia, *The Challenge of Africa*, Oxford University Press, 1962, cited by Dr Francis Deng in *(1965) SLJR*, p.535.
[27] Ibid.

married a wife for the deceased, and after the transfer of the balance of the estate to her. Even so, he will still exercise a supervisory role over the property and the newly raised family till some male children become mature enough to take over full responsibility.

2.3(c) *Exclusion of daughters from inheritance*
Daughters remain as members of the family as long as they remain unmarried. As soon as they are married, they become members of different families. Until they are married they enjoy all the necessary benefits of the family property, but they cannot inherit any part of the estate as they are potentially regarded as members of other families. To allow them to inherit part of the estate would mean that they were entitled to take this property to their new families. This would be incompatible with the principle that the property of the deceased (or of the family) must remain within the family.

2.3(d) *Exclusion of the divorced wife or wives from inheritance*
It is of course obvious that a divorced wife ceases to be a member of the family of her divorced husband, and so she cannot be entitled to inherit from the estate of the deceased husband. To be allowed to inherit would conflict with the principle of keeping the estate within the family of the deceased. Where she remains a wife at the time of his death, she is entitled to inherit. But if she later decides to divorce the deceased, she will have to give up the part of the estate which she has already obtained since she is leaving the family. She cannot inherit anything even if the deceased is her son. Nor can she inherit anything if the deceased is her daughter who died while married, and still remains married after her death.

2.3(e) *Testate or testamentary succession becomes less common*
No serious problems are posed if the head of the family or a person dies intestate, because the estate just remains within the family. Unless the family has grown large (i.e., if there are many wives with children) so that there exist smaller units of families within a larger family, there is no necessity to make a will. Where there are several wives with children, then it becomes necessary to divide the property among these small units. But in almost all cases the head of the family, when he is expecting death or sometimes when he is not expecting it, makes a distribution of the family property among his wives and their children. Although the whole property is kept by him, as the head of the whole family during his lifetime, each wife and her children have a specific property earmarked or assigned to them. The whole property, however, remains under the sole supervision of the head. There are

only few instances where it is necessary for a person to make a will when he is expecting death.[28]

2.4 Brothers and parents as alternative heirs

The idea of having parents or brothers as alternative heirs or successors presupposes the continuity of the oneness of the original family. Although the original family to which they belong (i.e., parents and deceased brothers) has grown larger and has fragmented into separate units, yet it is still closely tied by the strength of family bonds. In other words, the original family with its new components still remain one, although the ties may have become a little weaker. In fact, even if the deceased's wife or wives are alive, the deceased's parents, if they are alive, must exercise parental care over the deceased's family. Conversely, if these parents are too old to exercise the parental care, they automatically must fall under the care of the deceased's wives or/and children (if those children are mature). The deceased's parents (if they have ceased to have their own separate property, i.e., if they have relinquished control and passed their property to their children as they have become too weak to need ownership of property) must enjoy the benefits of the estate equally with the deceased's wife and children.

If the deceased has brothers but has no family of his own, his property will automatically remain under the charge of his brothers. The brother or brothers of the deceased normally hold the estate in two capacities. In one capacity, they hold the estate as trustees. As trustees they have certain social obligations which they must discharge for their late brother. These duties oblige them to exercise reasonable care for the safety of the deceased's estate and ultimately to marry a wife for him, since a person's main object in life (which is a joint responsibility of the whole family together with other close agnatic relatives) is to raise children to keep his lineage running perpetually. It is not the deceased's estate alone which will be used in the discharge of this obligation. His brothers' or parents' property, together with contributions from other relatives, will be used in raising a family for the deceased (if he died a bachelor or without a family).

The second capacity by which they hold the estate of the deceased brother is as the legal heirs (or successors). This does not mean the abandonment of their duty to raise a family for the deceased. They have the legal authority to dispose of the part or the whole of the

---

[28] Wills are often made when one is on the point of death. It is usually old people who make wills before their death becomes imminent. One appears to bewitch oneself if one makes a will.

estate of the deceased, provided that they are aware of their social obligation which requires them at any time to raise property, in order to marry a woman for the deceased. In many cases, if the duty to raise a family is not discharged during the lifetime of the deceased's brother, the latter's children or their grand-children will inherit the obligation and so they will still be bound in future to discharge this duty.

The same obligation is imposed on anyone else who takes charge of the deceased's estate as a trustee in circumstances where there are no parents nor brothers. The order of priority for persons who may be the trustees is set out in section 52 of the Dinka Customary Law Act, 1984. The priority goes to the maternal uncle; if he is not available, it goes to the paternal uncle. Each of these persons referred to in section 52 of the Act holds the estate only in one capacity, and that is as a trustee. He has no right to dispose of any part of the estate for his own purposes, unless the disposal is intended to improve the estate.

2.5 Property which constitutes part of the estate

At this juncture, we may discuss the nature of what may be regarded as 'part of the estate'.

In Dinka society, livestock is the most important property which constitutes the main part of the estate. In the first place, livestock is of great economic and social value. Because of this importance, it corresponds with currency as a medium of exchange and is commonly used for the discharge of very important social and economic obligations. Where a person has one wife and children, it will not be necessary for him to distribute the livestock. The livestock will pass to his family as a whole, since it is only one unit. If there is an elder son, he will hold the property as his property and as a trustee for the family. But, if there are several wives and children, as stated before, he must make a will to distribute the property among the units of his family so as to avoid future conflict. However, if he dies intestate while he has several family units, the whole family, with the assistance of other kinsmen, will take charge of the distribution of the livestock. Owing to the importance of livestock, there is always a will made for its distribution among the units of the family before the head expects his death.

The next property of importance is land (i.e. the home and farm land attached to it). There is often no conflict to be expected in the interests in land when succession becomes an issue. Because of the abundance of land, each wife and her children (or each unit of a larger family) have their own separate home and farm land. When the head of the family dies, each unit remains on its land. There will be no question of dispute over land with the other units. Each unit of family, which may consist of a wife, sons and daughters, will continue to live there. If the daughters get married, their mother and their brothers remain there. Each son who marries (the eldest is always the first to marry, followed by the next in order of birth) leaves the family home and builds a home for himself and his wife. This continues until, ultimately, the mother is left with her last son and young daughters who are not yet married.

If, ultimately, all the sons and daughters are married, the mother will choose to live with one of her sons or her daughters. The original home may remain with the last son to live in it if he is married, unless the land has been left because of infertility and the title has therefore been lost. Problems may arise nowadays in urban communities where a man with a number of wives owns one house and all of them live in it, because of the scarcity of land or due to the fact that a man may not be able to afford a plot and a house for every wife he has. The customary law does not have a provision for the distribution of such single estates. But, if the head of the family has not made a will as to its disposal, such a house or land may be regarded as part of communal ownership (according to the principle of communal ownership of family property). If there are several units within the larger family, the best way out of the difficulty will be to sell it and divide the proceeds in equal shares, or the senior wife or a wife with more children may get a bigger share.

Such a procedure may not be strange to the conception of the Dinka people, because there are circumstances where the head of the family may have several units within a large family, and he may have a single cow. If he dies, these units of his family will wait till the cow produces offspring which can then be distributed. Usually, the senior wife is entitled to a larger share and so she and her children may take the cow while its offspring are divided among the junior wives.

But it must not be understood that Dinka Law distributes the estate in fixed fractions, as is the case in Islamic Law, where a wife gets a quarter of the estate (if they are two wives, each wife gets one-eighth); the daughter gets one-half (if there are two or more, they each get one-third) while each of the deceased's parents gets one-sixth and the males, such as sons, get the residue, or, if there are no sons nor grandsons, the deceased's brothers get the residue.

The issue of fixing the shares in cases of succession is rendered less important by the conception that the property of the family (though there may be small units within it), in principle, must remain under communal ownership. Even in circumstances where each unit is entitled to own separate property, there must still be general control by the head. Further, all the major obligations facing the family must jointly be discharged out of the whole family property with assistance from the agnatic relatives and sometimes from the maternal uncles. All the kinsmen join to contribute property in the discharge of such general obligations, for example, marriage or payment of compensation for homicide. In short, the fact that the estate is not distributed in fixed shares is more a product of the principle of communal ownership. Further, the Dinka do not deal in property which may be divided into fractions. The question of selling property and dividing the proceeds may be a new phenomenon, which is a product of the introduction of currency with the advent of the modern Government, but it has not up to now become a part of the Dinka Law of Succession.

The other items of property which may form part of the deceased's estate are ornaments, such as *guen-jang* (precious beads usually worn in large numbers around the waist or neck by a suitor, as part of decoration); *tung-akôôn* (a carved elephant tusk worn as an armlet by a suitor or a man of noble character); *thienyē-cil* (a precious stick made from rhino's horn which is highly valued as a prestige booster). A person who intends to marry must have these things in order to bolster his prestige. *Guen-jāng* is a type of bead which was on sale during the Turkish Rule in the Sudan and ceased to be produced a long time ago. Since its sources of production have become extinct, it has become so precious that no one can correctly state its value.

These ornaments are essential parts of the deceased's estate. Where one dies without having made a will, it is usually decided that, in case of *guen-jāng*, it must remain the joint property of the sons, because it is not usually worn continuously by one person. It may even be lent to other relatives or friends if they have special occasions for which they want to decorate themselves. In the case of *tung-akôôn* or *thienyē-cil*, the owner may decide, during his lifetime or when he is nearing his death, to pass it to one of his sons, usually the eldest. But it is not an obligation that either of these should always go to the eldest son.

Other properties of minor importance, such as utensils or the household items in general just remain within the family. They cannot be the subject of any dispute.

2.6 Appointment of a trustee for the family
There is one other important point which must not be left untouched. It has been touched upon briefly before. Although the wife or wives and any children who are under age do not constitute part of the estate, the man must include them in his will. He must appoint a person or persons who will take care of his wife (or wives) and children. If the wife or wives are still at child-bearing ages, he must appoint a person, among his brothers, or among his agnatic relatives,

to take care of each wife and to continue the production of children with her. Of course, if he has several wives, they will not be entrusted to one man. If he dies intestate, his parents or brothers or other relatives will decide upon a person or persons to whom the wife or wives shall be entrusted for the purpose of procreation of children. Meanwhile the deceased's parents and brothers take the overall care of the whole family of the deceased, even if the wife or wives are entrusted to some distant relative or relatives.

2.7 The impact of tribal or public rights upon succession
There are two impacts imposed by public rights upon the question of succession, namely:

2.7(a) *rights which cannot be inherited*
As a member of a tribal community, a person is entitled to enjoy certain rights which are also commonly enjoyed by other members of the community at the same time. For example, he has the rights of fishing in tribal lakes and rivers; his cattle are entitled to graze in the tribal pastures; he is entitled to obtain various benefits from the tribal forests and so forth.

All these rights do not constitute part of his personal estate, which is subject to inheritance by his heirs. He cannot bequeath or make a bequest of these rights, because they are not his personal rights over which he has exclusive enjoyment. But his legal heirs can enjoy the same rights, not as heirs of the deceased, but as members of the same community. Precisely speaking, there are certain rights which a person may enjoy but cannot pass to his heirs, because they are also the rights of the public or of the tribal members.

2.7(b) *the estate may be inherited with restrictions imposed upon it through the rights acquired over it by others*
Members of the public may acquire certain rights over one's property. These rights may be in the nature of easements and profits. For example, the right of way over somebody's property may be acquired by members of the public. But the owner of the property cannot deprive them of this right. Members of the public may also be entitled to enjoy fishing in a '*kol*' owned by a family. When the owner of property dies, the property passes to the legal heirs with these restrictions imposed upon it through the acquisition of rights by members of the public.

3. THE LAND LAW

3.1 Statutory provisions

Part One of this chapter concentrates on the tracing of property and the transfer of title. In that part, 'cattle' is treated as the dominant property. But there is no reference to land as part of property. It must also be noted that land law is not embodied in the Re-statement of the Bhar el Ghazal Region Customary Law Act, 1984; nevertheless it must be included here.

The subject of land in the Sudan is regulated by the Land Settlement and Registration Act, 1925 and the Unregistered Land Act, 1970.[29] The latter Act declares that

> all waste, forest, occupied, unoccupied and unregistered land is deemed to be Government property and to be registered under the Land Settlement and Registration Act, 1925.

Although, according to this Act, the Government is the dominant land owner, the customary rules operate (within the frame-work of Government ownership) to regulate the use of land among the tribal communities. In practice, the statutory provisions operate in certain towns or developed areas. Government ownership of all the land in the country is merely theoretical. Among the rural communities, in many areas, rights over land are being regulated by customary rules. The operation of the customary rules, however, does not deprive the Government of its theoretical ownership. The Land Law in the Sudan also recognises private ownership.

> 'The Sudan Land Law, being influenced by Islamic Law and custom, recognises the doctrine of ownership of land. In this respect it is different from English Land Law where there is no doctrine of ownership of land; there is a doctrine of possession of land or seisin, the overlord being the Crown.'[30]

But the individual's right of ownership is a qualified one.

> 'The right of ownership of land is not exercised absolutely. Land

---

[29] This Act was repealed by the Civil Transactions Act, 1983. But concept of private ownership is incorporated in the latter Act, sections 519–521.
[30] Dr Saed Mohamed Ahmed El Mahdi *(1971) SLJR*, p.260. Dr Saed made this statement in his article which was published after the enactment of the Unregistered Land Act, 1970.

may be deemed to be subject to liabilities, rights and interests even without notification in the land register.'[31]

Some of these liabilities are: land tax, house tax, building, sanitary and other regulations, rights of way, rights of water and other easements and so forth.

After the enactment of the Unregistered Land Act, 1970, repealed by the Civil Transactions Act, 1984, ss 519–530 which lay emphasis on private ownership of land except that owned by the Government, some of the above liabilities may not have automatic existence. 'No easements, rights or title to land registered in the name of the Government, could be established nor acquired.'[32]

In fact, some of these liabilities have no practical application or do not operate in practice in rural areas but only among the urban communities. For example, regulations relating to buildings or sanitation do not affect the ownership of land in the rural areas.

3.2 Stagnancy in land development

In dealing with the question of 'property', the Dinka seem to give precedence to cattle, and, consequently, there is more development in branches of the law where transactions involve the use of cattle. The precedence given to cattle tends to give the impression that 'land', as part of property, has very little significance. This impression seems to be supported by the fact that there is either stagnancy or very little development taking place in the field of Land Law.

But it would be a wrong conclusion to state that land is of little significance to the Dinka. Land is very important to the lives of people as well as the lives of their domestic animals, such as cattle. The question of stagnancy or slow development in the field of Land Law is a result of two main factors. The first factor is connected with the predominant idea of communal usage or ownership of land.[33] This tends to limit the zone of individual rights or interests over land. As the zone of private rights or interests is reduced by the communal usage or ownership, disputes between private individuals become fewer. Consequently, civil litigation becomes less frequent and this

---

[31] Dr Saed Mohamed Ahmed El Mahdi *(1971) SLJR63*.
[32] Dr Saed Mohamed Ahmed El Mahdi *(1971) SLJR65*.
[33] In *(1965) SLJR 592*, Dr Francis Deng said:

> 'Mythologically, if not actually, the conquering Leader in a tribe is said to have distributed land among his original followers, and thereby formed the sub-tribe or sections, the heads of these sections redivided the land among their internal groups....'

factor contributes to the slow development of the law in this field. It is, of course, obvious that rapid development of the law is facilitated by the immensity of litigation.

The second factor which contributes to the slow development of the Land Law is that economic transactions involving the disposal or transfer of land are almost nil. For example, transactions such as mortgages, conveyances, sales or purchases of land, land charges, leases or tenancy and so forth are unknown to the Dinka. These economic transactions involving ownership or possession or interests in land contribute much to the development of the law, because a great deal of civil litigation is attributed to them. The courts' decisions on these issues create the expansion of the law. Apart from these judicial precedents, the State legislatures also enact statutes to organize the interests of individuals over land, and this adds to the increasing development in this branch of the law.

3.3 The two land divisions and their usage

In dealing with the subject of Land Law, there are two geographical features of land which must be taken note of. The territory of a Dinka tribal community usually comprises two geographical features technically known as *baai*[34] and *toc*. Each of these land divisions has its special significance to a Dinka life. The word *toc* has no exact corresponding term in the English language and it is also very difficult to define, but it may be better understood when described. *Toc* (often written by foreigners as *toich*) is generally a low land. This is the area where lakes or rivers over-flow their banks and flood the adjacent plains during rainy seasons. Most parts of the *toc* may be described as open plains or vast areas of land covered by a variety of water plants and grass. The lowest parts of the *toc* remain swampy throughout the year or for the most part of the year. Scattered trees may be found in areas which are relatively high. The 'Sud' region along the White Nile is a typical example of the *toc*.

Baai, on the other hand, literally means 'home'. It has other meanings, one of which is that part of the land or territory which is suitable for building homes or permanent settlements. It is also suitable for farming or agriculture. The latter meaning constitutes the context in which the word is being used here.

3.3(a) *The importance of the Toc*

Toc is very vital to the life of the Dinka for a variety of reasons. In the

---

[34] This is the area which Dr Francis Deng referred to as 'Arable or Residential land'. *(1965) SLJR 593*.

first place, the Dinka rear cattle in the *toc*. It is a very suitable area for their cattle to graze, as it consists of large and rich pastures. Besides the pastures, there is always plenty of water throughout the year for cattle use. Secondly, the fishing areas are in the *toc*. Thirdly, the *toc* attracts a variety of wild game because of rich pastures and water. It therefore constitutes a good hunting area. Owing to these three main advantages, the life of the Dinka is very much adapted to the *toc*. A Dinka person would imagine a life without *toc* to be a very miserable one.

3.3(b) *The importance of Baai*

On the other hand, the main reasons which give significance to the other land division, *Baai*, have in fact been stated before. These are its suitability for building homes or permanent settlements and farming. There are also many other advantages connected with *baai*, apart from those which have been mentioned. For example, as it is usually high land, there are forests from which many advantages are derived. But the legal importance of the distinction between these two categories of land use rests on the fact that in the *toc* area the whole land is subject to communal usage (with very few exceptions). Private rights in this area are overriden by communal rights. But in the residential area (*baai*), apart from those areas which are reserved for communal usage, private interests in land or rights are recognised and respected;[35] for example, the community does not tamper with the rights of an individual to have a residence, or agricultural land around his house. The details concerning communal and private usage of land will be discussed later.

3.4 Public and private interests in land

These will be discussed under the following headings:

(a) Modes of acquisition of land;
(b) The nature of individual's interest in land;
(c) The ownership of things on and under the land;
(d) Reserved lands for communal usage; and
(e) Rights of members of the public over the property of other persons.

As the nature of the individual's interest over land is not very clear, it requires to be determined separately. The modes of acquisition of

---

[35] There are also a few exceptions, e.g., right of way. The word 'absolute' means that as long as one remains the occupant of land, one's right of usage cannot be disturbed.

title to land, which hereafter follow, relate solely to acquisition by the tribal community.

3.4(a) *Modes of acquisition of title to land*
The following are the recognised modes of acquisition of title to land:

(i) by occupation;
(ii) by conquest;
(iii) by way of gift and inheritance.

It is to be remarked here that owing to the advent of modern Government with a system of public security, acquisition of land by conquest has become a matter of a historical interest only. A very brief explanation for each of these modes of acquisition of title may be given here.

3.4(a) (i) By Occupation
Where a piece of land has no owner,[36] its ownership or title may be acquired by occupation. The ownership or title passes to the first occupants of that land. Occupation is established if the occupants settle on the land with intent to remain thereon permanently. But this does not mean that any portion of the land of a tribal community which remains without settlements on it, or which is empty, can be regarded as land which has no owner.

3.4(a) (ii) By Conquest
Acquisition of title to land by conquest was most common in the past when the Dinka tribes were migrating from the east to the west or to the areas which they presently occupy. Most parts of the Dinka lands, west of the White Nile, were occupied by a certain Luo tribe known (by the Agar) as Gel or (by the Rek) as Jur-Luel. It is not clearly established where this Luo tribe went and settled after they had been dispossessed of their land by the Dinka tribes.

3.4(a) (iii) By Gift
A third mode of acquisition of title or ownership of land is by gift. One example which may illustrate this point is a case between the Dinka Agar and the Jur-beli of Rumbek.
The Agar tribe, under the leadership of Buoi Kuot, who was a

---

[36] In case of 'res nullis' or 'ownerless property', even in the cases of private individuals, the first to occupy a piece of land with intent to appropriate it is entitled to occupy it.

Banybith (Spiritual leader), were living with their cattle in the *toc* which they had acquired after the Gel had been driven out of it. This land or most of it remained covered with water for most or all of the year, and was therefore unsuitable for agriculture. The Jur-beli had a large area of agricultural land which remained dry throughout the year. Buoi Kuot wanted part of this territory to be given to his people, but there was already a feud between the two tribes. Buoi Kuot therefore decided to make a peace treaty with the new leader of the Jur-beli (called Lang Joro;[37] the former leader had been killed with his son Warnyany and others by the Agar). Buoi Kuot gave his daughter to the new leader so that peace could prevail between the two tribes and to enable him to obtain part of the agricultural land. Buoi succeeded. The Jur-beli moved further south, leaving a large territory to him and his people. The Agar therefore acquired the ownership of the land around Rumbek town as a gift from the Jur-beli.[38]

Having disposed of the modes of acquisition of title to land, the nature of the individual's interests in tribal land will now be considered. Land may also be acquired by inheritance.

3.4(b) *The nature of the individual's right or interest in land.*
The nature of an individual right or interest in land poses a serious problem of identification.

> 'The analysis of the clusters of rights and claims of privileges and liabilities which are related to the ways in which Africans hold and work the land, live on it and use its products is complex, on the one hand, because of the difficulties in evaluating the exact nature of the rights and claims and, on the other hand, because of the implications of economic, social, political and religious factors. It is therefore very difficult to characterise African systems of land tenure in terms of familiar legal and linguistic concepts.'[39]

These religious aspects may be seen in a number of cases. It is common to find most of the claims related to the residential areas or *Wuntheer* [40] (or in the plural *Wuot-theer*) based on religious or social

---

[37] The land around Rumbek town is now known as the land of Akon Buoi, i.e., the land Buoi bought with his daughter Akon.
[38] The pronunciation of this name may have been corrupted by the Dinkas.
[39] Biebuyck, *African Agrarian Systems*, cited by Dr Francis Deng in *(1963) SLJR*, 588.
[40] 'Wunther': these are ancient mounds which a certain Luo tribe built in the toc many years back when they were occupying the present Dinka land.

aspects. For example, if the claimant's ancestors died and were buried in the place, a strong claim of the land may be asserted by the descendants of those ancestors. It is believed that the spirits of the ancestors still remain in occupation and so no one else should occupy it. The frequency of claims on those bases differs from area to area. Among the Dinkas, there are other tribes however who acknowledge the loss of a private individual's right to arable land which he has already abandoned. More of this issue will be discussed below.

Dr Francis Deng, the only writer to deal with Land Law among the Dinkas (in an article published in the Sudan Law Journal and Reports),[41] like other writers on African law found himself in difficulty in stating whether the nature of the individual's rights or interests in land may be expressed in terms of ownership or not. It seems that it is the idea of communal rights in land which creates most uncertainty in determining whether the individual's interest (right) in land may, as in the case of livestock, be regarded as 'ownership'. This conclusion is clearly demonstrated by Dr Francis Deng in the following statement:

'The customs governing the cattle differ from those relating to land. *Whereas rights in land are more communal in nature,* ownership of cattle is more personal.'[42]

In an attempt to stay on the safe side, Dr Deng tries to avoid using the concept 'ownership' to describe the interest of a private person in land. Instead, he more often uses the term 'right'. But, on the whole, where he uses the term 'right', he implies that the private interest in land may be expressed in terms of ownership. This view is confirmed by the following quotation from his article:

'But in all the three tribes (i.e., Nilotes Dinka, Nuer and Shilluk) and in whatever manner the possession of *arable or residential land* is acquired, a man and his family have the exclusive right to use that land. It is inherited from generation to generation... the right of the individual member of the tribal community over his residential land is so strong that even if he abandons it, it must be kept unoccupied unless he gives consent to a relative to take it over.

---

[41] Dr Francis Deng, *Property and Value – Interplay among the Nilotes (1965) SLJR,* pp.592-595.

[42] Whether deliberately or not, Dr Francis Deng uses 'right' in the case of land and 'ownership' in the case of livestock. He seems to be using 'right' and 'ownership' as if they are synonymous or inter-changeable, or he is perhaps deliberately avoiding the common difficulty in choosing the correct concept (between possession and ownership) to express the nature of private interest in land.

Often a long-abandoned area is referred to by the name of the owner who has once occupied it but has long since deserted it.[43] Even if someone else be allowed to use the unoccupied land in the absence of the owner, on return it must be surrendered to him.'[44]

The exclusive right of a man and his family to use the land, the inheritance of such land from generation to generation, the right of the individual's member of the tribal community over the residential land even if such land has been abandoned, all point to the fact that the individual right in land (i.e., residential and arable land) may be expressed as a right of ownership. This is even more apparent in the last part of the quotation where Dr Deng uses the term 'owner' in reference to the person who once occupied the land which he abandoned subsequently.

However, in reference to the rights which are usually exercisable in the *toc*, Dr Deng seems to acknowledge their being communally enjoyed. He writes: 'Rights in land, grazing land, and fishing and drinking pools are held by those who are considered to be the descendants of the original occupiers of the area.'[45]

The descendants of the original occupiers (of these specifically mentioned areas) are in fact the community. These descendants may be described as a clan (but the word 'clan' may not be appropriate because a clan may be spread among many Dinka tribes. With the Dinkas, a clan is not a unit that always lives in one place). The term *wut*, used by Dr Deng, is more correct. In essence, he recognises the fact that the right or ownership of these places is vested in the community whose ancestors were the first to occupy those parts of the land. The complexity of the nature of the individual's right over land (not only among the Dinka but among the African communities) often baffles any writer on the subject. Consequently, he is often in a dilemma as to the correct concept to use to describe the individual's interest in land. Dr Deng is therefore not exceptional. He admitted this when he said: 'So complicated and intricate are the problems associated with the land tenure that to use words like 'ownership' so loosely is futile.[46]

---

[43] Such reference to the original owner as far as the old site (or *pantheer*) is concerned is usually made when the land remains unoccupied since the time it was abandoned by the owner. But, if there have been subsequent occupants of it, unless there is a special reason, reference need not be made to the first occupant.
[44] Dr Francis Deng, *Property and Value – Interplay among the Nilotes*, (1965) SLJR, pp.592-595.
[45] *(1965) SLJR 592*, p.592.
[46] Ibid., p.593.

On the customary law of the Aweil Dinka, Capt Cook Stubbs[47] expressed the same difficulty. Although he talked of the individual's claims of interest over land, he was unable to state confidently the nature of that interest – whether it is possessory right or ownership right. As far as the community is concerned, he acknowledged the vesting of 'ownership' in a clan; that is, the ownership of a territory vests in the community. The individuals, whether from the same community or another community, enjoy what appears to be a usufruct[48] or profit. They can remove a forest and make residences there.

> 'The ownership of cleared land is jealously guarded and vested in the clan and sub-divided among the heads of families... it may sometimes happen that a family who have left their land years before return and, finding it occupied, attempt to turn the new comer off. In the past the chiefs would have upheld the cause of the original *owner*, but by the government intervention it has been ruled that a man cannot be turned off the land he has cultivated for the past two years.'[49]

But despite the vesting of ownership of the 'cleared land' in the clan, Capt Stubbs indirectly regarded the family or the individual's interest over arable land as a right of 'ownership'. This was obvious when he said: 'In the past the chiefs would have upheld the cause of the original owner'.[50]

We mentioned earlier that the subject of Land Law has some peculiar features which require to be discussed separately. The difficulties involved have been made clearer in the above discussions. As far as the identification of the nature of the communal rights or usage of land is concerned, there has not been any difficulty. The consensus of opinion is that the right of ownership of a given territory is always vested in the community. The problem however is the identification of the nature of the individual's interest in land. The choice of the right concept by which his interest can be expressed poses some difficulties. These difficulties can be said to be the products of the communal rights of ownership of land. This however seems to give the appearance that the problem is one of 'a battle of words'. This battle of words relates to whether the individual's interest in land can be

---

[47] File No. *BGP/66-B-1, p.5*.
[48] The right of using and taking the fruits of something belonging to another.
[49] File No. *BGP/66-B-1, p.5*
[50] Ibid.

described as a 'right'. But 'right' may not, in this case, stand in isolation, and so one may go further to try to ascertain whether it is a 'possessory right' or a 'right of ownership' or whether it is a limited right which might appropriately be regarded as usufruct, and so on. The discussion here will be aimed at determining whether the interest of a private individual can be expressed or identified in terms of one of the concepts mentioned above.

But before we discuss this issue, we will first refer to one caution given by Dias:

'The formation of sound thinking habits is bound up with the meaning and use of words. Lawyers should be particularly concerned with this question since, as Lord Macmillan said, *'the Lawyer's business is with words. They are the raw material of his craft.'*[51]

Dias continued:

'Some of the difficulties that have arisen in jurisprudence are rooted in fallacies of language... In the first place, the idea that a word must necessarily possess some "proper" meaning should be abandoned. The same thing may be referred to by different words for different purposes... Secondly, although a word has no "proper" meaning, it may well have a "usual" meaning. But even in this it should be observed that some words have more than one usual meaning in which case the context may have to resolve which meaning is being considered... Thirdly, it is of the utmost importance that words should be accorded the interpretation desired by their user.'[52]

This passage has been quoted at length, since it constitutes a consoling caution in the circumstances where the search for the proper word or concept to be used in expressing a particular point of interest may tend to obscure the whole subject of discussion. The last point in the quotation is of special significance. It is helpful where writers on this subject seek to identify the nature of the individual's interest in land. It is an advisory opinion which may lead a writer to try to understand what people believe to be the nature of the individual's interest in land. The writer should not impose the use of a concept of

---

[51] R. W. M. Dias *Jurisprudence*, 2nd ed., Butterworths, London, 1964, p.146.
[52] Ibid.

his choice merely because he thinks it is a convenient term to use.

The references which we made did not state in clear terms what the correct concept should be in expressing the nature of a private individual's interest in land. There are three proposals to make here, in order to determine which should be the correct expression regarding the individual's interest in land: (1) a possessory right (2) a usufruct (3) an ownership right.

3.4(b) (i) Possessory right

It is established clearly that the ownership of a whole territory is vested in the community or tribal community whose ancestors were the first to settle on it as an empty land, or through conquest, or as a gift. All writers on African legal systems concur on this point. The question of reserved lands for communal usage within the tribal land is a subject of separate discussion below. In this section, the whole discussion is devoted to the nature of a private individual's interest in land as indicated by the three proposed alternative views.

The first proposal is that it is a possessory right because the occupant of land has both the *corpus* and *animus possidendi*. There is no doubt that an occupant of a residence with arable land around it has *corpus* (the custody of a thing or the thing under his physical control). He may also have the *animus possidendi*.[53] But this second element seems to give rise to a confusion as to the nature of his interest in land. The exercise of this element – *animus possidendi* – tends to equate a possessor of land with an owner. However, to base a judgement on the intention of the occupant of land is to apply a subjective test. It is not the maintenance of *animus possidendi* that makes him the owner. It is generally what the community believes that should be the basis for determining the nature of such interest, that is, whether it is a possessory right or a right of ownership. In other words the test should be an objective one.

The second argument in support of this point is that, since the ownership of the whole land or territory is vested in the community or tribe, it is impossible that a private person can simultaneously be entitled to acquire the ownership of it. While the owner (i.e. the community) has not relinquished the right of ownership, there is no room for an individual to exert a claim of title over somebody's property. As was shown in the definition of ownership, an owner[54] has

---

[53] 'Animus possidendi' refers to a mental element or intention to hold a thing as one's own (Salmond).
[54] The owner being the whole tribal community.

an exclusive right over his property, and so a private individual has no claim. It can therefore be stated that what he enjoys over the land under his physical control is merely a possessory right.

A third argument in support of the point is that, where the agricultural land within the individual's homestead has become exhausted or has ceased to be fertile after long continuous cultivation, the occupant may decide to move to new fertile land, where he settles by making a new home there. In this case, if the abandoned land has acquired fertility again and still remains empty, another member of the community is entitled to enter and make his residence there. This is where we have some reservations with respect to the extreme view – of indefinite exercise of exclusive right by the original occupant – put forward by Dr Francis Deng. This extreme view of exclusive rights will be subjected to further discussion below. In fact the new occupant acquires the right of occupation. There are a few exceptions where the original occupant is entitled to exercise exclusive rights over the abandoned land, but such right of exclusion is subject to some conditions also. However, I will reserve the discussion on these exceptional circumstances till later.

Fourthly, the possessory nature of the individual's rights or interests over the land is supported by the fact that the exclusive right of a person over the abandoned residential land is merely an exceptional case and not a general rule.

Fifthly, the community would not allow an individual to acquire the right of ownership while at the same time it allows free movement of its members in search on fertile lands. This would lead to scarcity of land if an individual were able to exercise exclusive rights (indefinitely, as Dr Francis Deng thought) over abandoned lands. He can also have many abandoned lands over the whole tribal land, since there is no restriction on movement, and, if he is entitled to maintain indefinite exclusive rights over the abandoned lands, he may acquire private ownership over a substantial part of the land of the whole tribe. If this is done by everybody, there will be very serious physical conflicts which would require the society to decide to prevent the abandonment of residential homes, or else to decide that no one is entitled to have exclusive rights over the abandoned lands. All these factors lead to the conclusion that an individual enjoys only possessory rights, which he loses as soon as he abandons the residence.

But it is not established that the community believes that the interest is in the nature of a possessory right. In view of the previous caution on the war of words, we must adopt a concept acceptable to the community. But the community's conception of the nature of private interest in residential and arable land does not seem to conform with the concept of possession, in which case another concept may be examined.

3.4(b)   (ii) Usufruct
The word usufruct is a Roman legal term. It means:

> 'the right of using and taking the fruits of something belonging to another. It was understood to be given for the life of the receiver, the usufructuary, unless a shorter period was expressed and then it was to be restored to the owner in as good condition as when it was given except for ordinary wear and tear.'[55]

The word 'fruit' in the definition does not literally mean fruit in the usual meaning. It means 'produce' or 'products' of property.

The involvement of a Roman term in the discussion of an African law may appear strange. But we must state here that certain concepts or practices have universal application. Many African customary laws, including the Dinka, have a system which is very similar to the Roman right of usufruct. The Dinka, and many African traditional legal systems embody a practice where an occupant of an area of arable land may allow another person to cultivate his land. It may be for one year or a number of years. The period is usually indefinite if the person cultivating the land of another has not yet made a home before acquiring arable land elsewhere. The technical word for such practice in Dinka is *oor* (usually expressed as *oor-dom*. *Dom* means 'farm' or field for cultivation). The one who cultivates the land of another (i.e. usufructuary) owns the farm produce but cannot claim any right or interest apart from his 'fruits' on the land. In other words, he does not maintain *animus possidendi* over the land. Nor can he be called a possessor of the land because the *corpus* is not vested in him. The main difference between '*oor*' as a system and 'usufruct' is that the latter is a right but the former is a privilege.

It has been proposed alternatively that, if the individual's interest in

---

[55] *Osborn's Concise Law Dictionary*, 6th ed., by John Burke, p.338.

Note: Under the definitions of the Prescription and Limitation Ordinance 1928, it is stated that 'unless and until the contrary is established upon settlement under the Provisions of Land Settlement and Registration Ordinance a person in possession, use, or enjoyment of waste, forest, or unregistered land with or without express permission of the Government shall be deemed to be an usufructuary'. But the same Ordinance (in fact now an Act) recognises the acquisition of ownership of land (by passage of 20 years in the case of non-Governmental land and 10 years in the case of Governmental land). But with the enactment of the 1970 Act, prescription of Governmental land may not continue.

land is not a possessory right it may be regarded as a usufruct. This proposal receives support from the fact that if the ownership vests in the community, the possession also vests in the community, unless the community decides to vest the possession in someone else while it retains the ownership; if this is so, the first alternative could be the correct expression of the nature of the individual's right.

We have mentioned before that in the Roman concept, 'usufruct' is a right, while *oor*, which is the Dinka term, is not a right but a privilege. The occupant of land can terminate this privilege at will at any time. Even if *oor* were a right as 'usufruct' is a right, it can be stated that such a right is very limited. It is only a right to the ownership of 'fruits'. Consequently, a private individual's right cannot be expressed as a 'usufruct' (or *oor*, which is even more limited in scope). Again the Dinka people do not view private interests in land in terms which are similar to usufruct. Hence this is not the correct concept to adopt.

3.4(b) (iii) Ownership right

The third view is that the individual's interest over the residential and arable land is a right of ownership. An individual may acquire the title to his residential and arable land in a manner which is the same as the modes of acquisition of land by the community (which have already been explained), except that he cannot acquire the title or ownership by conquest. He can also obtain it by inheritance. Let us examine the reasons which support this view.

In the first place, this opinion accords with the introductory statement of Dr Saeed to which we referred earlier on. It is also in conformity with the views of many other writers. The difficulty for most of these writers has been the lack of confidence in choosing the correct term or concept to use. Others[56] admitted defeat and expressed the difficulty of choosing correct concepts to express the African use of land. All in all, one can say that, despite the uncertainty, these writers generally express these interests in terms of 'ownership'.

Secondly, the conclusion that an individual owns the land can be deduced from the distinction between 'ownership' and 'possession'. As already defined, ownership (*dooc*) is a right of exclusive enjoyment of a thing. It also denotes a relationship between a person and a right vested in him. These characteristics or features are not part of possession. The usage of 'right' signifies a recognition by the community of a relationship between a thing and a person. It is not therefore a subjective expression or a claim by the individual

---

[56] e.g., Biebuyck.

concerned, but it is how the public understand it and describe it.

But according to Maine's definition, 'possession' (i.e. *muok*) is a physical detention coupled with *intention to hold the thing as one's own;* or, according to Salmond, 'it is the continuing *exercise of a claim to the exclusive use* of a material object'. In these definitions 'right' has not been used to denote the relationship between the person and the thing in question. Also, the *intention to claim exclusive use or to own a thing* is a subjective opinion and not objective. It is the person concerned who forms the intention and claims the exclusive use of the thing. Whether the community recognises such an intention to own or to claim the exclusive use as a right is not part of the definition of this concept. This is just the way the holder of the material thinks and not the way the public think. It is said 'possession is prima facie evidence of ownership'. This makes it clear that right of ownership is superior to the right of possession, and this is how *dooc* and *muok* are judged by the Dinka.

From this analysis, if we look at the interests of the occupant of residential land the correct conclusion is that the occupant is vested with the ownership of it. The community recognises the relationship between the person and the right vested in him. His exclusive right can be established by the use of an objective test. It is obvious from the public attitude that they recognise the relationship between the occupant and the land upon which he resides and which he cultivates.

The subject is in fact being discussed in a foreign language and not the language of the community whose custom is under discussion. If the subject were discussed in Dinka so that the Dinka concepts which correspond with 'ownership' (*dooc*) and 'possession' (*muok*) were used, a quick conclusion could have been reached. It is obvious that *dooc* is superior to *muok*. *Muok* clearly denotes that the holder is not the owner but that the owner is somewhere else (although of course the owner can also possess his property at the same time). But *muok*[57] is generally automatically associated with physical detention by a non-owner.

Thirdly, if the occupant of a homestead does not have ownership but only possession, it is possible that he could be evicted by the community at the expiry of a certain period or for other reasons. But this rarely happens.

We have mentioned in the above discussion that the community recognises that the interest of an occupier of a residential land or

---

[57] There is again the difficulty of getting a more appropriate word to correspond with foreign terminology. *Muok* as 'possession' in relation to land may not be the best word.

homestead is a right of ownership. This is the most important determining factor in choosing which concept to use, and we are therefore inclined to accept the use of 'ownership' as the correct expression of a private individual's right over residential land.

To conclude the discussion of this subject, it is necessary to make the following comments. It is often said that 'laws are made by man', but this is the common expression of laymen. Where there is a legislature (which is deemed to represent public opinion, i.e. of those who elected it), it has the power to pass statutes. Not all the people who participate in the enactment of statutes are lawyers; the majority of them are laymen. But whether the legislators are laymen or lawyers or a combination of both, they must have an intention which they must convey in certain and clear terms. However, not all the legal expressions in such statutes can always convey clearly the intention of the legislature (which is also deemed to be the intention of the populace). In this way, it becomes the task of the judges to carry out the interpretation of the words or expressions of certain concepts with the objective of trying, as far as possible, to ascertain the intention of the legislators. They must try their best to find out the intention of the law-makers and not what the judges or the lawyers think. Sometimes if the term is too vague to enable one to determine the intention, the judges have the advantage of reading certain terms into it in order to give efficacy to the legislators' intention.

In the case of customary law, the situation may in a way be said to be analogous to what has been stated above. There is no legislature that enacts the laws, but, as has been explained in the first chapter, customary rules grow out of practice. A particular custom or rule of custom must also have been adopted in practice in order to convey a definite intention. It is also the function of the lawyers or judges who apply these rules of custom to find out the intention. The customary rules may not convey clearly how the nature of the individual's interest in land can be expressed in precise concepts.[58] This has been the theme of the discussion all along. We have tried to examine the views of the writers quoted in the discussion, but it appears that there has been vagueness over the concepts used to express the nature of the individual's interest over land. However, despite this vagueness, the general opinion of almost all the writers is that an individual enjoys ownership rights over his residential and arable land.

We have also stated that, according to the Dinka conception, the

---

[58] Dias said that the custom 'must be certain and precise'. But difficulty in finding a latent meaning in a customary rule or the right concept to use would not amount to uncertainty.

correct concept to use is ownership or right of ownership. This conclusion on the nature of the individual's interest in land gives efficacy to the intention of the people. Further, this conclusion conforms with the previous caution quoted from Dias that it is of the utmost importance that words should be accorded the interpretation desired by their user or users. The users in our situation are the Dinka people. It is they who developed the custom and it is what they intend, if it can be identified, that should be adopted.[59]

3.4(c) *The ownership of things on and under the land*
It is generally understood that the ownership of things on and under the land belongs to the owner of the land. This means that the ownership of land goes with things on it and under it. But a distinction must be made here between the different things that can be found on land.

There is non-living and living material or property which may be movable or immovable, and there are living things such as animals. Domestic animals are excluded because every domestic animal has an owner. The animals referred to are the wild animals and fishes.

It is an accepted principle that an owner of land owns the things on it as well. For example, there are usually economic or fruit trees on the arable land of an individual. He may have a *rak*[60] (tree) or *akan* (Palm tree) on his land. He has an exclusive right over them. It is not necessary that he planted them himself. But he has exclusive right of ownership by virtue of the fact that he has the ownership of the land. If his neighbours come to enjoy the benefits of these things, it is through his express or implied permission.

Further, there are many herbs or plants or roots of certain trees or plants which are very useful as drugs or medicine. The herbs are usually dug from the ground or obtained from trees or plants. An owner of land under which these things remain buried, or on which they are fixed, owns them. There are two other cases which further

---

[59] (a) The case of *Macar Aeckoc and others* v. *Riak Dak and others* (See p.173), illustrates the conclusion that the conception of the Dinka as to the nature of private individual's interest in land can be expressed as ownership. The parties were claiming rights of ownership. Several decisions were made by many different courts on the same issue and these courts (except the one whose decision was appealed against) held that the ownership of land was vested in the appellants, whose grand-fathers, one after the other, had been living on that land continuously.

(b) The case of *guen-jang* (post), related by Makoi Ruai, does not establish only that an occupier of land enjoys the right of ownership but also that he enjoys the right to own things on it and under it.

[60] Rak – in Arabic language is known as 'lulu'.

Some Aspects of The Law of Property

illustrate this principle: (i) the case of *Guen-jang* and (ii) the case of *Aber* (metallic ore).

3.4(c) (i) The case of *Guen-jang*
Guen-jang has been explained before during the discussion of succession. Briefly, it is a precious type of beads.

The case of *guen-jang* is a good illustration of the rule that ownership of land goes with the things on it and under it. This was not a case contested in court. But rules of custom may be ascertained from the decisions of elders as well as from those of the courts. There was a unanimity of all the village elders on the existence of the rule that things which are found on land and under it are always the property of the owner of the land, and they continuously remain his property even if he has abandoned the land, provided that the land still remains unoccupied at the time the things are found or discovered.[61] The unanimity in reaching the decision was based on an existing custom. The facts of this case are as follows:

> The children of Pan-Kajo (i.e. the family of Kajo) were playing on *pan-theer*, the site of an old or abandoned home. The attention of the children was attracted by some objects lying on the surface of the land. They found that they were pieces of *guen-jang*. They started to collect them. During the collection, they began to search for more and they discovered some pieces of the precious beads buried under the earth. They dug them out. After they had finished digging, they ran home to their elders and announced their discovery. The beads were taken from them by the elders. From their appearance, the beads had been lying there for many years.

The question which faced the elders was where to find the owner. Neighbours were called and informed of the discovery. There was no one (after a reasonable search) who exerted a claim of title. In the absence of anyone who came forward to prove his title, it was generally concluded that they were the property of the original owner of the land. This conclusion was based on the rule that things found lying or fixed on land and those found under it are the property of the land owner. In fact the claim of title by the owner of land for the things on his land or under it can only be defeated if someone else comes forward to prove his title by showing how those things came to lie on

---

[61] There are of course some exceptions to this general rule, for example, where a person other than the land owner proves his title to the property found, he is entitled to claim it.

or under the land, or by other means proof. In this case no one did so. And as the original owner or his descendants could not be found or remembered by anyone, the beads were retained as foundlings. In the absence of the true owner, or the land owner, the founder had a better title than anyone else.

3.4(c)   (ii) The case of *Aber* (metallic ore)
Aber may also constitute a good illustration of the rule. Before the coming of the Government, metals were locally manufactured[62] by the people from what is known as *aber*; common among these were iron and copper ores. *Aber* used to be dug in order to make all sorts of implements such as hoes, spears, armlets or anklets. Where *aber* was discovered in one's land it was recognised as one's property by virtue of the fact that one owned the land.

3.4(c)   (iii) The ownership of animals on land
The animals here include fishes in rivers and lakes. In the case if animals on land, it is very difficult to state specifically that the ownership of land goes with the ownership of the animals (and the fishes) found thereon.

However, the difficulty in giving a positive or negative answer to this question lies in the case of wildlife or game and the fish in rivers or lakes. The difficulty in exerting a claim of title to wild game is that it does not remain in one place but may today be in the territory of one tribal community while tomorrow it may be in the territory of another tribal community. In the case of fishes in the rivers they also keep on moving. A tribal community owns that part of the river or lake which falls within its territory. Like animals on land, fishes also keep moving from one part of the river or lake to another part owned by another community. There is no clear answer to the question. What happens sometimes is this: a tribal community may decide, in rare cases, to exclude strangers from hunting within its territory or from fishing in its rivers and lakes. This seems to give the impression that community members have an exclusive right over the animals and fishes within their territory and that strangers or members of a different tribal community may, by implied permission, enter in order to get fish from the rivers or hunt the game within the territory. But it is not in fact established that the right of exclusion of others from hunting or fishing signifies the existence of communal right of ownership of those animals and fishes on the community's land, since the members of the

---

[62] Manufacture of metallic implements is one of the local industries destroyed by the advent of the white man's government in Africa.

community have no power of control over the animals and fishes. The right of exclusion derives from the ownership of land rather than the ownership of the animals and fishes on it.

In a chiefs' tribal conference in the early 1940s, the late Chief Macar Ijong claimed that where a member of his tribe injured an elephant in his territory and the wounded animal moved to the land of another tribal community, the animal was still his or the property of his people. If the members of the other tribe completed the killing of the animal, the tusks should be given to him. He then put a claim against the Chief, Deng Jok, of the Jur tribe, whose people killed the elephants which had been wounded by the Apaak people (i.e. the people of Chief Macar). The reply of Chief Deng Jok was that, if Chief Macar claimed the ownership of animals which had once been in his territory, he had no objection to giving up the tusks or parts of the animals, provided that Chief Macar and his people compensated his people (i.e. Chief Deng Jok's people), some of whom had been killed or injured by those wounded elephants or other animals. But Chief Macar refused to accept responsibility for the acts of those animals over which he had no control. The conference declared that Chief Macar was defeated in his claim. This was a rejection of the argument that a community owns the animals other than the domestic ones within its territory. It conversely means that if the land owners were entitled to claim the ownership of wild game on their land, they would also have to accept the vicarious liability for the tortious acts committed by the animals. Rights and duties must correspond.

It may be concluded that the community has a right derived from the ownership of land to exclude strangers from enjoying certain benefits over its land.[63] This means that the right to exclude others from fishing or hunting on land is not based on ownership of animals or fishes but derives from the ownership of land, which entitles the owner to exclude others from it. An owner or a legal possessor of property has a right to exclude others from his property or from enjoying certain benefits from his property, except in the circumstances which will be discussed under the next heading. It can therefore be stated that the ownership of land does not mean the ownership of animals and fishes on it since there is no physical control which can be exerted over them.

3.4(c)   (iv) The loss of title to land
The loss of title here relates to the individual's title to residential and

---

[63] Such exercise of exclusive rights over the areas reserved for common usuage, if resisted, may often result in a breach of the peace.

arable land. The community does not lose its title to the territory unless it migrates to a different territory with intent never to come back.

This is one of the difficult points where there is much variance of opinion. The importance of this point is that there are many factors which make a person or a family decide to abandon a homestead and make a home in a new area. The commonest reason is the infertility of the land.

There are two conflicting views on whether or not one loses the title to abandoned land. One view, advocated by Dr Francis Deng, is that

> 'The right of the individual member of the tribal community over his residential land is so strong that even if he abandons it, it must be kept unoccupied unless he gives consent to a relative to take it over'.[64]

In the fulfilment of this principle, it is contended that if someone else enters and occupies the abandoned residence, the original owner still retains his title and has the right to evict the new comer. In a sample survey of opinion which I made, the adherence to this rule is stronger among the Western Dinka (i.e. part of the Rek to the Tuic and the Ngok) but less among the Central Dinka. The Malual also adhere to it, but they are somewhat more liberal. One reason to justify this rule is the scarcity of land which is suitable for building homes and for cultivation. There are many Dinka tribes living in the *toc* and they use the few relatively high areas of ground in the *toc* as sites for homes. The greater part of the land is unsuitable for homes and agriculture because of floods. This lack of sufficient highlands in some areas makes it even more difficult to move frequently. Once a family obtains a highland they hang on to it, for they may not get another one. Hence the frequency of the abandonment of homesteads becomes much more limited. This is one of the strong reasons why the rule in question is strictly adhered to. But among the Central Dinka, there is no scarcity of arable and residential land and, consequently, there is no strict adherence to this principle.

There are questions which the advocates of the principle fail to answer. It is very common for a person or a family (except in the areas referred to above where the abandonment of land is not frequent because of the scarcity of land) to abandon their homestead and move to settle in a new place. They may remain in their new home for many generations. Sometimes this second homestead may be abandoned

---

[64] *(1965) SLJR*, p.594.

for settlement in yet another area. In many cases, the person or his descendants never return to the original land. The question which then arises is: can this person or his descendants be entitled to exercise exclusive rights over the abandoned land indefinitely? Further, if the same family has lived in more than one place, for example, two, three or more places, can it exercise exclusive rights over all these places? Again, when the family expands, there are new homes to be required. Will it not be possible for one family or its descendants to take control over a substantial tribal area of land? While this person or family is exercising exclusive rights over abandoned lands, many other families are also doing the same thing. Will such a rule not create serious conflicts within the community? These questions remain to be answered.

The other question which can be asked is: is the right of ownership of land absolute? In answering this question, we may once again refer to the definitions of ownership. The relevant parts of the definition are in the words of Salmond:

'Ownership is absolute or restricted. Absolute ownership involves the right of free as well as exclusive enjoyment, including the right of using, altering, disposing of or destroying the thing owned. Absolute ownership is of indeterminate duration. Land, in strictness, is not subject to absolute ownership because it cannot be destroyed, and because of the theory that all land is ultimately held of the crown.'[65]

We call this definition of Salmond into question, again, because the rule under discussion is whether an owner of a homestead has an absolute ownership over his land.

By referring to this definition, we are not attempting to interpret a principle of customary law by means of an alien rule. It is not strange to refer to this definition. The part which refers to the right to 'destroy' is scientific and is of universal application. One must have often come across a Dinka person expressing himself or herself in these words: '*Ekedie. Aleu ba rac. Aleu ba cuat-wei. Aleu ba gam*' (i.e. It is mine. I can destroy it. I can throw it away. I can give it away freely). This means that part of the definition is not alien to the Dinka Customary Law. The second point, that because the ultimate owner of the land is the Crown the individual is therefore prevented from exercising absolute ownership of it, also is not alien to Dinka Law.

Without referring to the provisions of the Unregistered Land Act,

---

[65] *Osborn Concise Law Dictionary*, by John Burke, p.338.

1970 (which as a territorial law is superior to a customary rule), there is an analogous answer from Dinka custom itself. The Dinka Customary Law recognises the over-all communal ownership of the whole territory. An individual's ownership is exercised within the umbrella of the communal ownership. This makes the position in Dinka Law more or less analogous to the position maintained by the Crown. Apart from the claims of ownership by the Government of the Sudan, the tribal community is in the position of the Crown. This position is also clarified by the restrictions imposed on an individual's ownership by the communal interest, for example, reservations of certain parts of the land for common usage or the exercise of rights by others over one's own land. These will be discussed below.

With all the difficulties and restrictions which we have stated, we cannot hold that an individual has absolute ownership of land, especially abandoned land. Even the advocates of the principle of absolute ownership of land (including abandoned land) are not certain about the correctness of this principle. They have no answers to the questions which have been posed above. Even Dr Francis Deng was only sure of absolute ownership over livestock and not over land, owing to the involvement of communal rights. Finally, the principle of absolute ownership of land is not of universal application throughout the whole of Dinka land. Sometimes there are cases where an individual may claim the exclusive right over land he has previously abandoned, but the outcome of each case depends upon its specific circumstances.

The general rule is that where an individual enters and occupies empty land (apart from other modes of acquisition such as gift or inheritance) he acquires a title, and he and his descendants or heirs will always retain that title as long as his or their possession of it is continuous. But where he voluntarily abandons his homestead and moves to settle in a new area, he loses his title to the abandoned land. However, if he intends to retain his title to the land he has abandoned, he must clearly and reasonably express his intention. It is not enough to express the intention of retaining the title, but it must also be clearly shown by the reasonable steps he has taken that he will resume the occupation of the land within a reasonable period, because no one can be allowed to exercise the right of excluding others for ever or for an indefinite period from abandoned lands when the right of ownership of an individual over his land is not absolute but restricted.

From the foregoing account, it is to be understood that the exception to the general rule is where the original occupier of land may be entitled to evict newcomers and to resume the occupation of the land.

The general rule may be illustrated by the case of *Macar Aweckoc and others* v. *Riak Dak and others, (RMRY/Civ.App/43/77.* This was a dispute over land between the two families represented by the above-mentioned parties. The Pakam Regional Court, which had the jurisdiction over the parties, made several decisions over many years in favour of the appellants. The facts of the case will appear below in the decision of the appellate court. But here I only intend to state precisely the general rules underlying the previous decisions of the Pakam Regional Court that were violated by the respondents.[66] This Court, at various times, held that:

(i) where a person enters and occupies a land which is free, he acquires the title and retains it as long as his occupation remains continuous. His children and grandchildren, and so on, will be entitled to acquire the title as legal heirs, provided there has been continuous possession. This condition was fulfilled by the plaintiffs (appellants);

(ii) any temporary dispossession of, or displacement of the owner from his land, through the act of an invading enemy or by other events which are beyond the owner's control does not deprive him of his title.

Hence the displacement of the tribe, to which the contesting parties belong, by their enemy (i.e. the Luac), did not deprive the plaintiffs (appellants) of their title. When the enemy was defeated the whole tribe returned to the territory and each person resumed the occupation of his original land.

The converse of this rule (in decision (i) above) was also expressed as follows:

where a person voluntarily abandons his residence and moves out to build a home in a new place he loses his title, as this (act of abandonment) constitutes evidence that he intends to abandon his home, and any other member of the community is entitled to enter and settle there and to acquire a title to it. But where an owner of land temporarily abandons his homestead, moves out and builds himself a home in a new area with the intention of retaining his title to the abandoned land, and with the intention of resuming the occupation of it within a reasonable period; and has, in furtherance of his intention to return, made arrangements which reasonably

---

[66] The last decision against which the appeal reached the district judge was contrary to the previous ones, for it ordered the partition of the land (post).

and clearly demonstrate to the public his intention of retaining the title and of returning within a reasonable time to resume occupation of the land, he does not lose his title. The new occupant cannot acquire the title; that is, the new occupant can be evicted from the land.

Accordingly, the court concluded that the appellants were entitled to the ownership of the disputed land because:

(a) the occupation of the land had been continuous throughout. When the appellants' father temporarily moved out of the land, he had made reasonable arrangements to manifest his intention of retaining the title to the land;
(b) the temporary displacement of the whole tribe from the whole territory did not mean loss of title to the land of either the tribal community or the individual owner.

But, from time to time, the defendants (respondents) continued to renew the case. At last the Pakam Regional Court varied its previous decision and ordered the partition of the land between the two families. The plaintiffs felt dissatisfied and submitted their appeal to the district judge in Rumbek.

The facts of this case must be stated in detail because of the importance of the history behind it. The detailed facts will also enable the reader to appreciate the previous decisions of the Regional Court. From these facts other deductions may also be made. The district judge stated the facts as follows:

This is an appeal against a decision passed by Pakam Regional Court concerning a dispute over land. The disputed land is called Ngaapagok. It is a dispute between the grandsons of Kuruai and the grandsons of Athian, the father of the famous warrior Wol. Pakam Regional Court partitioned the land between the two families. But the appellants are dissatisfied because they claim that the title to the whole land is vested in them exclusively. According to the appellants' argument, this piece of land was first occupied in the past by their grandfather, Kuruai. The land was later inherited from him by his son Arajab, then by another son called Monykuc. Mangong inherited the same from his father Monykuc. Once Mangong, owing to the death of most of his close relatives, abandoned the land temporarily in order to live in another village. He did not intend to relinquish his title to the land because his intent was to return to it. To make his intent to remain the owner of the land during his period of absence clear, he called the son of his sister, Mawut Wol Athian, and permitted him to live on this land until he returned to it. His fear was that if he left it empty, the sons of Wol Athian would move to it. After some years Mangong died, but his sons, Makueiakook and Ciman Arajab, returned to the land of their father. They built on the disputed land and used to cultivate there.

At this time certain sons of Wol (i.e. the respondents) and some of their relatives began to claim the title of the land. They attempted to occupy it by force and they destroyed the house of Ciman Arajab and Makueiakook Mangong. The case was tried by Kulang Marial Wol and Gai Mathiang Wol and they declared that the title was vested in the appellants. The respondents, who employed the use of force, were punished. After two years (i.e. in 1977), the respondents again occupied the land forcefully and asserted the claim of title again. This was tried by Pakam Regional Court and they decided on the partition of the land between the parties.

The respondents, on the other hand, still claim that the title is vested in them exclusively. But their statements are not unanimous as to whether the occupation had been continuous and uninterrupted throughout.

According to the first respondent, Riak Bak, the land had been occupied by their grandfathers continuously till his time. Athian, their great-grandfather, was the first to build his *Luak* there. After him his son, Dhal, lived on it and after Dhal his father lived on it, then his paternal uncle, Dut Dhoor. When the Luac chased them away they returned to it and resumed the occupation after the death of his father. He stated that the appellants' grandfathers and fathers never lived on the same land in the past. The statements of the next respondent, Deng Dhoor, are very inconsistent. At first he stated that Athian, and after him, his sons, Dhal and Dhoor, built on the disputed land and used to cultivate it. He altered this and stated that these people used to cultivate land near the disputed land and that the disputed land remained free and available for the use of anybody, including the appellants and other different people. The third respondent, Aluong Cuatgau, stated that the only grandfather who built a *Luak* (for cattle only) on the disputed land in the past is Athian and that this *Luak* ceased to exist a long time ago. He said his next grandfathers, Dhal and Dhoor, did not live on the disputed land, but they lived at some distance near the disputed land and even these homes were deserted a long time ago and big trees had grown on the place where they had previously built houses. He reiterated that none of his grandfathers built a dwelling settlement on this land but that it was a cattle camp[67] capable of temporary occupation by anybody at any time.

During the trial before the Regional Court, the appellants produced a number of witnesses but the respondents had no independent witnesses. The only person they called a witness to their case is an old blind man in Pakam area. This man could not even come to the Court at Maper in Pakam area because he is too old. Somebody had been sent by the Pakam Court to take his statement and that Court acted on that evidence in favour of the respondents. It is to be noted here that almost all the appellants' witnesses come from among close relatives of the respondents. They are the sons and grandsons of Wol Athian. This tends to make their evidence more weighty.

The first witness, Tueny Wol Athian, stated that by the time they grew up they found the mothers of the appellants, Ciman Arajab and Makueiakook, in occupation of the disputed land. When the same witness together with the other sons and grandsons of Wol Athian occupied the land, by show of force, their father, Wol Athian, who was a Chief, punished them and declared the title to be vested in the grand-parents of the appellants. Gai Mathiang Wol, the next appellants' witness, told the Court that he tried one case connected with the title to this land, together with President Kulang Marial, and that they came to the conclusion that the title belongs to the appellants. The third appellants' witness is Wol Mawut Wol. He went on to state that although he comes from the side of the respondents, he is bound to tell the truth that the disputed land belongs to the appellants. He narrated the history of the land and said that it had been in continuous possession of the descendants of Kuruai. He added that there was one period, in the past, when Mangong (father of the appellants) left the land temporarily but that he left his father on the land to keep other people away from it. His father, Mawut Wol, lived on this land by permission. He confirmed the fact that Kulang Marial, the President of Pakam Regional Court, with Gai Mathiang, once declared that the title belonged to the appellants. Ater Cier is not a witness as to who is vested with the title. He only expressed his doubt as to the validity of the evidence on which the last court relied in partitioning the land.

Judging from the evidence that I have taken down, it is well established that the appellants and their grand-parents have been in continuous and uninterrupted occupation of this land from the

---

[67] Cattle camps (or *wuot-theer*) are always reserved for communal usage.

Some Aspects of The Law of Property 177

past till this day. The period in which Mangong moved to another village and left Mawut Wol on it cannot be deemed as interruption, because Mawut Wol remained on the land by permission and left it when Mangong returned to live on the land. He did not make any attempt to assert an adverse claim of title.

The purpose of keeping Mawut on the land was to prevent other people from moving to the land.[68] Again, the period when the Luac chased away the Pakam from their land also cannot be deemed an interruption, because everybody in Pakam land escaped in order to save his life but there was no intent to abandon the land for ever. Even if the Luac came to live in Pakam area, they were not allowed to do so. The Pakam merely retreated in order to reorganise themselves; they came back and chased away the enemy. As the tribe returned to their territory everybody returned to his previous site, from where he had run away. Further, the possession of the appellants' forefathers had been public and peaceable.[69] The claim of title by the grandsons of Wol Athian came up recently after the title had long vested in the appellants' fathers.

The district judge reversed the last decision of the Pakam Regional Court which varied its previous decision. Further, the previous decision was upheld. The confirmation of that decision was based upon the reasons stated before.

From the decision and facts of this case, a number of conclusions can be deduced. Firstly, a person acquires a title of an empty land by occupation. Secondly, it is possible, under the customary law, for a person to live on somebody's land by permission, but this does not affect the owner's title. Thirdly, dispossession of a person of his land by an act of an enemy or other events beyond his control does not deprive him of his title. Fourthly, title to land may be acquired by inheritance. Fifthly, ownership of land is not absolute; and this is the reason why many references have been made to the question of 'continuous possession' of land by the family since the time of the grandfathers who first settled on the land when they found it empty. From the emphasis upon 'continuous possession', it is implied that if a person abandons his residence and moves out to build a home elsewhere, this constitutes evidence that he intends to relinquish his title.

But if he wants to retain his title, he must act as the appellants' father did: by doing something reasonable to demonstrate explicitly

---

[68] This was a manifestation of intention to retain the title to the abandoned land.
[69] It should not be understood that acquisition of title by passage of time is part of Dinka Law.

his intention to retain his title. If he permits another person to live on his land as a way of retaining his exclusive rights or control over the land, and as long as an authorised person continues to live on it, he may stay away indefinitely or even for generations and no one else can disturb his title. But if he merely demonstrates his intention of retaining the title by some other means short of leaving somebody on it by permission, his exclusive right will terminate at a certain time (although this is not fixed) when it can reasonably be inferred by anyone that he does not intend to come back.

There may be other ways of demonstrating one's intention of retaining one's title. For example, if a person's house remains intact on land and he continues to repair it from time to time, his exclusive right can remain indefinite. But this seems to be a very rare practice, if it is done at all. The most important result of this case is the rejection of the claim that an individual's ownership of or title to land is absolute.

It seems to be an accepted principle in many African traditional systems that a person loses his title when he, of his own volition, leaves the land where he has built his home and goes to settle in another land. This view is supported by Meek.[70] He states:

'In many African legal systems, it is an accepted principle that voluntary abandonment of the use of land should extinguish all prescriptive claims. And there may be a rule that no individual or group shall hold more land than can be effectively used.'

Apart from this principle, that is, that no individual or group shall hold more land than can be effectively used, there are other factors which support the loss of title to the land voluntarily abandoned. One reason is that there would be scarcity of land in a situation where the system of shifting cultivation is very common (due to the fact that there are no fertilisers to keep the land continuously fertile), if a person who has moved to another area were to be entitled to exercise exclusive rights over the land he has voluntarily abandoned. Another reason is that since the tribe or the community is the dominant owner of the land, a private individual does not have an absolute right which would entitle him to exercise exclusive rights over the abandoned land. Any other person, by his membership of the tribe or community, has a right to occupy a piece of land which is empty. We have already made some reservations in the cases of communities who live in the

---

[70] C. K. Meek, *Land Law and Custom in the Colonies*, Oxford University Press, 1946, pp.11-27.

toc, where residential land is very scarce or where religious beliefs are strongly adhered to. Nevertheless, exclusive rights over abandoned lands cannot be exercised forever.

But there is a situation where the claim of the original occupant to resume occupation of the land will take precedence over the claims of others: that is, if by the time he wants to resume the occupation of his original land which still remains fallow or empty he competes with other people's claims, his claim will prevail over the claims of others by virtue of the fact that he once lived there.

In certain cases the intention of a person to abandon the land for good becomes clear. He may express his intention that he is migrating to another land, or it may be reasonably inferred from the circumstances in which he abandons the land.

To conclude this controversy, the general rule which is acceptable is that the individual's ownership of land is not absolute but restricted. Consequently, he loses his title if he abandons his land and settles in a new area. But there are exceptions to this general rule and these have been made clear during the discussion.

3.4(d) *Reserved lands for communal usage*

The question of reserved lands for communal usage has been briefly touched on before. It is this issue of reservation of some lands for common use which, as was stated before, makes it necessary to explain the difference between the two land divisions, namely, the *toc* and the *baai*, and their significance to the life of the Dinka.

Because of the importance of the *toc* to the life of everybody in a tribal community, and the scarcity that might be created if private individuals were to be allowed to establish exclusive ownership of it, the community reserves the ownership to itself and permits its members to use all the benefits of this area communally or jointly. Consequently, the grazing grounds or pastures, fishing areas, hunting areas, *wuntheer* or *wuot-theer* (i.e. mounds found everywhere in the *toc* which were built or raised by the Luo who were the first occupants of the land), which are used as cattle camps are reserved for communal usage. The community accepts the principle of sharing all the benefits of these areas. With a few exceptions,[71] it may be stated that all the areas in the *toc* are reserved for communal usage. Even members of

---

[71] *Kol* or the deep part of a river may be owned by a family. But others are allowed to fish when the owners decide that it is time for fishing. *Wuntheer*, in certain instances, may be owned by a family but, as in the case of *Kol* such rights of ownership are not absolute. Members of the community or of other communities can occupy it temporarily.

other tribes may be allowed to enter and use these benefits, unless there are exceptional reasons why these strangers must be excluded. Members of other tribes are allowed to enter the land because there are reciprocal benefits involved here.

In the areas of permanent settlement (i.e. the *baai*), dancing places, foot-paths and the use of the benefits of forests and so forth are reserved for communal usage. The benefits to be obtained from forests may include fire-wood, wood for building houses, grass for thatching houses, fruits and so on. The communal use of these benefits is not confined to the members of the tribal community, but it is also, as in the case of the *toc*, extended to strangers or members of different tribal communities. But in the case of forests in agricultural lands, a person or a group of persons from the tribe may obtain parts of it and build their homes there, if their original lands have become less fertile.

3.4(d) (i) Restrictions on reserved lands for common usage
With respect to the reserved areas for communal usage, the tribal community may sometimes exercise their right to exclude strangers from the use of their pastures, if the cattle of these strangers are infected with disease; or the strangers may be excluded to prevent the exhaustion of the pastures or when there is a feud between the two tribes. A tribal community may also reserve its right to exclude others from fishing in its rivers or lakes. This right is often exercised if there is a pending dispute, or when relations are bad between members of the same community over claims of exclusive rights over parts of the reserved lands.

3.4(d) (ii) Claims of title as a cause of inter-tribal disputes over land
The previous discussions have established firmly that the ownership of a given territory is vested in the tribal community. Within the tribal land, members of the tribe acquire ownership of their residential and arable lands. There are certain lands, mainly in the *toc*, which are reserved for common usage. This common usage is usually extended to the members of other communities; that is, on a reciprocal basis, members of one community may, by express or implied permission, enter and enjoy the benefits of the land of another community. Members of another community may be allowed to build houses on tribal land. Such persons acquire title to their residential and arable lands. But their rights of ownership may be terminated by the host community if there are good reasons for doing so. An example of this is provided below by the case of *Wet-Duang* who were chased away by the Awan tribe.

Despite the acceptance of the principle of communal usage of land which may be extended to strangers on a reciprocal basis or through express or implied permission, inter-tribal disputes may arise if this implied permission turns into a claim of title to the land. Usage of land can be enjoyed by strangers, but under no circumstances can their claim of title be tolerated.

It is to be observed also that if there is any dispute over the whole territory or over the reserved lands for communal usage, it is always contested not on an individual basis but on a communal or tribal basis. Further, in most cases, they are contested on an inter-tribal basis. It has already been shown that communal rights are more exerciseable over the *toc* than the *baai*. The benefits in the *toc* are more attractive to the people and their domestic animals, and so inter-tribal disputes over the *toc* are frequent. Many wars have been fought as a consequence of such disputes. The following cases may show the nature of inter-tribal disputes:

3.4(d) (iii) Claim of title arising from the original occupation of land

A dispute may arise between different tribes or sections of a tribe, if each side claims that it has the right of ownership over the land,[72] on the ground that its ancestors were the first to occupy it. The protracted war between the Amakiir and the Lual (i.e. two major sections of one tribe) involved a claim of title to the lands in the *toc*, although this was not the actual or the original cause of the war. The claim of title later on was a result of bitterness.

The claim of title usually calls for the tracing of the history of the land, in order to establish whose ancestors were the first occupants of the land in dispute. In this case, the Amakiir claimed that during the Dinka migration from the east to the west, their great ancestor, Jôk Tong, was the first to discover the *toc* in the present Apuk land. He drove away the Luo and settled there with his people. He then sent for his paternal uncle's son, Riing-thii, to return to Pathuon (the name of Apuk land) because a rich *toc* had been discovered.

According to the history, Riing-thii, with his followers, had made a long journey, wandering up to the present land of Akuang-Ayat in Malual country in search of a certain Akuen alleged to have gone there years before. On the invitation of Jok Tong, Riing-thii returned to Pathuon. Jok Tong gave him part of the territory in the agricultural highlands *(baai)* and part of the *toc*, the dividing line being the Jur river.

---

[72] A dispute does not necessarily arise if members of one community enter the territory of another merely to enjoy its benefits without exerting a claim of title.

The Amakiir claimed title to the land on the ground that their ancestors, led by Jok Tong, were the first to occupy the land and by such occupation acquired the title which they, as the descendants of their ancestors, inherited. They claimed that Riing-thii and his followers received the land as a gift[73] and that, as a consequence of the bitter war, the Amakiir were prepared to revoke the gift of title. However, the Government at last intervened and made peace between the warring parties.[74]

A similar claim of title over certain lands in the *toc* between the Pakam (a section of the Agar tribe of Rumbek) and the Luac (from the Tonj district) brought about a bitter conflict which became a cause of a series of wars. For many years before, both tribes had been using each other's territory in common. But later on, when claims of title over lands in common usage in each other's territory began to be exerted, disputes developed at once and it became necessary to draw borders between their territories. But this proved difficult. Each side claimed that its ancestors were the first to enter and occupy the disputed areas in the *toc*. However, this, which would have determined which tribe had the title over the disputed lands, could not be proved.

In 1952, the District Commissioners of both Rumbek and Tonj initiated the convening of a special court (chiefs were among the members) to draw a boundary between their lands. As there were no natural witnesses to trace the history of the occupation of the land, the court found it difficult to decide which section had the title over the disputed lands. It was thought better to select two nearest points to the disputed land (one from the territory of each tribe) over which there was no dispute and then draw a boundary in the middle, making the two points equi-distant. This was accepted as a matter of convenience for there was no other reasonable solution which could be found.[75]

3.4(d) (iv) A community may exercise exclusive rights over its fishing areas

Despite the acceptance of the principle of communal usage of certain lands, which also extends to the members of other communities or

---

[73] But a gift of land which has remained undisturbed for centuries or many decades poses serious doubt as to whether it may be revoked or not by the original owner.

[74] *Note:* After the settlement of the dispute by the Government, each tribe was able to know the area which it had ownership. They then resumed the common use of their territories normally.

[75] Ref. Report of The Fact Finding Committee on the Apuk Tribal Conflict, 1975.

sub-tribes, landowners may sometimes reserve to themselves exclusive rights. They may decide to exclude members of other communities from the use of their land; for example, they may prevent strangers from using pastures or fishing areas. There are alsways various reasons why a community may exercise its reserved rights of exclusion. It may be a result of the scarcity of grass in grazing lands caused by conditions such as drought which, at the same time, bring about scarcity of water and fish. The exercise of the right to exclude strangers may be a result of deterioration of relations between members of two communities. Sometimes the owners of a river or a lake may control the fishing rights in their waters till certain ceremonial rites are performed, or fishing may be suspended up to a certain convenient period. If these restrictions imposed by the landowners are infringed by the non-owners this may result in a physical confrontation.

An illustration of this point is the 'Tong Akeu' battle which took place between the Panyon and the Athoi (both sections of the Agar tribe) in 1948 over lake Akeu. The lake belongs to a family known as Pan-Makat from the Panyon section. It is the members of this family who decide when fishing in the lake must be allowed, usually after they have conducted ceremonial rites.

The Athoi were very impatient. They did not want to wait for the completion of the rites. One day, the Athoi, in large numbers, decided to march to the lake before the Panyon had lifted the restriction. A fight was the result. Several members of the Athoi were killed by the Panyon, and the attempted violation of the imposed restriction on fishing rights in the lake was stopped.

3.4(d) (v) Where permission to settle on a tribal land develops into an adverse claim of title

A tribe or community may allow an individual or family or a few families from a different community to settle on its land by permission, implied or expressed. It may happen that the members of these families increase or they are joined by many other members of their community. They may attempt to turn the permission into an adverse claim of title for their community; or a large-scale migration of members of a different tribe into the land of the other for settlement may cause alarm. This large-scale migration may create a fear in the minds of the landowners that these immigrants are adopting tacit methods of trying to appropriate their territory. In each of these cases, the landowners, out of fear, may withdraw their permission and resort to the exercise of their reserved rights of exclusion. If the newcomers, backed by their community, resist their rejection and exert their own claim of title, this again is likely to be the cause of an inter-tribal dispute. These examples may be illustrated by the following cases.

(a) *The dispute between Awan Chan Section of Gogrial and Lou of Aweil.*

As these cases relate to disputes over claims of title to land, the versions related by either side often differ from each other. According to the Awan's version, the dispute was over an area north of Awan Chan, now known as Ameth Wet-Duang. It happened that, a long time back, a certain family from the Payii clan, in the area of Chief Riiny Lual Dau of Aweil, left their home because they had killed a person in that area. They went to Awan Chan and settled among the Payii clan of Awan Chan. A member of that family married a girl from Awan and, in order to consolidate this marriage relationship, the people of Awan allowed that family to occupy Ameth as their area. All the same, they still continued to be part of the people of Aweil and they paid their taxes to Aweil. This family multiplied and became known as Wet-Duang.

When the boundary between Aweil and Gogrial was drawn, part of the area occupied by Wet-Duang was given to the Lou section of Aweil and the other part remained as part of Awan Chan. Yet Wet-Duang of Awan continued to pay their taxes to Aweil.

When Ameth developed as a commercial centre, the local traders went and obtained licences from Aweil local authorities. The Aweil local authorities also decided to establish a Police Post in Ameth and provided a dispensary for the people. This was seen by the people of Awan Chan as absolute usurpation of their land by people whom they had long considered as no more than squatters.[76] The Awan people, of course, decided to chase Wet-Duang back to Aweil area, but the Lou of Aweil would not allow this, and therefore recurrent wars between the two sections have been going on.

(b) *The dispute between Awan Mou and Amuol (Gogrial Area).*

The dispute between the Awan and the Lou is the same as the dispute between the Awan Mou and the Amuol of Gogrial over Riau. A member of Amuol section married a girl from Awan Mou. He was allowed to live in Riau; but when he had long settled there comfortably he was joined by some of his relatives and friends from Amuol, thereby making the area

---

[76] According to this version of the story, Wet-Duang live in the land of the Awan Chan by permission; and they turned this into an adverse claim of possession.

predominantly occupied by the Twic people. Their social service taxes are still paid to the Twic Rural Council. However, this large-scale influx of the Twic people became the cause of continual fights between the Awan Mou and the Amuol sections.

The Awan believe that, through tacit methods, part of their territory has been appropriated by Amuol, whose members settled in their land by permission. In both cases the two sections of Awan believe that they are genuinely exercising their exclusive rights since their good faith had been subject to abuse. Of course the other combating parties have their own version as to their claims of titles to these lands.

3.4(e) (vi) Rights enjoyed over the property of another person
The Customary Law allows members of the public to enjoy some limited specific rights over the property owned by another person. These rights are analogous to easements. Foot-paths always pass over the lands occupied by other people. Any member of the public is entitled to use the path despite the fact that it passes over somebody's land. In negative terms it may be stated that a landowner is not entitled to prevent members of the public from the use of that part of the path which goes over his land. A second example is that a member of the public is entitled to go over somebody's property in order to obtain water from a well.

There are also rights enjoyed by others over the property of another which are analogous to profits. An example is where members of a tribe enjoy hunting rights over the land of another tribe, or where they enter to obtain fish in a *kol* which is owned by a family. However, a family which owns a *kol* may impose restrictions on fishing there at certain times. But when the time comes for fishing, any member of the public will be allowed to enter to obtain fish. The right of the owners of the *kol* is that they are entitled to collect one fish from every member of the public who fishes there. In other words, every member of the public who goes to fish in a *kol* is bound to contribute a fish to the owners of the property.

CHAPTER FIVE

The Law of Obligations

Introduction
An obligation may be a duty to do something or it may be a liability to pay or discharge an obligation. According to the definition in *Osborn's Concise Law Dictionary*,[1] page 239, obligation means

> 'A duty: the bond of legal necessity which binds together two or more determinate individuals. It is limited to legal duties arising out of a special personal relationship existing between them, whether by reason of contract or a tort, or otherwise; e.g. debtor and creditor – see liability.'

Owing to the existing relationship between the two terms, namely, obligation and liability, the dictionary directs reference to be made to the definition of liability which it defines as

> 'subjection to a legal obligation or the obligation itself. He who commits a wrong or breaks a contract or trust is said to be liable or responsible for it...'

It is clear from these definitions that an obligation is either a duty or a liability. It is to be understood, further, from the definition that obligation amalgamates contractual and tortious duties or liabilities. Hence the law of obligations is an amalgamation of the two branches of law. (i.e. contract and tort). The distinction between contract and tort is that the duties in contract are fixed by the parties themselves and are owed to a particular person or persons, whereas in tort the

---

[1] By John Burke, (Sweet and Maxwell).

Some Aspects of The Law of Property

duties are imposed by law and are owed to the public generally.

In his daily activities, a man may subject himself to the burden of a number of legal obligations (or liabilities) through the physical acts he undertakes or through the statements he publishes. Further, such obligations or liabilities may be imposed upon him vicariously through the acts of others with whom he has some special relationship, or through the acts of the animals he keeps. An obligation may fall into the field of contract law if it promulgates from the agreement. On the other hand, it is regarded as tortious obligation if the person concerned is under a duty to exercise reasonable care towards the public.

A few subjects have been selected in both laws (contract and tort) for discussion in this Chapter. For the law of contract, '*amuk*' (security or guarantee) has been selected. In the field of the law of tort, homicide,[2] liability for animals and defamation are selected.

1. AMUK (OR AMEC)

Amuk is a security or pledge for the repayment of debt. It is one of the commonest transactions among the Dinka people in the field of contract law. It is defined under section 64(a) of the Re-statement of the Bhar el Ghazal Region Customary Law Act, 1984, as follows:

(a) '*Amuk* or *Amec* is any property delivered by a debtor *(raan-koony)* to a creditor *(raan-kony rande* or *amekony)* as a form of security or guarantee for the repayment of a debt *(keny)* or discharge *(cuot)* of existing obligation *(keny)*.'

(b) 'If the debtor fails completely to repay the debt at the fixed time, the secured creditor is entitled to own the property he possesses as *amuk* at a reasonable period after the expiry of the said period or at the period which the court may consider to be reasonably long in the circumstances, if no fixed period for the discharge of the debt was agreed upon at the time of the contract.'

From the definition, it is to be noted that the creditor obtains the legal possession while the ownership remains vested in the debtor. The creditor, who has the legal possession is under an obligation (or duty) to exercise reasonable care for the safety of *amuk* (or the safety of the property held as security). Section 66[3] of the Act provides:

---

[2] The reasons for classifying homicide as tort are given below.
[3] *Note:* Section 66 also embodies that a lienee must exercise reasonable care, and so the dots represent the provisions connected with lien.

'Any person who retains possession of a cow or other property as *amuk* (pledge)... is bound to exercise reasonable care for it. If such a cow or property perishes or disappears through his negligence or the negligence of his successor or agent,... and in case of *amuk*, the property or cow which has perished or disappeared in his possession through such negligence shall be deemed as full satisfaction of his claim against the debtor.'

The provisions of this section put the creditor into the position of a trustee of property, in so far as the duty of care is concerned. But strictly speaking, the degree of care imposed on the creditor is more than the degree of care imposed on a trustee. The difference is due to the fact that there is a contractual relationship between the debtor and the creditor which imposes mutual obligations on both parties.

But, in the case of trust (*kuei*) there is no contractual relationship although some agreement is involved. The owner of property makes a decision to transfer its possession to a person who accepts to hold it in trust. By this agreement, there is no benefit to go to the trustee from the owner of the property. A trustee may enjoy the 'fruits' of the property he holds in trust, but this is only an incidental benefit. It is not a benefit resulting from any agreement. The duty of care imposed on a trustee of property is implied from his acceptance of the property to remain under his dominion. It is not a duty imposed by a contractual agreement. This makes the difference between the degree of care exercised by each of these people, namely, the creditor and the trustee. The latter takes possession of the property and exercises care without any benefits accruing to him. He is a volunteer of a kind.

Amuk or *Amec* is one of the subjects which involves extensive litigation in the courts. The equivalent term to *amuk* or *amec* in the English legal system is security or guarantee or pledge. 'A' may obtain a loan from 'B'. 'B' may demand an immediate delivery of some property to him as a guarantee for the repayment of the debt, because there may be a doubt as to whether 'A' will ultimately fulfil his obligation. 'A' will then be bound to deposit some property with 'B'.

As cattle is usually the most important medium of exchange, *amuk* transaction is mostly carried out in cattle. It has been stated before that the creditor is bound to exercise reasonable care with respect to the *amuk* property. If such a property (or cow) perishes or disappears through his negligence, or through the negligence of his successor or agent, the property or cow which has perished or disappeared through such negligence shall be deemed as full satisfaction of his obligation against the debtor. On the other hand, the debtor is bound to repay the secured debt at the end of the fixed period, if there was any period fixed; otherwise, the secured creditor is entitled to own the property he possesses as *amuk* at any reasonable time the court may fix after the expiration of the agreed period. In the circumstances where the parties did not fix a time for the refund of the debt at the time of the agreement, the court has discretion to determine that a certain time is reasonable for the repayment of the debt, and, if the debtor is still unable to pay, the creditor will be entitled to appropriate the *amuk*.

The law may sound as straightforward as stated above, but the parties may land themselves in all sorts of problems which will necessitate complicated legal contests before the courts of law. Most of the conflict is brought about by the fact that, in almost all the transactions related to *amuk*, the parties fail or neglect to fix a period by which the debtor ought to refund the loan and the creditor to redeliver the security to the debtor. The indefiniteness of the period is always a source of serious legal problems. When the period is indefinite the debtor sits back without making any attempt to discharge the debt until the creditor makes a demand. Even after such a demand, it is difficult in many cases for the debtor to respond readily. The creditor, on his part, may not make a demand at a reasonable time, especially when the debt is secured. During this unreasonably long time, the *amuk* may continue to reproduce. By the time the dispute arises and goes to court, the debtor will be entitled to recover the *amuk*, together with its produce or offspring, after he has discharged the debt in conformity with the order passed by the court. No interest is to be claimed against the debtor however long he delays in refunding the debt. The property promised to be paid in discharge of the debt always remains the same. The creditor may claim an increase or interest, but the courts adhere strictly to the original terms of agreement.

Another conflict may arise when the secured creditor is dishonest or unfaithful. He may, without notifying the debtor, dispose of the security for his own purposes, even before the time for the repayment of the loan has become mature. Sometimes disposal of the security may be made by the creditor, if the debtor's failure to discharge the debt has taken such a length of time that it creates a belief that he has foresaken the security. This may be illustrated by the case of *Col Mathet* v. *Mathiang Yang and Agree Miith*[4]. It was held that according to the terms of the agreement the plaintiff was entitled only to one heifer. The term of the agreement could not be varied by passage of time. The first defendant was ordered to pay only a heifer, as he originally promised, to the plaintiff and no more. The plainiff's argument that, due to the passage of time, he wanted two cows

---

[4] RMRY/Civ.App/77 – the facts have been previously stated.

instead of one was rejected. He appealed to the district judge against this decision, but the decision of the court of first instance was upheld because it conformed with the provisions of the agreement.

It may be argued that the court's decision was harsh to the plaintiff (appellant) and to the third party, who received the property for value from him in good faith. But the court's decision is justified by the following facts: (a) the plaintiff (appellant) had contributed to the delay in the discharge of the debt because he remained silent throughout; (b) further, he disposed of the cow to the third party without ascertaining whether the first defendant had actually failed to discharge the debt or not. By law, if this had been ascertained, the *amuk* would have become the property of the plaintiff (i.e. the creditor) and he would have been entitled to dispose of it at will. The *amuk* becomes the property of the creditor when the debtor fails to discharge the debt at the fixed time; or if there was no fixed time, then after the passage of a time which the court considers to be reasonable in the circumstances of the case.[5] The decision as to what period should be regarded as reasonable must be made by the court and not by the creditor.

Thus, in the case of *Nyilueth Puou* v. *Ruai Makoi (RMRY/ Civ.App./15/77)*, the defendant (respondent) contracted a debt from the plaintiff (appellant). The former obtained a bull from the latter and promised to pay a heifer for the bull in an unspecified future period. Meanwhile he secured the debt with a cow. After the passage of a considerable period, the plaintiff (i.e. the creditor), sued the defendant to discharge his obligation. The court gave the defendant six months to find a heifer with which to discharge the debt so that he could recover his cow which was held as security. He failed to produce a heifer after the passage of the period which was fixed by the court. The plaintiff returned to the court. It was held that a reasonable time had already passed since the court gave the defendant six months to pay. The six months constituted an additional reasonable period to give the defendant a further opportunity to discharge the debt; yet he failed again. This second failure to discharge the debt (although he had many cows) was a clear manifestation of his intention not to discharge his obligation. The court ordered that the *amuk* cow remained the property of the creditor (i.e. the plaintiff).

The defendant appealed to the district judge against the decision of the court of first instance but to no avail. The creditor in this case was aware of his right. He was also wise to bring the matter before the

---

[5] Section 64(b) of the Act (i.e. Re-statement of Bhar el Ghazal Region Customary Law Act, 1984).

court to determine the question of 'reasonable time'. He was unlike the creditor in the previous case who determined the 'reasonable time' for himself.

The debtor's failure or refusal to discharge the debt may be inferred from his exercise of dishonest conduct. The exercise of dishonest conduct entitles the court to order the appropriation of the security (*amuk*) by the creditor.

A similar case was contested between *Akec Ayiel and Marial Makuac (RMRY/Civ.App./17/77)*. The defendant obtained a loan of Ls.50.000 m/ms in 1976 from the plaintiff and promised that he was going to pay to the said plaintiff a named heifer – *nyanyom*. But there was no date fixed for the delivery of the named cow; nor was it stated why the named cow should not be delivered straightaway so that the transaction could just become a contract of sale. The defendant (i.e. debtor) secured the debt with a cow called *diing*. It was also agreed that if the defendant discharged his debt by delivering *nyanyom* to the plaintiff, the latter would pay to the former an additional sum of Ls.10.000 m/ms. It was further agreed that the *amuk* would become the property of the plaintiff if the defendant failed to discharge his obligation.[6] Again, there was no time fixed as a deadline for the discharge of that obligation.

Sometime later, the defendant, instead of producing the cow he had named for the discharge of the debt, went and recovered the cow which was being held as *amuk* without the plaintiff's consent or knowledge. The plaintiff (creditor) sued him for the recovery of the same cow. It was held that the defendant ought to return the *amuk* to the plaintiff. Further, it was held that the defendant's conduct clearly demonstrated his refusal to discharge the debt and so the ownership of the *amuk* passed to the plaintiff.

In conclusion, I would like to mention that the immense litigation in this field of the law is a product of the following factors:

(a) the usual failure of the parties to fix a deadline for the discharge of the debt;
(b) the creditor's usual failure to press for the discharge of the debt at a reasonable time; and
(c) the strict adherence by the court to the terms of the agreement, without putting into consideration some reasonable circumstances which justify the creditor's claim of interest over and above what had been promised to him in discharge of the debt.

---

[6] *Note:* It was superfluous to make such a clause since that is what the law provides anyway.

For example, the unnecessary delay in the discharge of the debt may be purely the responsibility of the debtor (i.e. if he refuses or neglects to pay despite the creditor's attempts to get paid). If many years pass and the debt is not discharged, the court should fix a reasonable time within which the debt should have been paid. Any delay beyond this period should entitle the creditor to receive interest. If, according to the agreement, the debt is to be discharged by paying a cow, the number of offspring the cow could reasonably be expected to have produced (if the cow were paid at a reasonable time) should be calculated and awarded to the creditor). The courts should, however, make allowances for unforeseen events while assessing a reasonable number of cows to be awarded to the creditor.

A reasonable argument against this suggestion is that if the courts are given such power, they will be interfering with the freedom of the parties to make contracts. The parties are free to choose their own terms. As this may be the case, a better way out is for the parties themselves to include a term or a clause in the agreement to cover the payment of *interest* by the debtor in case of unreasonable delay in discharging the debt or after the passage of an agreed period.

2. LIABILITY FOR ANIMALS – DAMAGES FOR PERSONAL INJURY CAUSED BY ANIMALS

Tortious acts are committed by human beings, and thereby they impose obligations or liabilities upon themselves. Another source of such obligations or liabilities upon human beings is through the acts of the animals they keep. This section deals with the liabilities imposed on human beings through the acts of their animals.

The following questions may be asked: why should a person be held liable for a tortious act committed by an animal he keeps? If there is any justification at all for such liability, is it based on the keeper's knowledge of the animal's mischievous propensities or is the liability strict and absolute? Further, is the keeper of animals liable for the acts of all the types of animals he keeps or is there any distinction made by the law? Finally, to whom is the keeper of an animal liable?

These are the questions which require to be discussed in this section. It may be more convenient to start with the classes of animals for whose acts the keeper may be held liable. For this purpose the classification of animals in Dinka Law differs from the Roman Law classification, which was later adopted by the English Common Law.

For the purpose of liability for the acts of animals, the Roman Law divided the animals into two classes: (i) Ferae Naturae and (ii) Mansueta Naturae.

The animals of class (i) are deemed to be naturally dangerous, for example, the lion, the leopard and so on. The examples of the animals of class (ii) are cows, dogs, cats and so on. An animal of this class may, as a special case, develop dangerous propensities. Under the English Common Law, liability for the acts of the animals of class (i) was absolute. Since the animal is naturally classed as dangerous, the keeper of this kind of animal could not pretend or be heard to state, in his defence, that he did not know that the animal was dangerous.

The English Common Law rules were replaced with statutory provisions, when The Animals Act, 1971 was passed. The Act retains the classification under the Common Law but makes some alterations in the rules relating to liability. Under the Act, where damage is caused by an animal of a dangerous species (i.e. ferae naturae) the keeper of the animal is generally liable. In the case of an animal not of a dangerous species (mansueta naturae), the keeper is liable for the damage which that particular animal causes (s.2 of the Act). By section 5(3) of the Act, a trespasser cannot, as a rule, recover damages for the injury inflicted by a dangerous animal. The keeper of a dog is, as a rule, liable for damages, if it kills or injures livestock – Dogs (Protection of Livestock) Act, 1953. By the Criminal Justice Act, 1967, s.92, schedule 3, Part I), straying animals may be detained and the damage caused by them is recoverable together with the expense of keeping them.

For the purpose of liability for their acts, the Dinka Law classification of animals markedly differs from the classification which exists in English Law or Roman Law. The animals which are classified as 'ferae naturae' are not contemplated by the law since they are not kept by the Dinka people, and so there is no question of liability of a person for their acts.[7] They are enemies of every human being, since they are dangerous. The animals classified as 'mansueta naturae', commonly known as domestic animals, are the ones in the contemplation of the Dinka Law.

For the purpose of liability for the acts of these domestic animals, they are divided into two categories. The first category consists of animals which the Dinka people regard as having more social and economic value. This class comprises cattle, goats, sheep, and so on.

---

[7] Classification of animals is provided for by s.68 of the Act. Class (i) consists of animals of economic and social value while class (ii) consists of others such as cats, dogs, horses.

They are regarded as first class domestic animals because of the reasons stated above. The second category consists of domestic animals which render some limited services to man. This class includes mainly dogs, cats, donkeys, horses and so on. There are no social and economic values attached to them by the Dinka people, although the protection afforded by the dog cannot be under-rated. Also, in some areas, horses and donkeys discharge heavy duties for man; nevertheless, they are not given any social or economic importance.

The question now is: what is the basis of the liability of the keeper or the owner of an animal for its acts? It seems that the importance of the animal to man appears to be the basis of liability. A keeper of an animal may be held liable for the act of his animal in three ways: firstly, if the animal causes damage to the property of another person. According to the provisions of section 79 of the Dinka Customary Law Act 1984, the keeper or owner of an animal is bound to pay damages if the animal causes damage to the property of another person (i.e. property other than another animal). The liability is strict. The mental element of the keeper is immaterial.

Secondly, if the animal causes injury or the death of another animal kept or owned by a different person, the keeper or owner of the animal that caused the injury or death may be held liable. But his liability depends on a number of factors, and these are:

1. whether the animal killed or injured was within the premises of its owner or keeper; and
2. whether the animal that caused the death or injury was trespassing or was a wandering animal.

If these two grounds are established, the keeper or the owner of the animal that committed the tort is liable (s.80 of the Act). But, if the two animals were trespassing on the premises of a third party; or, if the animal killed was the trespasser; or the two animals met in a no-man's land, for example, in a grazing place, the keeper or the owner of the animal that committed the tortious act is not liable (s.80 of the Act).

In paying damages or compensation, the keeper or the owner of the animal that committed the tort is bound to hand over the same animal. This means that, it is the same animal that causes the death of another animal (of the same kind, of course) which has to be handed over to the claimant. But if the tortious act causes injury which does not amount to the death of the other animal, damages will be paid – nowadays, in the form of money.

The provisions of sections 79 and 80 of the Act relate to the animals of the first category only. They do not include the animals of the second category.

Thirdly, the keeper or owner of an animal may be liable if the animal inflicts injury on a person. This again depends on a number of factors. In relation to the injury caused to a person by a domestic animal of the first category, the liability of the owner depends upon whether the victim is a trespasser or a lawful visitor. If the victim is not a trespasser but a lawful visitor, he is entitled to obtain the same animal that inflicted the injury on him or her as damages, unless the amount of damages proportional to the injury is less than the value of the animal; for example, if the injury is not serious. In this case, money can be paid, or some property which has value proportional to the injury. If the injured person or the victim was a trespasser, for example, if he were a thief or an invader, he deserves no damages.

Where the injury is inflicted by a domestic animal of the second category, whether the victim was a trespasser or a lawful visitor, he is not entitled to damages from the owner or the keeper. It appears in both cases as if the animal is the one to be held responsible for its own acts.[8] But, in the case of an animal of the second category, it seems that the victim does not need the animal as damages, probably because of no value attached to it. However, in the situation where the injury was inflicted by an animal of the second category, the owner of it may be ordered to pay damages, if the animal had, for some time, shown dangerous tendencies and the owner knew it. He thereafter keeps it at his own risk.

We may summarise the answers to the questions which were posed at the beginning. We begin with the classification of animals.

2.1 Whether the animals are classified; and, if so, whether the keeper or the owner is liable for the acts of the animals in both classes

Unlike the English or the Roman Law which classifies animals for the purposes of the keeper's liability in tort, the Dinka Law classifies animals, for the same purpose, according to whether the animal has or does not have social and economic value attached to it by the society.

---

[8] This opinion derives from the fact that the owner (in the case of the animals of the first category) or keeper is bound to surrender the animal which has committed the injury to the victim. It may be stated that the animal is liable for its own act. However, since the animal is the property of the keeper, he is the one actually liable as he is bound to surrender it. In the case of the second class animals, the owner or keeper is not liable. But if the victim claims the same animal, it seems there is no reason why it should not be surrendered to him by the keeper. However, the injured person will not claim it since there is no social and economic value attached to it by the society.

In general, the keeper of an animal which has social and economic value (e.g. cow, goat, sheep, etc.) is liable for its tortious acts. Whether the liability is absolute or not is to be answered separately below. Further, in general terms, the keeper or owner of an animal which is classified as having no social and economic value (e.g. dog, cat, horse, etc.) is not liable for its tortious acts. There is, however, an exception made by the law. If the keeper of the animal which is classified as having no social and economic value has observed that the animal has for some time shown dangerous tendencies, the keeper or owner is liable for its tortious acts.

2.2 Whether the liability for the torts committed by these animals is absolute or whether the mental element of the keeper or owner is a necessary requisite for his liability.

(a) Under section 79 of the Act, where an animal of social and economic value causes damage to the property (other than another animal) of another person, the mental element of the owner or keeper is immaterial. The liability is strict or absolute. The animals which have no social and economic value are not in contemplation under the provisions of this section. The reason for non-contemplation of the said animals has been mentioned during the discussion.

(b) Where the injury or death of an animal owned or kept by another person has been caused, the liability of the keeper of the animal that caused the injury or death of another animal depends on the following factors:
    (i) whether the injured animal or the killed animal was, at the time of the injury or death, within its keeper's premises or not; and
    (ii) whether or not the animal that inflicted the injury or caused the death was at the time a trespasser or was wandering.

If it is proved that the victim was within its keeper's or owner's premises and that the other animal that did the act was trespassing or wandering, then the keeper or the owner of the animal that inflicted the injury or caused the death is liable. The proof of these two factors makes the keeper or owner of the aggressive animal liable absolutely.

2.3 Exception

Where the animals referred to above were both trespassing within the premises of a third party or where both met in a common place (i.e.

no-man's land), the keeper of the animal that caused the injury or the death of the other animal is not liable. Again, the animals in contemplation here are those which have economic or social value attached to them by the society.

Where an animal of category (i) (e.g., a cow or a bull) inflicts injury on a person, the liability of the keeper or owner depends on: (a) whether the injured person was a lawful visitor, or (b) whether he was a trespasser.[9] If the victim was a lawful visitor, the owner or the keeper of it is liable strictly. But he is not liable if the victim was a trespasser.

However, if the injury is caused to a person by an animal of class (ii), for example, a cat or a dog, the keeper is not liable, unless he knows that the animal has been showing dangerous character previously.

The legal position is not clear if the animal causes the death of a person. Anyway, this issue relates only to the nature and the extent of the amount of damages to be paid. As for liability, there is doubt whether the keeper of the animal is liable, unless the victim was a trespasser. But a case was tried in Rumbek in the late 40's after a boy was killed by a cow he was milking. The owner of the cow was the one being tried. He denied having been in any way negligent. The boy was doing his duty, that is, milking the cow. It was held that the cow was the one to be paid to the relatives of the deceased as *apuk* (compensation).

2.4 The basis of liability for the acts of animals

(a) The first reason is the restoration of the status quo, or to put the claimant in the economic position he was in before the act was committed.
(b) A person keeps at his risk an animal or animals (i.e. animals of economic and social value). The keeper of an animal of this kind owes a duty of care to the members of the public and their property. If one of the animals causes injury to a person or damage to his property, there is a breach of this duty of care on the part of the keeper; consequently, he is liable to pay damages. The keeper is under a duty to prevent his animals from causing tortious acts to people or their properties.
(c) The third reason is that the keeper or owner of an animal or

---

[9] Liability of the keeper for personal injuries caused by the animal is provided by s.68 of the Act.

animals enjoys the economic and social benefits from the animal or animals, and so he must accept the liabilities for its or their tortious acts. The keeper or owner cannot be expected to enjoy these benefits and then refuse to be held liable for their actions.

2.5 To whom is the keeper of an animal liable?
The keeper of an animal is liable to:

(a) the lawful visitor injured (or killed) by the animal he keeps (this excludes liability for a trespasser);
(b) the owner of the damaged property (i.e., property other than an animal); and
(c) the owner of the animal injured or killed when the keeper's animal that did the act was trespassing on the premises of the owner of the injured or killed animal.

In general terms, the keeper (or the owner) of an animal of the first category, or an animal of the second category which he knows to have been showing dangerous propensities, owes a duty of care to members of the public and their property. Property, in this context, excludes animals of the second category.

3. LIABILITY FOR HOMICIDE (NAKĒ-RAAN)[10]

3.1 Why homicide is classified under the Law of Obligations
It may look strange to find homicide *(nakē-raan)*, which is a crime, classified as a tort or part of the Law of Obligations. The reason for this is that an act may constitute a crime and, at the same time, a tort. This means that there are criminal and civil aspects simultaneously involved in an act. It depends on the individual victim which remedy he intends to obtain. If he chooses to obtain a civil remedy, he can sue for damages and, if he intends to prosecute, he can take up criminal proceedings. Another reason for the classification of homicide as a tort is that the objective of Dinka Law, as was stated before, is the restoration of the social equilibrium which has been disturbed. Since African law is largely positive and not negative, that is, since it is concerned not with punishment but the restoration of the social equilibrium, Dinka Customary Law treats homicide as an ordinary

---

[10] Liability for personal injuries is provided for by ss.67–68(i) of the Bhar el Ghazal Region Customary Law Act, 1984.

tortious liability. 'The principle of a life for a life rarely leads to a permanent peace.'[11] Social equilibrium is restored through the payment of damages or *apuk*. In cases of homicide damages or compensation is always paid in cattle (i.e. 30 cows for a person).

Dr Francis Deng seems to believe that the payment of compensation (in cattle) is based on the principle of getting property to marry a wife for the deceased.[12] He derives this belief from Howell's statement that 'It (i.e. compensation) involves the fundamental principle that a deceased person must be "married a wife" so that the wife's children, begotten by some kinsman on his behalf, will bear his name, belong to his branch of the lineage, and may concern themselves with his interests in posterity.' But this statement can be refuted. If the need to marry a wife for the deceased were the basis of the compensation, there would be no need for the deceased's relatives, after obtaining the compensation (*apuk*) cattle, to share those cattle among themselves. Marriage may perhaps be only an incidental aspect of the compensation. Of the thirty cows paid as compensation, there are usually two cows specifically selected for two purposes: one for the 'head' and the other for the 'legs' of the deceased. These cows are not subject to distribution; they are reserved for the close relatives of the deceased, who would be bound to contribute cows for compensation if it were the deceased who had caused the death of another person.

The other point which goes against Howell's statement and therefore Dr Deng's belief is that the obligation to pay compensation still exists even if a married person who has no need for more children (because he already has many of them) is killed. In this case, if marriage were the sole reason, the realtives of the killer would not be bound to pay anything to the deceased's relatives, because the murdered man was already married and had children of his own, so that there was no longer any need for them to find property to marry a wife to bear children for him. Therefore, the fundamental reason for the compensation is, as has been stated before, to restore the social equilibrium which has been destabilised by the wrongful act.

3.2 The basis of collective responsibility for homicide or certain torts
Responsibility for homicide or certain torts is collective. This statement raises three questions: (i) what is meant by collective responsibility? (ii) who are liable to pay the damages? and (iii) what is the actual basis or philosophy of the principle of collective responsibility?

---

[11] P. P. Howell, *A Manual of Nuer Law*, Oxford University Press, 1954, p.41.
[12] SLJR, 1965, p.559.

3.2(i) *Collective responsibility*

If a person commits homicide, liability to pay damages or compensation for the offence is not his sole responsibility but the responsibility of others, such as his family or relatives, his clan or tribe. This does not, however, mean that everyone who is socially or legally obliged to contribute towards the payment of compensation is to be tried together with the perpetrator of the tort. The tortfeasor is tried alone. The responsibility of other people enters the picture when the tortfeasor is found guilty of the offence and is ordered to pay compensation. Arrangements for contribution by others are not essentially a part of the judicial proceedings; they may be made outside the court. The chief whose kinsman has caused the death of another person deliberates with his people (who are bound to pay) to arrange the amount to be contributed by each person or family towards the compensation.

It has to be borne in mind that it is not every tortious act or civil wrong committed by an individual that demands the application of the principle of collective responsibility. Collective responsibility or liability relates to cases of homocide and very serious personal injuries. In the latter case, it is the degree of the injury inflicted and the quantum of damages ordered to be paid which determine whether or not other people are to contribute. Other torts, especially sexual offences, are the sole responsibility of the wrongdoer.

3.2(ii) *Persons who are liable collectively for the tortfeasor's act*

Liability for the act of an individual may fall on each or some or all of the following bodies:

(a) the family of the tortfeasor;
(b) the kinsgroup to which the tortfeasor belongs;
(c) the tribe or the sub-tribe, whichever the case may be, to which the tortfeasor belongs; and
(d) maternal uncles, if the tortfeasor is not a redeemed child.[13]

The liability of persons in categories (a), (b) and (c) above, depends firstly on the nature and degree of the act committed; and secondly on the circumstances in which the act was committed. These may be explained in some detail:

The nature and the degree of the act
Where the act committed is of a nature that does not impose a social

---

[13] *Note:* For the definition of 'redeemed child' see Chapter III – Family Law.

or legal obligation or liability on other people, for example, the publication of a defamatory statement or the infliction of a simple injury (which does not require a hefty compensation to be paid), it is the tortfeasor alone or he and his family who will be liable to pay compensation. The family is regarded as one unit and it holds its property communally. The liability of a member of the family, therefore, has to be charged against the family property. If the tortfeasor has a separate property, then the liability will be charged against his own property.

But, where the gravity of the act demands collective liability, for example, where grievous injury has been inflicted on another person or homicide has been committed, the family and the kinsgroup of the offender will be collectively liable, irrespective of the circumstances in which the act was committed. However, the liability of the kinsgroup has to be qualified. It is not always necessary that the whole kinsgroup or all the blood relatives (or paternal relatives) of the tortfeasor should be collectively responsible for the homicide or grievous injury. Among the relatives or kinsgroup of the tortfeasor, there are families who (through affiliation or cooperation) share in common their social and economic benefits. On the other hand, they also share in common liabilities for grave offences or tortious acts which require heavy payments of compensation. Where a group of agnatic families collectively shares cattle paid as compensation if one of them is killed by an outsider, the same group of families also shares the liability if one of them causes the death of an outsider.

There is another qualification to make in the case of grievous injury. Contributions from members of other families may not be required, unless the amount of compensation is great. In fact, not all grievous injuries are of the same degree; some are more serious than others, and so the amount of compensation required may be the same as the amount payable when death is caused. In such a situation, the liability should not be left to the family of the tortfeasor alone; other families within the kinsgroup must also contribute.

The circumstances in which the act is committed
The circumstances in which the act (e.g. homicide) is committed may determine whether the liability will be shared by the whole kinsgroup together with the tribe or sub-tribe of the tortfeasor.

Liability for causing the death of another person is the sole responsibility of the tortfeasor's family and their relatives who are socially bound to contribute towards the compensation. However, a person of one tribe or sub-tribe may grievously injure or kill a member of another tribe or sub-tribe in a tribal fight. In certain circumstances, the person who causes the death or who inflicts the injury may deny the act (although he may secretly confide it to his relatives so that he may be purified) and it may, at the same time, happen that the person alleged to have committed the act and all the people from both sides involved in the fight may sincerely not know who caused the act complained of. In such circumstances, section 70 of the Bhar Ghazal Region Customary Law Act 1984 provides:

> 'When two tribes or more enter into a fight and some people get killed on either side, the payment of *apuk*[14] to the relatives of the deceased person or persons shall be confined to the killers with their relatives, but, where the killer is unknown (or the one who caused hurt), the tribe involved in the fight against the deceased's tribe is bound to pay the *apuk*.'

From the provisions of this section, it is clear that the payment of compensation is the sole responsibility of the tortfeasor's relatives, even if he caused the death while he was defending the whole tribe against an external enemy. The whole tribe is liable only when the doer of the act is unknown.

In fact there is an element of unfairness in confining the liability for the act to the relatives of the killer alone, when the act was done for the defence of the whole tribe or sub-tribe. The whole tribe should be held liable in such circumstances. The only consolation is that it is a rule which is likely to affect any group of families (of one tribe) at any particular time when there are inter-tribal fights.

In the case of category (b) above, where an unredeemed child causes the death of another person, the liability falls on the maternal uncle or uncles and his or their relatives (i.e. paternal relatives of the maternal uncles); or upon the tribe to which the killer's maternal uncle belongs in the cases referred to in section 70 of the Act.

3.2(iii) *The basis or philosophy of the principle of collective responsibility*

The basis or philosophy of the principle of collective responsibility may be found in the following quotation from Dr Francis Deng:

> 'It is in homicide that the broadest family identification comes into perspective in tort cases. In traditional society where the effectiveness of the social control did not provide sufficient security for the individual and the nuclear family, such broad group solidarities

---

[14] Compensation or damages.

were vital. Among the Dinka and the Nuer, for instance, an act of homicide immediately gave rise to a blood feud between kinsgroups, or other groups, depending on the circumstances of the homicide.'[15]

The reason why liability, especially in homicide cases, should be collective is based on the solidarity or oneness of the family. All the members of a family regard themselves as one body. Further, people of common descent[16] (or of one blood) still retain a sort of a loose union. Their common descent enables them to regard themselves as branches of one original family. Blood-relationship is expressed in many ways; for example, in the maintenance of strong social bonds, in rendering necessary mutual services or in the maintenance of a common defence against an external enemy or enemies or dangers and so on. Put differently, the maintenance of strong social bonds (or relationship), the rendering of mutual services and the maintenance of a common defence are founded upon blood-relationship.

Since the family or group of families which claim common descent (or kinship) regard themselves as one body, any external danger against one member, or one family, which belongs to this group of families is regarded as a danger against all the families. Consequently, they face the danger collectively.

While the families which have common descent or kinship render mutual services to one another and mount a common defence against external dangers, they also equally accept the sharing of responsibility in cases of major liabilities, such as contributions towards compensation for an act of homicide committed by a member of the kinsgroup.[17]

As stated before, there is no collective liability where the act committed and the amount of damages to be paid are trivial, or where the act, by its nature, does not impose collective liability, for example, cases of sexual offences which are individualistic in nature. The wrongdoer alone is liable. It is not in the interest of the community to render him collective assistance. To do so would encourage the commission of sexual offences in the society. Further, it is not the type

---

[15] SLJR, 1965, p.558.
[16] In this context, 'common descent' does not include the original ancestors or very distant common ancestors. The degree of relationship must be near or close. The descendants of the original ancestor or the very distant ancestor might have become too many to be able to maintain unity.
[17] Other areas of collective liability or responsibility include contributions towards bride-wealth in marriage or in cases of grievous injury where the amount of compensation is high.

of wrong which one can claim to have committed in the name of the community.

Strictly speaking, the liability of relatives to contribute cattle towards compensation is not legal but a social dictate which the law recognises. Section 70 of the Act declares that liability to pay compensation for the commission of homicide is confined to the relatives of the killer, even if the death was caused by the wrongdoer while he was defending his whole tribe in an inter-tribal fight.

Before bringing this discussion to a close, we may summarise the grounds for collective liability of the relatives, where one of their members commits homicide as follows.

The first important ground is the solidarity of the kinsgroup or the group of families which are closely related on the paternal side. In the words of Dundas,[18] the ground is the 'unity of clan'. But 'clan' to the Dinka is too wide. Some clans are too large even to know their own members. They may trace their kinship only through a totem. Members of one clan can also be found spread among so many Dinka tribes that they really cease to have any practical links among themselves.

The second ground which justifies collective liability in cases of homicide is the principle of reciprocity whereby fortunes and misfortunes are mutually shared. There are many instances where the relationship between certain families may be very close and yet they do not share liabilities in cases of homicide. The reason is that (due to the lack of affiliation or for some other reason) such families may have ceased to maintain social bonds which would enable them to share benefits as well as obligations or liabilities. In many cases, such situations where close families cease to share benefits and obligations may not be the outcome of explicit decisions, but they may be the result of practices stemming from disputes among the families.[19]

It is to be noticed that reciprocity itself imposes obligations on persons. Where there has been no sharing of benefits, there cannot be a duty or obligation to share liabilities. Hence close families may not necessarily share the liability for homicide where they do not share benefits. For example, where a relative is bound to contribute towards compensation for homicide, he is also entitled (or, as of right, required) to take a share in the blood-cattle, if one of the family's relatives is killed by an outsider; and so it is not the relationship alone which is the determining factor. However, it is not altogether true to

---

[18] Readings in African Law, Vol. I, Frank Cass, London, 1970, p.178.
[19] However, the blood-relationship still enables them to discharge some other obligations together, for example, common defence against an external enemy or danger.

say that the obligation imposed by the principle of reciprocity ignores the question of solidarity of families or the unity of kinship. Such reciprocity derives from the blood-relationship. Non-relatives are not required to share liabilities for homicide.

The third ground appears to be the collective responsibility of the kinsgroup to control the acts of its members. The relatives of a person killed regard all the agnatic relatives of the person responsible for the killing. If compensation is not paid, any agnatic male relative will be exposed to the risk of vengeance by the relatives of the deceased. This imposes collective liability on agnatic relatives to avert the danger by collecting cattle to pay the compensation. If the liability is left to one person (i.e. the killer or his family) and he fails to discharge that liability in full, it is anybody's guess which member of his kinsgroup will be killed in revenge. The enemy may decide to kill a person other than the actual killer.

Finally, sharing liabilities in cases of homicide promotes the maintenance of a common defence against external enemies. If a person knows that he cannot receive any assistance towards the compensation cattle after causing the death of another in a fight in defence of a relative, he will refuse to take part in it; and this fact undermines the solidarity among the relatives. Blood-relationship itself, without the benefits or assistance derived from it, would be meaningless. This would encourage individualism and selfishness.

3.3 Whether the mental element is a necessary requisite for liability in homicide cases

A person may cause the death of another person in consequence of premeditation, or in furtherance of a conspiracy or a common intention, if others are involved with the wrongdoer. He may cause the death as a result of grave and sudden provocation or while exercising the right of self-defence. It may be caused through negligence or when the doer of the act intends to cause injury. Death may be caused accidentally or in good faith. The killer may be a madman or a person who has not yet reached maturity in age, and so on.

The general rule is that the mental element is immaterial in cases of homicide, in so far as the claim of damages is concerned. Section 71 of the Bhar el Ghazal Region Customary Law Act 1984 provides that:

> 'A person who has caused the death of another is bound with his relatives on the paternal side to pay *apuk* (i.e. compensation) for thirty (30) cows to the relatives of the deceased, although death might have been caused while the killer was exercising the right of self-defence.'

In view of this provision, the mental element is immaterial in connection with the payment of damages in homicide cases. One reason for payment, which has been stated earlier, is the restoration of the social equilibrium or the status quo (although damages for loss of life does not really restore the status quo). But the basic reason, in fact, is the maintenance of absolute peace. Even if the deceased was the aggressor and the killer was exercising his right of self-defence, the bitterness generated by the killing is never removed from the family of the deceased. The family of an aggressor who is killed during the exercise of his aggression cannot stop lamenting the loss of their relative just because the killer was exercising his right of self-defence (or was suddenly and gravely provoked or was intending to cause injury only). As the bitterness remains despite the fact that the killer's mental attitude at the time of the killing could exonerate him completely from liability or serve as a mitigating factor, there is fear that another life could be lost in revenge at a future time. To prevent such an event from happening, the mental element is overlooked and the killer and his relatives are ordered to pay compensation. The law regards the maintenance of peace and the prevention of further loss of life as of paramount importance. If these objectives can be achieved by ordering the payment of damages or compensation, and the society accepts it, so much the better.

This cannot, however, be construed as a total elimination of the mental element from homicide. It was not by mere accident that self-defence was specifically mentioned in the provisions of section 71 of the Act. It indicates the existence of the mental element in the law, but damages are only paid on the stated grounds. Cases will be discussed below where the mental element is considered in ordering the payment of compensation.

This question of mental element has created much conflict of opinion among many writers on African law. Some writers argue that the mental element is absent in African law. But others, including T. O. Elias, vehemently maintain the existence of the mental element in African law.

In discussing 'motive' and 'intention', J. H. Driberg pointed out that:

'There is some conflict of evidence as to how far intention is taken into account. In strict theory it is obvious that, if the object of the law is to restore the status quo, intention cannot come into the matter. The offence has been committed and has to be adjusted. But what I have said of theft applies here too, as the circumstances may be as important as the offence. This particular applies to acts of homicide.'[20]

The same writer went on to enumerate many examples of tribes in Africa who consider the mental element in homicide. He said:

'The Baluba, for instance, distinguish, according to Colle, between voluntary and involuntary homicide; among the Basonge drunkenness is a palliative circumstance.'[21]

T. O. Elias also argued that:

'There is a notion of mens rea in African Law... When people deny that motive, intention, etc., play any part in African Law, they seem to be arguing from the particular to the general – from the single instance of homicide and its treatment to the whole African Law. They forget that all African Law is neither homicide nor even crime in general, and that there are large areas of civil law in which these concepts (i.e. motive, intention etc.) are fully regarded by the elders in their adjudication of dispute.'[22]

The argument which T. O. Elias pursues is in fact true of the Dinka Law too. In cases of homicide, intention, self-defence, negligence, grave provocation, or causing death while the intention is to inflict injury are all said to be immaterial, and thus liability becomes absolute. This is not, in fact, a denial of the existence of mens rea or the mental element in the law. At this juncture we must refer to cases where the mental element is considered in acts of homicide.

3.4 Cases where damages are mitigated
There are two cases where the state of mind of the killer amounts to a reduction of the number of *apuk* cattle that may be paid. These are cases of accidental killing, where death is caused in good faith, and the causing of death through the killer's mental incapacity, for example, if he or she is an idiot, an insane person or a minor. Their agnatic relatives are still liable but the *apuk* or amount of damages to be paid is only ten cows. Such payment, strictly speaking, is not based on any legal liability. It is made to satisfy some ritual requirements only.

---

[20] Readings in African Law, Vol. II, Frank Cass, London, 1970, p.165.
[21] Ibid.
[22] Ibid.

3.5 Cases where relationship or a particular circumstance exists

3.5(a) *Where a person causes the death of a relative*

The general rule is that where a person causes the death of a relative intentionally, the killer and some other closer agnatic relatives are bound to pay *apuk* in full. In fact, if the killer is an agnatic relative of the deceased, the payment of *apuk* and the amount to be paid depend very much on the degree of relationship and also on whether these agnatic relatives – the deceased and his killer – belong to the families who are bound always to contribute jointly to *apuk*. If the degree of relationship between the deceased and the killer is very close and they come from the families who are bound to contribute jointly towards the payment of *apuk* when their relative kills an outsider, *apuk* will not be paid, but a few cows may be paid to the parents of the deceased in order to 'wash away the blood' or to 'appease' the soul of the deceased. No payment is involved at all if the person whose death has been caused is the father, mother, sister or brother of the wrongdoer on the ground of the unity of the family. The family cannot compensate itself. It is important to note the relevance of the mental element in this instance.

The converse rule is that where a person causes the death of a relative unintentionally, no *apuk* is to be paid, except the few cows for the appeasement of the soul of the deceased. However, this depends on the degree and nature of the relationship between the killer and the deceased. If the deceased is a maternal relative to the killer, full *apuk* must be paid by the agnatic relatives of the killer. (But it is doubtful whether *apuk* is always payable in similar cases.) Further, if the deceased is a distant agnatic relative, the full amount is payable.

3.5(b) *Where the wife causes the death of a person*

The general rule is that where a married woman (except in accidental killing) causes the death of a person who is not a relative[23] of her husband, *apuk* shall be paid by her husband and his agnatic relatives (see section 73 of the Restatement of B.G.R. Customary Law Act, 1984). The liability falls on them because the married woman is a member of their family, as long as the marriage remains in force. However, if the marriage subsequently breaks down, the general rule is that the husband and his relatives are entitled to be reimbursed by the relatives of the divorced woman for the cattle they had paid as *apuk* to the relatives of the deceased. The occurrence of the divorce

---

[23] *Note:* If a married woman causes the death of a relative of her husband, mens rea becomes material.

shifts the liability for *apuk* to the relatives of the woman. There are many details connected with these rules, but there is no space to state them all here. However, suffice it to say that, if the person killed by a married woman is a relative of her husband, the situation is the same as mentioned in (a) above. The rule is not very clear where a married woman kills her blood relative, for example, her father, mother or brother. Although I cannot remember such a case having happened before, it is very improbable that the husband and his relatives would be required to pay *apuk* to her relatives, for if this happened the marriage would be likely to break down. This point, in fact, raises a very controversial argument which cannot be discussed here for lack of space.

3.5(c) *Where the wife kills her husband*

Where a married woman intentionally causes the death of her husband, the rule is very straightforward. The marriage is automatically dissolved and the relatives of the deceased are entitled to claim *apuk* cattle in full from her relatives. It follows also that all the rights which had been passing from one side to the other while the marriage was in force will have to be adjusted too. Again, the mental element becomes relevant in this case. It follows therefore, that if the causing of death was unintentional, *apuk* will not be paid and the marriage will still remain valid. A few cows may be paid by her relatives to the relatives of the deceased in order to satisfy the ritual requirements such as the 'washing of the blood' or the 'appeasement of the soul.'

3.5(d) *Where the husband kills his wife*

Where it is the husband who intentionally causes the death of his wife, the marriage is also automatically dissolved and the bride-wealth cattle which was paid to her relatives at the time of the marriage will be regarded as *apuk*. No new cattle will be paid as *apuk*, unless the bride-wealth cattle was less than 30 head, in which case, the deficiency will have to be made up. It also follows that all other rights which had accrued to each side of the marriage will have to be adjusted to the satisfaction of both sides (see section 76 of the Restatement of Bhar el Ghazal Region Customary Law Act, 1984).

4. DEFAMATION

4:1 Duty of care owed to the public

A man owes a duty of care to the public with respect to the statements he utters or publishes. He commits a breach of this duty if he publishes a defamatory statement against another person or persons; and, consequently, he is liable to pay damages to the aggrieved person or persons.

> 'Spoiling a man's name by an unjustifiable defamatory statement is considered a serious matter in African societies. Such solidarity as African societies cherish can only be maintained in an atmosphere of mutual respect which defamation tends to destroy. In as much as solidarities in Africa centre in the family, as we have seen, it is clear that defamation is necessarily contrary to family interests. Equally significant is the fact that the maintenance of one's name is the primary purpose of the family in African thought, and anything which spoils a man's name threatens to reflect on his family. Protection of the family is therefore an important factor in the law of defamation.'[24]

In Ashton's words:

> '... A similar type of offence is defamation. This is the spoiling of a person's reputation by maliciously attributing something evil to him, misrepresenting his words or actions or spreading false rumours... The action is brought primarily to vindicate the plaintiff's reputation rather than to obtain damages.'[25]

It is common that 'malice' prevails in cases of defamation, but its existence is not a necessary requirement in determining the liability of the publisher. This point will be elaborated later.

The equivalent terms to the English word 'defamation' or the phrase 'injurious falsehood' in Dinka are *lētē-guop* or *yor-guop*. Defamation may elaborately be defined as: a publication of injurious falsehood by one person or persons against another person or persons or against a family or families, which has a tendency to destroy or harm in the society, the prestige or the character or reputation of that person or family.

The statement published must be false and it is immaterial whether or not the publisher knows it to be false. If the publication is true, it does not amount to defamation or *lētē-guop*. Hence, truth is a defence to charges of defamation.

---

[24] Dr Francis Deng, SLJR, 1965, p.560.
[25] H. Ashton, *The Basuto,* extract published in *Readings in African Law, Vol. II,* Frank Cass, London, 1970, p.146.

4.2 Damages for defamation

Where a defamatory statement or injurious falsehood is published against a person, the victim of this injurious falsehood is entitled, according to section 78 of the Act, to recover damages against the wrongdoer, as follows:

(i) if the defamatory statement or injurious falsehood is published in an ordinary conversation or discussion, the victim is entitled to obtain a heifer as damages;
(ii) if the injurious falsehood or defamatory statement is published in a song, the victim is entitled to obtain one pregnant heifer provided that the court may pass, in addition, an appropriate sentence of imprisonment or fine or both against him, in accordance with the provisions of the Sudan Penal Code.

In fact, the amount of damages to be paid to the victim according to the order of the court may increase, depending on the gravity of the injurious falsehood. It is also important to note here the difference between publication of injurious falsehood in a conversation and such publication in a song. The difference is that the latter publication spreads very fast, far and wide. Publication in conversation or discussion spreads slowly and may be confined to a limited community. Publication in a song also has the character of remaining permanent and in constant repetition. For example, if the publication is made in a dance song, it is capable of being repeated every now and again in dancing places or by individuals in public places over a period of years.

4.3 What constitutes defamation in a locality

We have just noted above that the publication of the truth against a person does not constitute *lētē-guop* or defamation. But certain beliefs may exist among local communities: for example, among the Dinka, the belief exists that certain families possess some dangerous supernatural powers. Some families are believed to be possessed with *wuuth* or *peeth*.

Wuuth or *peeth* is the power and the person alleged to possess it is called *wuth* or *apeth*. The *wuth* or *apeth* is believed to have the power of killing others with his or her eyes or by staring at them, and this is, according to the belief, inherited. The problem which arises is this: suppose a member of the clan or families locally believed to possess the power of *wuuth* is affected by a publication that he or she is a *wuth* or *apeth*, does such imputation or publication constitute defamation?

It is my submission that what amounts to defamation should be understood according to the belief of the local population. For example, what the Western or the Eastern people consider as defamation should not necessarily be so to the Bantu or the Dinka and vice-versa. Hence, although I do not believe that there are people possessing such power, I would submit that imputation of *wuuth* or *peeth* to one of the families locally believed to possess such power would not amount to defamation. Similar cases are often contested in courts and the publisher of the statement confidently insists that he has published the truth. He may be ready to take an oath before a *Banybith* that his accusation is true.[26] He may also call witnesses who will support his case. But such a statement would constitute defamation if it were published against a member of a family which is

---

[26] As the cases of *wuuth* or *peeth* cause serious sensations, I refer to the parties in the following case by the first letters in their names. The case comes from Aweil district of Bhar el Ghazal. It was contested between 'G' and 'A' CS/117/71 (Wet-wel Court). One day in 1971, 'A' – a lady – disclosed in the company of her close friends that: 'the repeated death of the children of 'R' is known to 'G', whose mother came from a notorious family in the land of Paliet (tribe) in the east. That family destroyed much of Paliet land. It was responsible for the death of many children. 'G's' mother could not find any man to marry her in Paliet land and so her father brought her down to the country of Gomjuer in the hope that she would find a man, among the people who had no knowledge of their evil power, to marry her. The unfortunate father of 'G' married her in ignorance of the notoriety of 'G's' mother's family, with very few cows. But she was really a mistress of beauty.' One of the ladies took up the discussion and said: 'My friends, are you not aware that the descendants of *apeth* (the evil-eyed people) are the champions of beauty on earth?' 'A' later picked up the conversation and said: ''G' is merciless and cannot pity poor 'R' by sparing him some children.' 'But this is the tradition of his maternal uncles – how can he abandon it?' said one of the ladies.

The contents of this conversation leaked out later to 'G', who then threatened to take the law into her own hands, unless her conduct was sufficiently vindicated through court processes. The chiefs intervened and the dispute went to Chiefs' Court at Wet-wel in 1971. 'G' said the publication against her and her family was false and it constituted a defamation. 'A' and her supporters contended that it was a publication of the truth and so they were not wrong in any way. They were prepared to prove their point either through taking an oath before a *Banybith* or by calling the local people who knew that 'G's' family possessed the power of *peeth*. They said that it was widely known in their locality that 'G's' mother came from a family possessed of this power.

At a later stage of the trial, the court adjourned the hearing and referred the parties to a *Banybith* for the oath. 'G' at first agreed to go, but afterwards he declined without giving any satisfactory explanation. It was understood that he feared taking the oath and this was construed to be an admission of the truth of the imputation made against him. The court held that 'A' was justified when she published the imputation. The case was dismissed as far as the civil claim was concerned. But 'A' and some of the ladies accused with her were fined for causing a breach of the peace.

not locally known to possess such power. Cases where *wuuth* or *peeth* or *rooth*[27] has been imputed are often brought for trial in the courts. Despite the existence of the local belief that the families complaining possess these powers, the publishers have been punished in criminal courts conducted by chiefs. The reason is that either the publishers intend to provoke a breach of the peace or that their publications, usually in songs, are likely to result in breaches of the peace.

4.4 The corrective element

There is another important aspect which must be discussed in connection with the publication of defamatory statements, and that is the general attitude of the Dinka people towards such publications. Publication of a defamatory statement is an offence, but it has one very important positive aspect in the society. It tends to promote a high standard of morality. Such publications form a part of general or public criticism in the society. They put pressure on everybody to be of good character, even though he or she is not directly affected by the publication. A person must try his or her best to maintain a good reputation, so that critics do not get the opportunity to make defamatory publications against him or her.

For these reasons, litigation in the field of defamation has not been common. Sometimes there is even an element of prestige involved in defamation, unless the imputation is seriously injurious to one's character. There is a tendency to publish defamatory statements against chiefs or persons of noble families. But, in such cases, the public do not believe the truth of what is published. It is understood that it is the outstanding character or status of the person which attracts the criticism. Such a criticism, if found to be groundless, boosts one's prestige. Nobody wastes time or trouble on criticising a poor man or a person of low status in a song. 'You look very important or noble when many people tend to criticise you, whether rightly or wrongly.'[28]

The best step which the affected people usually take is to reply to the criticisms with similar publications in songs. However, in many instances, the continuous publications of more and more critical songs against one another leads to high tension and breaches of the

---

[27] *Rooth* is a power which affects the skin or causes other bodily sickness. As the belief goes, it is transmitted by physical contact.
[28] This was expressed by many chiefs in the Conference in Tonj in 1975. This Conference was convened (as repeatedly stated elsewhere in the book), for the re-statement of the customary rules which were codified and passed as The Re-statement of the Bhar el Ghazal Region Customary Law Act, 1984.

peace. When this happens the courts step in to stop the publication of those defamatory songs and punish the publishers.

There is, in fact, divided opinion among the Dinka as to whether or not the publication of defamatory songs should be penalised. This divided opinion was obvious during the Conference of Wanhalel (at Tonj district) in 1975 to draw up the Dinka Customary Law. Such publications are deemed to have both harmful and useful aspects. The latter aspect seems to enjoy more weight in the society's opinion. In circumstances where there is no press or other mass-media where public criticism or criticism against particular individuals can be expressed, a sizeable majority of the Dinka community believe that publication of general criticisms which may hurt others should not be totally hampered, if the society is to maintain high moral standards. What should be guarded against is the degree or gravity of harm the injurious falsehood inflicts. Although such falsehood causes suffering to particular individuals, the people, as a whole, are put on the alert to adjust their conduct accordingly.

4.5 Distinction between defamation and insult
In the discussion of this subject, it is important to determine whether Dinka Customary Law makes a distinction between insult and defamatory statement. Further, whether the mental element of the author of the statement is material to his liability or not.

The two concepts, namely, 'insult' and 'defamation' or 'injurious falsehood', originate from one root. They have one common factor: they portray the bad character of a person. But their legal effects are not the same. It is more difficult to explain the distinction between the two concepts than to establish whether a particular statement amounts to defamation or insult. The legal effect of defamation is that the publication or the imputation of a particular character to a person destroys or harms his reputation or status in the society. The status or reputation of a person suffers harm when the society has been made to believe the truth of the published falsehood. But if the society believes that the publication is false, it will not amount to a defamation but will be regarded as an insult. The effect of insult is that it merely tends to provoke the other or to cause a breach of the peace.

Apart from the belief of the society as to whether or not the statement is true, the circumstances in which it is published may help to distinguish whether it constitutes defamation or insult. If the publication is, for example, motivated by a spirit of revenge or a reply to a similar statement made by the other party, for instance when the parties are quarrelling, it must, in most cases, be regarded as an insult. Apart from the spirit of revenge, there is also the question of provocation. The society is unlikely to believe the truth of the publication in such circumstances. But it cannot, of course, be ruled out that a publication made during a quarrel may be a defamation. If, by its nature, the publication convinces people that it is true, when it is false, then it will amount to defamation. The distinction between the two concepts is a question of fact and not of law; and so there is no general rule of law which can be formulated as a guiding principle, and no boundary can be distinctly drawn between the two concepts. And the court will not call members of the public to answer whether they believe the truth of the statement or not. Whether a particular publication amounts to defamation or insult will be determined by the court itself, according to the circumstances of each case.

4.6 Whether mens rea is necessary in determining liability

The next question to determine is whether or not mens rea or the mental element is essential in holding a person responsible for publishing defamatory material. As has been stated before, the aim of Dinka Customary Law is to restore the social equilibrium or to repair damage which has been done. It is therefore irrelevant whether or not the publisher of a defamatory material knew that the statement was false or whether he intended to harm the reputation of the person affected.

It is the attitude of the society towards the publication which is material to the determination of responsibility. The defendant is not expected to state, in his defence, that he did not know, at the time of the publication, that the imputation was false. If, by the nature of the material or the circumstances in which it was published, the court could come to the conclusion that there was a tendency to make the public believe the truth of that material, the publisher would he held liable for defamation.

CHAPTER SIX

Procedure

Introduction
It has been doubted, perhaps, by a good many people whether a customary law, which is relatively an undeveloped or a less developed traditional law, has any definite system of rules of procedure. However, it is undoubtedly true that every legal system has its procedural rules.

Relevant at this juncture, however, is the question: why do people waste a great deal of time and resources in studying or developing legal procedure, a subject which is very dry, tedious and indeed superfluous as there are rules of substantive law? But before I pursue an answer to this question, I must first ask another question: how do people differentiate between the rules of procedure and the rules of substantive law?

One of the differences between the two systems is that the rules of substantive law define rights and duties or liabilities of people, while the rules of procedure regulate how the rules of substantive law are to be defended and enforced by a court of law. It is easier to describe the law of procedure than to define it. It regulates the steps which must be taken by the parties in a litigation from the time when the plaintiff commences his proceeding to the time when, if he has been successful, he wishes to enforce the judgement he has obtained against the defendant; what formal document he must employ in order to set the machinery of the law in motion; how he must bring it to the notice of his opponent; how the area of dispute between the parties must be defined; the various steps that must be taken before the case comes to trial; how the trial itself is conducted, and how any judgement given is enforced.[1]

---

[1] P. St J. Langan and D. G. Lawrence, *Civil Procedure 2nd ed.*, Sweet & Maxwell, 1976, p.1.

The rules of procedure mostly answer the question 'how' – for example, how does a litigant open his case or enforce his right against a defendant? – while the rules of substantive law answer the question 'what'? For example, what is the right of an original owner when a thief who stole his property has been convicted? Or, what are the rights of a landlord under s.II of the (Sudan) Rent Restriction Act, 1953?

It must be stated at the outset that justice cannot effectively be achieved if there are no rules of procedure to regulate how the rules of substantive law are to be applied. Hence, a system of law whose objective is undoubtedly the administration of justice must embody some form of procedure, however rudimentary it may be. Rules of procedure provide a court of law with an effective mechanism to enable it to achieve a qualitative judgement in a given case. Procedure is the lubricant of the functional effect of the rules of substantive law. A machine operator who works a machine without lubricating oil risks the complete break-down of the machine. Likewise, the application of the rules of substantive law, unregulated by rules of procedure, may produce the wrong result. Procedure makes it possible for a court of justice to fulfil the objective of the general principle which provides that 'not only must justice be done but it must be seen to be done.' In this respect the rules of procedure provide that a court or trial must be open to the public unless, for reasons connected with security or privacy of family relations or secrets, the court has to sit in camera. Hence the rules of procedure are a means to justice and not the end. They also make for efficiency in the administration of justice.

Before we conclude this introductory discussion, it is essential to state here that procedure and the law of evidence belong to one class in contrast with the substantive law. Nevertheless the law of procedure and the law of evidence are distinct branches of law, which some writers call the adjectival law, in contrast with substantive law.

One of the traditional ways of classifying the law is that which involves the distinction between substantive and adjectival law.

> '.... Adjectival law is in its turn divided into the law of procedure and the law of evidence. Broadly speaking, the law of evidence deals with proof of facts in court, for example, what persons are competent as witnesses, rules relating to the evaluation of testimony....'[2]

---

[2] P. St J. Langan and D. G. Lawrence, *Civil Procedure 2nd ed.*, Sweet & Maxwell, 1976, p.1.

But the rules of procedure, as stated before, regulate the steps to be followed.

1. THE GENERAL PRINCIPLES REGULATING THE OPERATION OF THE RULES OF PROCEDURE

The operation of the rules of procedure under customary law is governed by certain fundamental principles which are designed to achieve or fulfil the objectives of the substantive law. Some of these fundemental principles require discussion here.

1.1 The functional role of the judge or the court during a trial

The judge or the court is required to behave as a referee or umpire under the English common law procedure known as the Adversary System[3] when the trial of a case is being conducted. The judge or the court does not take part in the judicial contest which is raging between the litigants. The judicial contest is the sole responsibility of the litigants and their pleaders. It is the function of a litigant and his pleader to elicit evidence in support of their claim and with the intention to defeat the opponent's case, without assistance from the judge. The neutrality of the judge or the court is aimed at the attainment of impartiality, which produces a high degree of public confidence in the law and prestige for the judges. A judge may put questions to a litigant or witness only in order to clarify certain points or to obviate particular doubts in their minds.

But, contrary to the principle of the Adversary System, the procedure under the customary law makes the judge or the court the investigator of facts during a trial. This process of investigation per se cannot be construed as amounting to partiality of the judge or the court. It is the duty of the judge (or court) to elicit the best evidence from the litigants in order that he (or it) may pass a correct judgement ultimately in the case. If there is any failure to produce the best evidence during the trial, the responsibility for such failure is attributed to the court. The failure may be regarded as an indication of inefficiency on the part of the judge or the court.

This investigatory system is justified on several grounds. In the first place, this duty of investigation is bestowed upon or imposed on the court by law, because there are no trained pleaders to assist the litigants. The system of advocacy is, in fact, unknown or is not part of

---

[3] '....The parties before the court are wholly answerable for the conduct of their own cases. Litigation is a game in which the court is umpire' (Pollock). *Osborn's Concise Law Dictionary*, 7th ed., by Roger & Bird, Sweet & Maxwell, 1983, p.191.

the law. Secondly, the parties or litigants prepare or caution their witnesses to agree on what evidence they must give to the court and what evidence they must withhold.[4] As this type of cautioning to filter the evidence to be received by the court is expected to take place on both sides of the litigation, the consequence is that the court or the judge is likely to be misled or induced to pass a wrong judgement.

Of course, sometimes, the preparation of the witnesses may not be done with the objective of misleading the courts by means of concocted stories or evidence, but to help the witnesses to acquaint themselves with court procedure, which they must follow, or how to give evidence when they appear before the court. But there are many instances where a party and his witnesses deliberately prepare false evidence for the purpose of inducing the court to make a decision which is favourable to him. Litigants may be aware of the fact that where a number of witnesses present their testimony in the same way, or when each witness corroborates the evidence adduced by the other, it is more probable that the court will give its judgement in favour of the party who called them, on the ground that the case has been sufficiently proved. Common knowledge of the fact that the judge or the court would not attempt to go behind the witnesses to question the validity or the genuineness of their evidence could make the judge or court a victim of deceit by unscrupulous litigants. However, this danger is either averted or minimised by the system of investigation.

A falsely prepared story is unlikely to prevail against the system of interrogatories or investigation administered by the court, because questions may be put in a way which does not invite answers consistent with the artificially prepared evidence or story. Hence the prepared sequence of events may quickly run into confusion, and there is bound to be a great deal of inconsistency in the evidence given. But a true story, as one understood or witnessed the facts, must remain firmly engraved in the mind of a person in logical order of the natural events; and, accordingly, the system of interrogatories from the court should not produce any substantial degree of inconsistency.

The system of investigation or interrogatories by the court differs from cross-examination. The former takes place while the party or the witness is delivering his testimony, whereas the latter system is conducted when a party or witness has completely said all that he wants to state during the examination-in-chief. Cross-examination takes place only when the witness or party has completed the delivery of his prefabricated evidence or story. If he is intelligent, he will try to

---

[4] This type of arrangement is even more exaggerated in a system in which advocates plead for parties.

be consistent with what he has already stated when he is subsequently subjected to cross-examination.

The system of investigation, under the customary law, is administered simultaneously with the examination-in-chief or during the delivery of evidence by the party or the witness, although the court must try to avoid throwing his story into a state of confusion. In other words, the objective is not to confuse the party or the witness but to get material facts established before they get buried in a long subsequent narrative.

The third point in support of the system of investigation by the court is that the interrogatory system affords the judge the best chance of fulfilling his duty of unveiling the truth and administering justice. The fourth point in support of the system is that a judge or court member may not be idle when a trial is in process. Fifthly, a judge or a court must not allow himself or itself to be dragged to a conclusion by logical and sufficiently corroborated evidence which may be false, but he or it must be satisfied that it is the evidence of truth. This satisfaction is attained through the involvement of the judge or the court in the investigation. Sixthly, respect for the judges or courts results from a good judgement which is the outcome of a thorough investigation.

1.2 The principle of conciliation

One of the main objectives of the customary law is that peace and harmony should be restored between the contesting parties, through compromise and reparation for the wrong committed. Hence, in order that this objective may be achieved, the court procedure is greatly influenced by the process of conciliation. This process of conciliation is substantially responsible for the flexibility of the whole procedure. A rigid procedure, apart from other defects it carries, would make it difficult for the courts to attain the desired conciliation between the parties or litigants.

The desire to bring about a conciliation between the parties sometimes equates the court with a system of arbitration. The court may adopt a persuasive role in order to induce an agreement, compromise or settlement between the parties. This persuasive role of the court is very common in cases which involve family relations. It may be contended, in other words, that the aim of the principle of conciliation is to prevent or avoid enmity or ill-feeling which a judicial decision might produce between the parties. This is the moment when the value of human relations is put to the test. Of course, there is an inherent belief in the value of a good relationship, which must not be submerged or allowed to be eroded by some material interest which gives rise to a claim in a civil suit. Blood or social relationship must be maintained, as far as possible, at the expense of material interest. The process of trying to achieve conciliation between the parties has always made it possible for the courts to revise their own judicial decisions, and in many cases, such revisions find favourable responses or welcome from the litigants, except when a revision has been made with a motive to achieve an adverse result against one party.

1.3 Settlement of disputes outside the court

It is compatible with the process of achieving conciliation between the parties that all legal disputes must, as far as possible, be settled out of court. In fact, the majority of the cases which appear before the courts should have been subjected to consideration by some sort of arbitration council outside the courts. A judicial proceeding is usually regarded as the last resort, when there is a deadlock which the council of elders cannot resolve. Even when the case reaches the court, the door to the settlement of the case outside is not closed. Those elders who take part in an attempt to reach a settlement outside the court may still insist on the point, and they may endeavour to persuade the court to refer the matter for settlement outside the court, or they may urge the court to persuade the parties to make some compromise. The court on its own motion may initiate a settlement of the dispute outside the court or urge a compromise.

Of course, there are certain cases, by nature, which cannot be settled outside the court or be subject to compromise. An example of such cases is where there is no blood or social relationship between the contesting parties, or where the relationship between them is purely economic. In fact the concept of litigation as it is understood today by litigants, for example, in the Western world, is alien to the Dinka or is a new phenomenon in Dinka society. It is an alien concept which foreigners imported to the Southern Sudan at the beginning of the condominium rule in the Sudan. The concept of litigation which traditionally prevails under the customary law is one which is geared towards conciliation. Litigation in the Western sense is a judicial contest which must end in favour of one party and against the other. The court is absolved or relieved from its duty, once it has passed the judgement and the execution is completed.

But, according to the traditional concept of litigation under the customary law, the court must look beyond legal rights of the parties to see what type of relationship is likely to prevail between them after the adjudication. The court must try to find a solution that does not leave feelings of enmity behind. The idea is that the unsuccessful party should not be made to feel that he is a loser while the other is the victor. Accordingly, the purpose of settling legal disputes outside the court is to achieve conciliation.

1.4 Simplicity of procedure

Since the rules of procedure regulate how the rules of substantive law are to be defended and enforced, they should not be made very difficult and complicated. They must be simple and comprehensible to every litigant of any level of understanding and to the court members themselves. This simplicity of procedure is compatible with the principle of conciliation, which has been discussed above. The objective of conciliation is to remove the conflict between the parties and to restore harmony. This objective cannot be achieved through a complicated procedure, which prolongs the litigation and is liable to frustrate the litigants. Further, simplicity of procedure facilitates speedy administration of justice, without too much waste of physical effort and expense. Complex rules of procedure are justified on the grounds that they are rules designed to meet, in many instances, complicated situations, and that framing simple rules to control complicated situations results in ambiguity and uncertainty.[5] But, as stated above, common experience shows that, in every legal system where the procedure is very complex, litigation is much more protracted, and a single case can be contested by the parties for several years. Parties to this protracted litigation grow weary, impatient and disappointed.

The procedure under customary law, which is very simple, enables speedy settlement of disputes; it minimises physical effort and expense and, for these reasons, this type of procedure suits the litigant.

2. THE CONSTITUTION OF CHIEFS' COURTS

The Constitution of the Chiefs' Courts, which governs the traditional or customary laws of the people of the Southern Sudan, was established by means of a statutory instrument called The Chiefs' Courts Ordinance, 1931. This was the first time the State machinery got involved in the constitutional organization of the traditional judicial system in the Southern Sudan. S.4(1) established the Constitution of the Chiefs' Courts as follows:

'There shall be the following classes of Chiefs' Courts:

(a) a Chief sitting alone;

---

[5] Dr Nand Lal, *Code of Civil Procedure, Vol. I, 2nd ed.*, Allahbad, 1980, p.9.

(b) a Chief as President sitting with members;
(c) a Special Court as provided in s.8 of the Ordinance.

Chiefs' Courts under (a) and (b) above, are permanently established by means of warrants called the Warrants of Establishments[6] of Courts under the hand of the Chief Justice.[7]

The class of courts under (b) above, has been implemented in the following hierarchy:

(i) a Chiefs' Court called Branch Court (A-Court) with a chief sitting as President with members;
(ii) a Chiefs' Court called Regional Court (B-Court) with a chief sitting as President with members;
(iii) a Chiefs' Court called Main Court, sometimes called Court of Appeal (C-Court); it was later abolished, however.

In the order of seniority which their powers indicate, the Branch Court is the lowest court, while the Main Court was the highest. Both the Branch and Regional Courts are only courts of first instance, while the Main Court had the appellate authority. It was also a court of first instance in major cases in which the other two courts were incompetent in terms of powers to adjudicate.

3. JURISDICTION OF CHIEFS' COURTS

The jurisdiction of the courts is one of the most important subjects in any system of judicial procedure. Whenever a case appears before a court of law, one of the most important issues which the court must determine in a preliminary stage is whether it has jurisdiction to entertain the case or not.

Jurisdiction has been defined as:

(a) the power of a court or a judge to entertain an action, petition or other proceeding;
(b) the district or limits within which the judgements or orders of a court can be enforced or executed.[8]

---

[6] Before 1956 the present powers of the Chief Justice and of the Province Judge were vested in the Governor-General and Governor of a Province respectively. But s.76 of the Self-Government Statute 1956 vested the powers of the Governor-General in the Chief Justice and of the Province Governor in the Province Judge.
[7] See s.5(i) of the Chiefs' Courts Ordinance, 1931.
[8] Osborn's Concise Law Dictionary, 7th ed., by Roger & Bird, Sweet & Maxwell, 1983.

Jurisdiction is further defined by Dr Nand Lal, as follows:

> 'Jurisdiction of a court may be defined to be the power of a court to hear and determine a cause, to adjudicate and exercise any judicial power in relation to it; in other words, by jurisdiction is meant the authority which a court has to decide matters that are litigated before it or to take cognizance of matters presented in a formal way for its decision.[9]

In several instances, there are restrictions placed upon the jurisdiction of the courts. Accordingly, it is determined with reference to: (i) value or amount; (ii) nature of property which is the subject of litigation; (iii) persons; (iv) territory within which the court may exercise its powers.

The jurisdiction and powers of the Chiefs' Courts are always defined by the Chief Justice in the warrants of their establishment, in accordance with the provisions of s.5 of the Chiefs' Courts Ordinance, 1931, which provides:

(a) Chiefs' Courts of the classes specified in (a) and (b) of s.4(1) shall be established by a warrant under the hand of the Chief Justice at such places or within such areas as it thinks fit.
(b) The warrant shall define the power of the court and the limits of its jurisdiction.

Further, the authority for the jurisdiction of the Chiefs' Courts is stipulated under s.6 of the Ordinance, as follows:

1. Subject to the provisions of sub-section (2) every Chiefs' Court shall have full jurisdiction and power to the extent set out in this Ordinance or in its warrant and in its regulations in all civil cases in which each of the parties is a native and in all criminal cases in which the accused person is a native, provided that:

    (a) in civil cases in which one or more of the parties, and
    (b) in criminal cases in which the accused person is a Government official or is a native not domiciled or ordinarily resident in the Upper Nile Province or in Equatoria Province or in Bhar el Ghazal Province the court shall have jurisdiction only – in case (a) with the consent of such

---

[9] Code of Civil Procedure, Vol. 1, 2nd ed., Allahbad, 1980, p.703.

party or parties, and in case (b) with the consent of the District Commissioner (but now it is the Resident Magistrate or District Judge of first grade).

2. A Chiefs' Court shall have no jurisdiction in criminal cases over a Government official who is not a native of or domiciled either in the Upper Nile Province or in Equatoria Province or in Bhar el Ghazal Province.

With regard to the question of jurisdiction as defined by the warrant of establishment of the court in terms of the value or the nature of the subject-matter of the suit, and in reference to a defined territory, there is little or no difficulty for a court to determine its jurisdiction. However, the determination of the question of jurisdiction over persons poses more difficulties which give rise to many controversies. In view of this, the question of the court's jurisdiction over persons needs a little more discussion.

The wording of s.6(1), which confers the jurisdiction over persons on Chiefs' Courts, is somewhat clumsy and not easy to comprehend. In this respect, it requires to be paraphrased in simpler expressions. The section confers jurisdiction over persons or Chiefs' Courts where:

(a) each of the parties in all civil cases is a native;
(b) the accused, in criminal cases, is a native;
(c) consent is given by one or more of the parties, in civil cases involving a Government official or a native not domiciled or ordinarily resident in any of the Southern Provinces of the Sudan;
(d) consent of a District Commissioner (now Resident Magistrate or District Jude of first grade) is given in criminal cases in which the accused person is a Government official or a native who has no domicile or ordinary residence in any of the Southern Provinces of the Sudan.

The term 'native' is defined by s.3 of the Ordinance as 'any native of Africa other than a native of Egypt.' Further, it may be remarked here that the jurisdiction of the court is qualified in (c) and (d) above, on the ground that the party or parties, or the accused person, has no domicile or ordinary residence anywhere in the Southern Sudan, otherwise the court would have full jurisdiction as in (a) and (b) above. The other qualifying ground is the fact that the accused, in criminal or civil cases, is a Government official who is not a native, domiciled or ordinarily resident in any of the provinces of the Southern Sudan (ref. s.6(2)).

Without any contravention of the statutory provisions of the Ordinance, as stipulated in s.6(1), and in conformity with the contents of the warrants of establishment, the Chiefs' Courts, through long years of practice, have developed supplementary rules for the purpose of regulating among themselves problems of conflict of jurisdiction over persons. The following rules of practice, *inter alia*, have been developed by the Chiefs' Courts: A Chiefs' Court (let us say, Court 'A') assumes jurisdiction over persons where:

(a) in civil or criminal cases, all the parties or the accused person or persons are subjects of Court 'A';

(b) in civil or criminal cases, the parties or the accused person or persons, who are subjects of another court (let us say, Court 'B') are ordinarily resident or domiciled within the territorial jurisdiction of Court 'A'. But where the legal dispute involves only the subjects of Court 'B', who are resident or domiciled in the territory of Court 'A', and these subjects want to refer their legal dispute to their own Court 'B', then Court 'A' will have no jurisdiction over them on that matter. But, where the dispute involves at least one of the subjects of Court 'A', then the parties cannot deprive Court 'A' of its jurisdiction;

(c) consent is given or submission is made to the jurisdiction of Court 'A' by the parties (i.e. plaintiffs and defendants) who are subjects of Court 'B' and who are not domiciled or ordinarily resident within the territorial jurisdiction of Court 'A'. It is to be noted here also that the consent may be given by Court 'B' on behalf of its subjects. Court 'B' is entitled to give consent on behalf of its subjects because, in the last analysis, it is itself the custodian of the jurisdiction over these subjects, since they are its citizens.

It may also be stated, at this juncture, that the Ordinance further advanced supplementary solutions to some of these questions of conflict of jurisdiction. Section 8(1) of the Ordinance provides that:

'The Province Judge may convene a Special Court if he thinks that the end of justice will be served thereby in any of the following cases:

(a) where the accused is subject to the jurisdiction of one chief and the complainant is subject to the jurisdiction of another chief;

(b) the accused is himself a chief;
(c) the alleged offence is of such gravity that the powers of any other court established under this Ordinance having jurisdiction appear to be insufficient.'

Precisely speaking, special courts were therefore stipulated under the Ordinance in order to solve problems:

(i) of conflict of jurisdiction where the parties to a case belong to different courts by creating a court of common jurisdiction. For example, border disputes have always been solved through special courts;
(ii) where a court which has greater powers to deal with very serious cases is needed; and
(iii) where a certain class of persons, by virtue of their authority or influence over the ordinary inferior Chiefs' Courts, need a superior court to try them.

To conclude the discussion of the question of jurisdiction over persons, it may be mentioned that the problem of conflict of jurisdiction also confronts the Chiefs' Courts at the stage of execution of decrees and judicial orders. The property which is the subject of execution proceedings may be situated in the jurisdiction of another court, or the judgement debtor may be the subject of another court or has his ordinary residence or domicile in the jurisdiction of another court. If the execution of decrees or judicial orders is carried out by a special court in such instances, then no problem of jurisdiction arises, since this is a court of common jurisdiction, as far as the parties are concerned. But if the execution is conducted by a Branch or a Regional Court, conflicts of jurisdiction are bound to arise, since each Court, according to its rules of practice, does not allow its territory to be invaded by the agents of an external court in pursuit of the execution of decrees, unless it has consented to it. More will be stated about this point later, when I come to discuss the subject of execution of decrees and judicial orders.

4. CAUSE OF ACTION AND RIGHT OF ACTION

4.1 Cause of action

Where a litigant indicates, by means of an oral or written petition, that he intends to bring a civil action or suit against another party, he must present facts which reasonably disclose a cause of action. Cause of action presupposes the existence of a *prima facie* case against the other party or defendant. Where a litigant or a plaintiff opens his case by stating facts which clearly show a baseless claim, it means that there is no cause of action, and his claim may be dismissed without any need to invite the defendant to answer. A court must not waste its valuable time on claims which are baseless at the beginning of the proceedings.

In fact, a person who intends to raise a judicial suit must, in most cases, seek the advice of experienced friends. If his claim is groundless, he will be advised against taking a court action. But, sometimes, a party may proceed to raise a suit or a civil action to test the court's wisdom, or to gamble his chances; he may hope that he will be able to outwit the court or the other party. However, the courts are aware that such gamblers are common, and so a party who petitions a court is always required to answer a series of questions before his petition is admitted as a suit. This examination is aimed at disclosing the cause of action, if any.

4.2 Right of action

Where a person has a cause of action, that is, where he can show that there is a *prima facie* case against the defendant, he is legally entitled to raise a civil suit against that defendant. This right to recourse to the court against the defendant is technically known as the right of action. This may be expressed by means of a general maxim which states that 'for every cause of action, there is a right of action.'

But, under modern legal systems, for example, the English Common Law system, the right of action does not prevail indefinitely in favour of a party. There is a period of limitation of actions imposed by statutory provisions. The right continues to exist in favour of a person, but if it is not exercised within a period prescribed by law for each type of action, the party is barred from exercising it at the expiry of this specified period. In this respect, the relevant statute in the Sudan was the Prescriptions and Limitation Ordinance 1928. This Statute, which embodied common law rules, was repealed by the Civil Transactions Act, 1984. It must be stated here, however, that this common law doctrine of limitations of actions is unknown to the Dinka Customary Law. A person's right to recourse to court against a defendant cannot be rejected by a court because of the lapse of a certain period. Right of action must always prevail against passage of time, except in certain circumstances, such as the following:

(a) where, in the circumstances of a particular case, the court may reasonably construe the failure of the plaintiff to exercise his right of action as an absolute forbearance of such right;

(b) where the right is so old that it can hardly be proved, for example, if all the necessary evidence cannot be produced because the contemporary witnesses are all dead; or where no evidence of any kind may be reasonably traceable to prove the claim;
(c) where the right was due to a person who is dead and who never, during his lifetime, made any attempt to exercise it. In such a case, his heirs or legal representative cannot be permitted to exercise the right, for it must be construed, in such circumstances, that the deceased person abandoned his right for good and no one else is entitled to reactivate it;
(d) where the plaintiff is trying to re-open cases which he expressly abandoned.

5. NON-RENEWAL OF DECIDED CASES (BERÉ-PINYÉ LUÔK)

The doctrine of *res judicata* operates under s.11 of the Chiefs' Courts Ordinance, 1931.[10] Where a case has been finally decided by a court between the parties, the same case or cause of action cannot be the subject of litigation again in the future between the same parties or between their successors or trustees of their estate and families. Although the decision of the court in the case may be questioned by an appellate authority or on application for revision, no party is entitled to raise the case again as if it were a fresh suit or as if it had not been the subject of a previous litigation between the same parties or their predecessors. This process of renewal of cases (i.e. *beré-pinyé luok*) is often confused with revision (ie *beeré-lukic*). Renewal (or *beré-pinyé luok*) means starting the case afresh as if it were a new case. However, revision (or *beeré-lukic*) is done on the ground that a new fact has been discovered after the passing of the first decision which is being revised.

6. WHO ARE THE PARTIES TO A SUIT OR A CASE?

The question, who are the parties to a civil suit or a case calls into consideration the question of solidarity or unity of the family or

---

[10] S.11 provides: 'No matter, whether criminal or civil, that has been adjudicated on under the provisions of this Ordinance, shall be cognizable by the ordinary courts of law so long as the judgement is subsisting, and no court established under this Ordinance shall adjudicate upon any case which is being or has been dealt with by any ordinary court or law except with the consent of such court.'

families. Under the customary law, a suit or a case raised by or against a family member is a suit or a case for or against the whole family or a group of families which are related. Every member of the family or families is a party, and is entitled to attend the court hearing. But, since it may be impossible for all the family members to appear before the court, those who actually attend and contest the case do so as representatives of the whole family or families. So, the action is a representative action. Where any one member of the family involved in the legal dispute appears before the court at any later date of the proceedings, the court cannot turn him out on the ground that he is not a party to the suit, nor will it be necessary to join him as a party at that moment. He is already a party to the suit by virtue of his membership of the family. But there are a few instances where this rule will not operate. One of the instances is where the member in question has no interest in the case, due to some changes in the family structure or relations.

In claims of damages in adultery suits, it is the husband or his representative, if the husband is dead, who is entitled to sue. But, although the relatives of the husband may not initiate or take the lead in the raising of an adultery suit, they will rally behind him during the process of litigation. The husband is the first party and his relatives become the second parties.

Further in conformity with the principle of solidarity or unity of the family, decrees or judicial orders may be executed against persons who do not appear as parties in the case. Such persons cannot, however, resist the execution of the decree or order on the ground that they had not been joined as parties in the suit.

7. SURVIVAL OF ACTIONS

Survival of actions prevails under the customary law. Where a party to a suit or a case dies while the suit or the case still pends before the court, his legal representative or heir is entitled to take it up. This rule is in harmony with the other rule which entitles every member of the family to be a party in the case. Hence the death of the parties to a case does not mean that the judicial contest has come to an end.

8. PAYMENT OF SUBJECT-MATTER OF THE SUIT INTO COURT

Before the hearing of the case commences, a court may order the defendant to produce the subject-matter of litigation or its equivalence in court. This order may be issued by the court if one of the following grounds exists or is suspected to exist:

(a) where there is a likelihood of the defendant transferring the subject-matter of the dispute to a third person, or where there is a likelihood that such property may be concealed by the defendant with the intention of evading the execution of any decree or order which the court may pass; or

(b) where it is likely that the defendant or the accused (whichever the case may be) is likely to disappear.

If the defendant or the accused neglects or declines or disobeys the order to produce the property, this must be treated as a contempt of court, for which he will be liable for any suitable form of penalty. Apart from any penalty that may be inflicted, the court must order the bailiffs or retainers or other court's agents to execute the order through the seizure of the said property or its equivalence.

When the property is produced, the court will appoint a reliable person as a trustee to keep the property, until the court issues its final order, after the disposal of the case. The trustee may be the court's President himself or a reliable local resident.

This procedure for producing the subject-matter of the legal dispute in court before the hearing takes place has some additional advantages. In the first place, it promotes speedy disposal of suits or cases, since it eliminates the process of execution of cases after the passing of judgements. Secondly, it ensures that any decree or order that the court may pass after the hearing will be executed.

9. COMMENCEMENT OF JUDICIAL PROCEEDINGS

A party may begin the proceedings by means of an oral or written petition addressed to the court or to the court's President or even to a member of the court. There are no formal requirements with which the petition must conform. But it must show a cause of action which gives rise to a right of action, otherwise it will be rejected. Further, there is no strict procedure in the presentation of the oral or written petition. The petition may be presented in any one of the following ways:

(a) the plaintiff may present his petition to the court's President or member, either in court or at home, even during his leisure hours, because a court or a chief may sit anywhere at any time of the day to determine cases, or to arrange them for a subsequent sitting;

(b) the petition may be presented, if it is written, or communicated, if it is oral, through the court clerk;

(c) the plaintiff may appear before the court and seat himself where complainants or aggrieved parties are seated in court. He will be asked to state the nature of his complaint or cause of action and the name of the accused or defendant;

(d) plaintiffs may prepare written petitions addressed to the local District Judge or Inspector of Local Government who has judicial powers.[11] The District Judge may refer these petitions to the relevant Chiefs' Court within the territorial jurisdiction of his court (i.e. District Court);

(e) until recently, a litigant or an aggrieved party could begin his case by offering some services, by way of labour, to the chief or court's President at the latter's home. But this practice has almost stopped now.

10. SUMMONS

When a litigant has presented his petition in any one of the forms or modes mentioned above, the court or the President will subject him to a brief examination, for the purpose of ascertaining the existence of a cause of action. If the court or the President is satisfied of the existence of such cause of action, the case is admitted and orders are issued to summon to court the defendant and his witnesses, if any, on a fixed day. If the defendant lives near the court centre, he may be produced on the same day.

Orders to produce or summon parties and witnesses are executed by retainers or other agents or employees of the court. But where the use of force may be expected, the retainer (who is a kind of semi-policeman at the court) will be required to execute the order. When summons are issued by the court, the appearance of the parties or witnesses before it is compulsory. Hence a defendant or a witness who has been summoned must appear before the court, otherwise he will be subjected to an arrest and produced. If he absconds, his property will be liable for seizure to compel his appearance. Apart from court's agents, summoning may be done by any person who has been so delegated or directed by the court. He may be a friend or a relative, or a person who knows the party or the witness being summoned.

The appearance in court of the defendant is compulsory, because

---

[11] The Distict Judge is a professionally trained lawyer while the Inspectors of Local Government are the successors to the authority of the former District Commissioners.

there is no system of passing default decrees if he fails or neglects to appear when he has been duly summoned.[12] Where the defendant does not appear on the fixed day the court may adjourn or suspend the hearing till he is produced at any time. But, if it is established that he is absconding, the court will issue an order for the seizure of the subject-matter of the suit, or other property of his which is available. If he continues to abscond despite the seizure of his property, the court may deliver the said property to the plaintiff when the court is reasonably convinced that the defendant will not appear or cannot be found.

However, if the defendant subsequently appears and states reasonable grounds why the court ought to revise its order or decision, the court may then order the hearing to take place. A final order will be issued at the end of the hearing as to who shall be entitled to take delivery of the property.

11. THE HEARING

The proceedings during the hearing are very simple. There are no pre-trial proceedings. Once a petition has been presented and admitted by the court, a date is fixed and on that day, and if all the parties appear, the trial or hearing begins. But before we embark on the trial proceedings, it may be necessary to know something about the seating arrangements of the people in the court, as this is also a part of the procedure.

11.1 The seating arrangements of the people

11.1(a) *The court President and members*

The court President and members are seated in a semi-circle or in the form of an arc at one side of the court centre. The President sits in the middle. The members sit on both sides of the President, according to their order of seniority, till the line ends on each side with the most junior member. Traditionally, court membership is very elastic. Its size may increase or decrease according to the number of chiefs who are present in the court. But with the advent of the Chiefs' Courts Ordinance, 1931, and with the introduction of the warrants of establishment of the courts, made under the hand of the Chief Justice, the constitution of the Chiefs' Courts has been fixed. At present, in Bhar el Ghazal Region, the constitution of each Chiefs' Court comprises

---

[12] Nor can a suit be dismissed for non-appearance of the plaintiff. But in this situation it will lie in abeyance till it is afterwards re-activated if the plaintiff appears.

five members, including the President. Three members, among whom is the President, constitute a quorum.

11.1(b) *The court Clerk or court Police*[13]
At some distance in front of the court, the court clerk and police are seated at the table and facing the court. They put on record the summary of the proceedings or the evidence given during the hearing.

11.1(c) *Agam-long*
Agam-long is seated in the middle between the court members and the clerk. *Agam-long* is a very important man in the court. No trial or hearing takes place unless he is present to play his traditional ceremonial role. His participation provides the court proceedings with the necessary formality and seriousness. Every person who speaks in court, including the President and court members, speaks through him. *Agam-long* repeats aloud the words of each speaker in the court. He is an orator who has a command of the language of the court. He is capable of reducing the long and clumsy statement of a speaker into a precise and comprehensive sentence. Apart from repeating the words aloud and precisely, it is a part of his duty to direct the parties, witnesses and the court as to what steps to take at the next stage of the proceedings. He is well-versed in court procedure.

11.1(d) *The parties and their witnesses*
The plaintiff (or plaintiffs) and his witnesses sit in front of the court at one side of *Agam-long*. At the same time the defendant and his witnesses are seated on the other side of *Agam-long*, and they all face the court; witnesses are not withdrawn till they are invited to speak by the court. They must sit in court with the parties who call them.

11.1(e) *Retainers and agents or employees of the court*
The retainers and court's agents, who help the retainers in maintaining order, do not sit but stand around the court centre and behind the court members to maintain order.

11.1(f) *The audience*
At the outer ring or around the court centre, the large audience or members of the public, who are always attracted by court proceedings, sit or stand. Court centres, in fact, are places of large gathering for many reasons. For example, (a) they are places of information collection about all the events that have taken place in the whole area;

---

[13] 'Police' here refers to State police, not the retainer. He presents criminal cases.

(b) they are centres of cultural and literary learning; and (c) they also serve as recreation and socialisation centres, etc.

12. WHO MUST OPEN THE CASE?

Upon the completion of the seating arrangement of the people and the instilling of order, a voice comes from among the court members calling out: '*Agam-long* invite the plaintiff, please, to state his case.' In response to the call from the court, *Agam-long* must always state or mention the name of the speaker from the court (whether the speaker is the President or a court member). The mention of the speaker's name, preferably his bull's name, is made by *Agam-long* as a ceremonial demonstration of respect for the court. *Agam-long* then proceeds to call the plaintiff by name (sometimes his bull's name) and says: 'I have been directed by the court to invite you to state your case; now begin.'

The plaintiff must take the oath before he begins to state his case. The oath is done by means of a spear.[14] The spear is held with the right hand and the one swearing the oath makes the following prayer to God: 'Almighty God, I am going to state the truth to the court. If I add or include any lie or false statement, I pray that you kill me with this spear.' After this statement of oath, he kisses the spear and puts the blade on his head. He kisses it for the second time and puts the spear blade on his right shoulder, then the left shoulder. The spear is then laid down on the ground and the party taking the oath crosses over it three times. With this done, the oath-taking ceremony is completed. The plaintiff now moves back to take his place and open the case.

While the plaintiff is delivering evidence in support of his claim, *Agam-long* transmits, in a louder voice, every statement he makes. The court allows him to state his case fully. The court must not restrict a party or witness when he is giving evidence, on the ground that part of the evidence stated is irrelevant, unless such irrelevance is substantial indeed. There is no fair hearing if a party or a witness cannot be given the opportunity to state what he knows about the case in full detail. Sometimes a long-winded narrative of the details of a case makes the trial very tedious. In some cases material facts are buried or blurred by the long narrative.

But the party (or witness) must be prepared to answer a series of

---

[14] An accused person must also take the oath. The reason is that the sanction for perjury is not human but divine. Where a person makes a false oath, he knows that he is taking the risk of inviting God's wrath. The oath, therefore, induces the truth to be told.

questions from the court while he is giving his evidence. Where a party or witness is trying (knowingly or unknowingly) to skip over or evade certain material points, or where a material point does not receive a clear explanation, a series of questions will be asked by the court and he will have to suspend the delivery of his story or evidence in order to answer each question satisfactorily. Where the court doubts the truth of a certain answer, the opposite party or opponent may be asked to confirm or contradict the point in question. When he has answered the questions, he will be directed to continue his evidence or story, if he has more to state.

This process of investigation, while a party or witness is giving his evidence, makes the system of cross-examination unnecessary. After the party or witness has completed relating his case or evidence, all the questions which would necessarily be asked during the cross-examination will have been answered already at the time of the examination-in-chief. The plaintiff may also be interrupted when he is delivering his case by inviting one or more of his witnesses to confirm or deny certain material facts which appear in his story or evidence.

When the plaintiff (or complainant) has completed giving his evidence, his witnesses will be required to confirm the whole of, or material points in, his story. The witnesses must also answer interrogatories from the court when they are giving their evidence in support of the plaintiff's or complainant's case. The court may also give the defendant (or the opponent) the opportunity to contradict certain points in the evidence given by the plaintiff's witnesses. The plaintiff's case is closed if his witnesses have completed giving their evidence.

13. THE DEFENCE CASE

When the plaintiff or complainant has completed stating his case, it is the turn of the defendant (or the accused), after taking the oath, to present his defence, if any. If he has no defence, or if he admits the claim or the charge against him, the court will no longer proceed with the hearing or trial. *Agam-long* will then direct the court: *'Cuat-ka ukum'*, meaning, 'Deliver the judgement'.

However, if the defendant contests the claim or the charge against him, he will be invited to state his defence at once. After him, his witnesses will be asked to give evidence in support of his case. The procedure is exactly the same as in the plaintiff's or complainant's case. The defendant or the accused will be subjected to answering interrogatories from the court and the plaintiff (or complainant).

When both sides have completed their cases, the court may allow any member of the public (among the audience), who makes a request, to comment on the case or ask questions directed to anyone of the parties. His comments or questions may be allowed by the court because he may be able to elicit some material evidence which the parties and the court overlooked during the hearing. This member of the audience may have sufficient knowledge of the background of the legal dispute and will be best placed to assist the court with that knowledge; such opportunities are always given to the elderly people among the audience. But the court is mindful about opening the door too wide to the audience, for fear of inviting some disorder or contempt of court. The court is capable of identifying the elders among the audience who have the ability to give the necessary advisory opinion or assistance. Those elderly members of the audience who are given the opportunity to comment on the case have the liberty to suggest what decision is reasonable in the circumstances of the case. The advisory opinion may be persuasive to the court, in which case it is likely that it will be adopted in whole or in part.

Members of the audience are allowed to take part, though in a restricted sense, in passing judicial decisions or orders, because the administration of justice is not regarded as the monopoly of the court. Justice is best administered if any person who claims to be in possession of some material knowledge or information is allowed to state it and to propose any solution he thinks is reasonable.

14. THE JUDGEMENT

Agam-long directs the court to deliver its judgement, when the hearing or the investigation of the case is completed. He will pronounce the statement: *'Cuat-ka ukum'*. Each member of the court, starting always with the most junior one, gives his judgement briefly, after analysing the evidence and stating the reasons which support his judgement. When, at last, it is the turn of the President to deliver his judgement, *Agam-long,* at the top of his voice, calls for the attention of the whole court and asks every member of the audience to keep silent and to listen. The retainers must now be on the alert to silence any act or noise which might constitute a disorder. *Agam-long* then invites the President to deliver his judgement. The President starts to analyse the evidence adduced on both sides and makes references to the judgements already delivered by his colleagues, and then passes his judgement. He must also give reasons which support his judgement.[15]

---

[15] During the analysis of the evidence when a judgement is being passed, the character of the party or the accused person is brought up for discussion. His previous offences or his conduct on previous occasions may be analysed by the court President or members to justify any decision to be passed.

The decision of the court is reached when there is a consensus of opinion on all the points in all the judgements delivered, or when a majority of the members, which includes the President, concur in their judgements. But it is hard to recall any case in which the judgement of the President was defeated because he was in the minority group. However, one thing is very clear: the President has an influential role which must induce other court members (who have already delivered their judgements) to acquiesce in his judgement. If the President is of a different view, or when the entire membership of the court is sharply divided on material issues, the parties and the audience are asked to withdraw from the court so that the court can discuss its judgement. When it arrives at a decision by consensus (after such discussion), or by a majority which includes the President, the parties and the audience are called and a single judgement is delivered by a spokesman of the court as though there was no dissension.

The court clerk now puts on record the summary of the facts and the judgement. The names of the parties and their addresses, as well as the names of their chiefs are also put on record. The serial number of the case is inserted and the names of the President and court members are recorded and each signs or puts his seal against his name. The judgement is then dated.

15. APPEALS

The concept of systematic organization of appellate hierarchy in judicial institutions is, strictly speaking, a new phenomenon which was mainly introduced by the Chiefs' Courts Ordinance, 1931. Under the traditional system, which existed before 1931, each chief or judicial authority (who was also the administrative leader), whether he was a *banybith* or a chief, was the final authority in his own area over judicial matters. His judicial decisions or orders were final, as there was no appellate authority beyond him. However, if a decision of a judicial nature was made by some inferior body or person, an appeal could be made by an aggrieved party to the Chief or *Banybith*, who, in most cases, used to sit with a council of elders to assist him; and this was the end of the ladder for applications. Decisions of *Banybith* were and are still now almost unquestionable, partly because of the psychological belief that he is always right, and partly because no one dares to raise an objection to a decision of a person believed to have divine authority.

However, with the enactment of the Chiefs' Courts Ordinance in 1931, there were two important results. Firstly, the process of appeal became the right of any litigant and not something in the nature of a privilege. Secondly, the range of appeal or the range within which the right of appeal was to be exercised by aggrieved litigants became extensively wide. Litigants have been provided with ample opportunity of presenting their appeals to higher courts through several stages in the judicial hierarchy.

This right of appeal is conferred by s.9 of the Chiefs' Courts Ordinance, 1931, as follows:

> 'There shall be a right of appeal in any civil or criminal case tried by a Chiefs' Court of the classes specified in (a) and (b) of s.4(1) to the Governor or to the District Commissioner authorized by the Governor to hear appeals.'[16]

Before the abolition of the Main Court, which was partly an appellate court and partly a court of first instance for cases which needed a court with greater powers or a court of common jurisdiction for the litigants, the system of appeals was as follows:

(a) Appeals from Branch and Regional Courts used to go to the Main Court.
(b) Appeals from the Main Court used to go to the District Commissioner.
(c) Alternatively, appeals from Branch and Regional Courts went straight to the District Commissioner, who, in many instances, referred them to the Main Court. District Commissioners had the power to entertain appeals by the authority of the Governor, who derived the same from the Governor-General.
(d) Appeals against the decisions of District Commissioners went to the Governor of the Province.

But, due to changes in both the Chiefs' Courts Ordinance of 1931, and the system of appeals and the hierarchy of the State Courts, the current stages of appeal are as follows:[17]

(a) Appeals against the decisions of Branch and Regional Courts (or, say, Chiefs' Courts), go to the Resident Magistrate or the

---

[16] Now, the Province Judge exercises the powers of the former Governor, while the Resident Magistrate or the District Judge of first grade exercises the powers of the former District Commissioner.

[17] The Chiefs' Courts Ordinance organized the stages of appeal up to the Governor. The Civil Justice Act. 1929, later replaced with the Civil Procedure Act, 1974 and now the Civil Procedure Act, 1983, regulated the appeals for all courts, except the Chiefs' Courts and former Native Courts under the Native Courts Ordinance 1932.

District Judge of first grade or to the Province Judge.
(b) Appeals from the Province Judge or the Resident Magistrate or the District Judge of first grade,[18] go to Court of Appeal. Decisions of Court of Appeal are final except on points of law.
(c) Appeals go from Court of Appeal to the Supreme Court, but only on questions of law. However, appeals from Chiefs' Courts have not yet climbed in considerable numbers the long ladder up to the Supreme Court.

15.1 Time for appeals

Under the customary law, there is no time limit specified for making appeals. An aggrieved party or a judgement debtor may be required by the court (Chiefs' Court) to execute the decree or judicial order before he appeals. He must however appeal within a reasonable time. It is the court which makes the computation of what time must be regarded as reasonable.

But, under sections 177 and 192 of the Civil Procedure Act, 1983, the right of appeal exists or is operative only within 15 days from the date of judgement or judicial order, if the party appealing was present in court at the time of its judgement, or had been duly summoned to attend the court but failed to appear without any reasonable excuse. If the party appealing was not present in court at the time of the pronouncement of the judgement or order, and he had not been duly summoned, then 15 days start from the date he received the notice of such judgement or order.

Whether the time within which the right of appeal must be exercised by litigants who contest before the Chiefs' Courts ought to be governed by the Civil Procedure Act, 1983 (which is a general territorial law), remains the question. Without any doubt, of course, a provision of a State law or general territorial law prevails where there is conflict with a provision of subordinate legislation or customary law. But the following points could be considered by anyone who is considering the question of time for submitting appeals.

In the first place, customary law is recognised by State law and Constitution as the personal law of the indigenous Sudanese communities. Hence, unless a provision under it is contrary to justice, equity and good conscience, it cannot be disturbed, merely because of its difference from a provision of State law. Secondly, the Chiefs'

---

[18] Up to September 1983, appeals from the Resident Magistrate or the District Judge of first grade used to go to the Province Judge, then from the Province Judge to the Court of Appeal. But now an appeal can be made directly to the Court of Appeal by evading the Province Judge.

Courts Ordinance, which was enacted in 1931 after the Civil Justice Ordinance of 1929 (now Civil Procedure Act, 1983), did not prescribe any time for making appeals (against decisions of Chiefs' Courts) in conformity with the time prescribed for appeals by the Civil Justice Ordinance itself. Hence it was not meant that there must be uniformity on the question of time. Thirdly, in a system where professional lawyers are not available to assist litigants, any legal provision which establishes or fixes a time for appeals is likely to lead to serious miscarriages of justice. Adherance to such time limits would defeat the good objectives intended by the law makers.

15.2 Rationale behind making appeals

When an aggrieved litigant makes an appeal to an appellate authority, the general presumption is that the decision of the court against which he is appealing is wrong and must not be allowed to stand. It must either be varied or reversed totally. Accordingly, the applicant must state the grounds where and why he thinks the lower court went wrong. He must then state what relief he was denied of and which should be awarded to him by the appellate authority. But he must not include in the appeal what he did not raise in his original claim, otherwise it will cease to be an appeal.

The appellate authority may allow the appeal and reverse or vary the decision against which the appeal is made, or it may dismiss the appeal and confirm the decision of the lower court. But the respondent must be heard before the appellate authority takes its decision.

But readers may be reminded here that when these appeals reach State courts, these State courts have always followed the general principles and procedure prescribed by the general territorial law. This results, sometimes, in the importation of alien rules of procedure into the customary law and in unsatisfactory decisions.

16. POWER OF REVISION

The Chiefs' Courts Ordinance, 1931, conferred the power of revision of cases on the Governor and the District Commissioner. As stated earlier, the powers of the Governor are now inherited by the Province Judge while those of the District Commissioner are inherited by the Resident Magistrate or District Judge of first grade. S.10 of the Ordinance provides:

'The Governor or District Commissioner may of his own initiative intervene to quash or revise the decision of any chiefs' court of the classes specified in (a) and (b) of section 4(1) or may transfer the case to his own court or to any other chiefs' court of competent jurisdiction at any stage of the proceedings and shall take one or other of these courses if the chiefs' court has exceeded its jurisdiction or powers.'

The Ordinance conferred this revisional power on the Governor and the District Commissioner in order to interfere with the jurisdiction or decisions of the Chiefs' Courts for the purpose of correction. Revisional power is exercised on the following grounds:

(a) to correct the errors of facts in judgement;
(b) to correct the errors on point of law; for example, when a chiefs' court lacks competence to entertain a particular case because it assumes the jurisdiction which it does not have, or it tries a case which should be tried by a court which has greater power, and so forth;
(c) to correct decisions made in excess of the court's jurisdiction or powers. For example, a court may have competence to try a particular case, but it may pass a judgement which exceeds the powers conferred on it under its warrant of establishment;
(d) apart from the grounds which are explicitly stated under s. 10 of the Ordinance, there are a number of other instances in which the revisional power may be invoked. For example, where (i) the procedure adopted by the court constituted a serious abuse of law which affected the court's decision; or (ii) when fundamental evidence has been subsequently discovered, it will be justifiable to exercise the revisional power.

This power of revision is not the creation of the Ordinance, as far as the customary law is concerned. The power existed under the customary law before the enactment of the Ordinance. Under the customary law, revision may be made by the same court or chief who passed the decision which is the subject of revision.

A request for a revision is well received in contrast with an appeal. It is well received because the litigant does not question the efficiency of the court or the chief who made the decision. The litigant may state: 'I call for a revision of the case because a new fact which could not be found before has been discovered or has revealed itself.' A request for a revision looks humble, while the appeal looks aggressive as it tends to label the court or the chief as inefficient or biased.

17. EXECUTIONS OF DECREES AND ORDERS

Section 12 of the Chiefs' Courts Ordinance, 1931, provided the power for the execution of decrees and judicial orders. It conferred the power for the execution of the decrees and orders passed by the Chiefs' Courts on the Governor and the District Commissioner. The section provides:

> 'The District Commissioner or the Governor may enforce the execution of any judgement or decision of a chief's court at the request of the chief or the aggrieved party as if it were the judgement of an ordinary court of law.'

Hence, under the Ordinance, there is no power created and conferred on the Chiefs' Courts to execute their own decisions. Nevertheless, the Chiefs' Courts rely on their traditional procedure of executing decrees and judicial orders through certain agents, namely, the bailiffs (i.e. *Banywuot*), retainers, and sometimes, by the Chiefs themselves.

When a court passes the decree or judicial order, the litigation is not yet brought to an end until it has been executed. Executions are conducted by seizure of property and its delivery to the judgement creditor or decree holder, unless the judgement debtor willingly produces or delivers it to the said decree holder or judgement creditor. Decrees or orders are allowed to accumulate and when they have become many, the bailiffs or the retainers or a combination of both, together with all the decree holders or judgement creditors, are briefed and ordered to carry out the executions. The whole team moves from area to area looking for judgement debtors and the properties which are to be seized. This is a duty which takes many days or months, as long distances have to be covered.

When a judgement debtor is found with the property which is to be seized, the head of the team orders him to deliver the property to the decree holder. If the judgement debtor obeys the order and delivers the property, then the process of execution simply comes to an end. However, if he refuses to obey the order, the execution will be conducted by seizure of the property concerned. A reasonable amount of force may be exercised to overcome any resistance by the judgement debtor. It may also be necessary, in certain cases, to charge the judgement debtor with contempt of court for resisting the execution of its order, or he may be charged with obstructing the agents of the court in the conduct of their lawful duties. Once a charge is brought against the judgement debtor, he will be liable for immediate arrest, without any prior need to obtain an order of arrest from the court.

The team then continues to search for other judgement debtors, until all the decrees required to be executed in this single mission are completed.

18. EXECUTION OF DECREES AND ORDERS IN OTHER TERRITORIES

It may be necessary to execute decrees or orders in the territorial jurisdictions of other chiefs or courts, in the following instances:

(a) where the property which is the subject of execution is situated in the jurisdiction of another chief or court and in the custody of a subject of that chief or court;
(b) where the judgement debtor is a subject of another chief or court and is ordinarily resident or domiciled in the jurisdiction of that chief or court;
(c) where the judgement debtor is a subject of the court conducting the execution but he is ordinarily resident or domiciled in the jurisdiction of another chief or court.

The court which is conducting the decree (in (a) and (b) above) may undertake one of the following courses:

(i) the decree may be referred for execution to the chief or court within whose jurisdiction the property is situated, or the chief or court to which the judgement debtor is subject, and in whose territory or jurisdiction the said subject has his ordinary residence or domicile; or
(ii) the agents of the court conducting the decree may conduct such execution with the permission and assistance from the chief or court in whose jurisdiction the execution is being carried out, or the court to which the judgement debtor is subject.

In (c) above, the court conducting the execution may:

(i) obtain permission from the chief or the court within whose jurisdiction the execution is to be carried out. This permission may be expressed or implied;
(ii) directly carry out the execution of decree without permission from the chief or court within whose jurisdiction the execution is being conducted in certain cases.

Procedure

Where the pastoral communities from different territories are in the habit of crossing their borders from time to time, in search of pastures, it may cause delays and inconvenience to obtain permission in every instance. Further, where a subject of court 'A' is ordinarily resident or domiciled in the territory of court 'B' and the said subject remains under the sole administrative and judicial authority of court 'A', then court 'A' cannot seek permission from court 'B' to execute a decree against him. Since court 'B' has no protection over him, it cannot resist the execution being carried out by court 'A', which has absolute control and protection over the subject.

Table of Cases

1. *Gilbril Barbare* v. *Reen Abdel Massin Khalil* — 19, 20
2. *Pan Akoc Majok* v. *Manoah Pabeek* — 21
3. *Bamboulis* v. *Bamboulis* — 22
4. *Kattan* v. *Kattan* — 22
5. *Abdulla Chercheflio* v. *Maria Bekryorellis* — 22
6. *Mogul Steam Ship Co.* v. *McGregor Gow & Co.* — 34
7. *Jacob Mabor Agany* — 37
8. *Hyde* v. *Hyde* — 57
9. *Maliyabwana* v. *Abdullah* — 68
10. *Magot Kok* v. *Dorin* — 70
11. *Deng Kac* v. *Nyuon Makuac* — 74
12. *Not Pet* v. *Gac Nyol* — 74
13. *Maguek Atony* v. *Marial Dorin and others* — 82
14. *Adut Puouwak* v. *Tiera Macar, Maker Macol* — 83
15. *Macuny Kalok* v. *Sol Amiro* — 85
16. *John Gum* v. *Martin Makuek Abol* — 85
17. *Bona Mou Ngot* v. *Alek Nyang Dhieu* — 87
18. *Maguek Atony* v. *Marial Dorin and others* — 88
19. *Thokmer and others* v. *Malual Cindut* — 88
20. *Maguek Atony* v. *Marial Dorin and others* — 89
21. *Manyiel Cindut and others* v. *Marial Manok and others* — 89
22. *Angelina Gabriel* v. *Cyrillo Malou* — 94
23. *Mabor Adhel and Buoi Ajak* v. *Amon Mon* — 96
24. *Buol Yuol* v. *Irneo Dut* — 98
25. *Bamboulis* v. *Bamboulis* — 108
26. *Farida Fuad Sameer* — 108
27. *Gilbril Barbare* v. *Reen Abdel Massin Khalil* — 108
28. *Bamboulis* v. *Bamboulis* — 109
29. *Joseph Athian Deng and his sister Maria Deng* — 111
30. *Joseph Athian Deng and his sister Maria Deng* — 115
31. *Hollins* v. *Foweller* — 120
32. *Hollins* v. *Foweller* — 120
33. *Chief Majak Malok Akot* v. *Nyadiyiel and others* — 124
34. *Majak Akok* v. *Dut Cuot Ager and Riak Ager* — 124
35. *Col. Mathet* v. *Mathiang Yang* — 126
36. *Moses Abaker* v. *Issa Makuac* — 128
37. *Marial Reec and Manhon Gol* v. *Meen Makerlill* — 128
38. *Mabur Abiel* v. *Makur Dhuol* — 130
39. *Mageer Makoi* v. *Yang Majok* — 131
40. *Maker Mabor* v. *Daniel Marial Buot* — 133
41. *Maker Mabor* v. *Daniel Marial Buot* — 134
42. *Macar Aweckoc and others* v. *Riak Dak and others* — 166
43. *Macar Aweckoc and others* v. *Riak Dak and others* — 173
44. *Col. Mathet* v. *Mathiang Yang and Agree Miith* — 189
45. *Nyilueth Puou* v. *Ruai Makoi* — 190
46. *Akec Ayiel and Marial Makuac* — 191
47. *'G' and 'A'* — 212

Glossary

Abar The heir.

Aber Metallic ore, e.g. iron-ore or copper-ore. Before the advent of the Condominium Government in the Sudan, the Dinka (like other natives of Southern Sudan), used to dig the ore and other metals from which they made weapons, implements, ornaments, and so on. But this industry was gradually destroyed, during the Condominium Government, by the introduction of ready-made implements.

Adooc Property which is the subject of ownership.

Agam-long *Gam* means 'accept' or 'accept and communicate,' e.g. *Gam-wet*: accept and communicate the word or statement; or *gam-long*: communicate the legal order or the law or solemn statement of the law or of the legal order.

Agam-long is a person whose duty it is to admit every statement made by any party, person or court member during the process of trial, and communicate it aloud to the hearing of everyone in the court. *Agam-long* reduces long, clumsy or incomprehensible expressions into precise and comprehensible statements. *Agam-long* is not, strictly speaking, a substitute for a loudspeaker, but he is a symbol of sacred or solemn deliberations. His role during legal transactions or sacred social agreements, such as court proceedings or a marriage agreement, provides the occasion with an authentic character; otherwise, his absence on such occasions raises the question of the formal validity of the marriage or court proceeding.

Akan A type of palm tree with large sweet fruits.

Akeeth Incest; sexual intercourse between a male and a female who have a blood relationship either from the paternal or the maternal side. Sexual intercourse of this nature is believed to affect the health of the woman and of her offspring afterwards, unless some religious purification is undertaken. Purification rites are only conducted when she has confessed the identity of every male relative who has had sexual intercourse with her (Ref: s.14 of the Re-statement of the Bhar el Ghazal Region Customary Law Act, 1984).

Akor (i) *Akor* means (a) adultery with a married woman; (b) cattle or property payable as damages by a man who commits adultery with a married woman, to the husband or his successor or agent or trustee.

Glossary

(ii) In the sense of adultery, *Akor* means commission of sexual intercourse between a married woman and another man without the husband's consent (Ref: s.10 of the Re-statement of Bhar el Ghazal Region Customary Law Act, 1984).

Aleu ba cuat wei 'I can throw it away.'

Aleu ba gam 'I can give it away.'

Aleu ba rac 'I can destroy it.'

Ame-kony Creditor.

Amuk (or Amec) Pledge or security for the repayment of a debt.

Animus Possidendi (Latin): Intention to possess a thing exclusively. *Animus* means intention; *possidendi* (possessio) means legal possession.

Apeth An evil-eyed person. A person who has super-natural power to kill or cause the death of other people by look. He or she is believed to have the ability (through the power of the eye) to burn the heart of a person he or she intends to kill.

Apuk The act of paying cattle or other property as damages (or compensation) by the accused or the accused and his relatives to the relatives of the person whom he has killed or injured (Ref: The Re-statement of the Bhar el Ghazal Region Customary Law Act, 1984). *Apuk* also means the damages or compensation itself.

Arueth The property or cattle payable to the husband and his relatives (i.e. by the husband's in-laws) in a certain proportion to the bride-wealth (which the husband and his relatives have paid to the in-laws); cattle or property after the conclusion of the marriage (Ref. s.9 of the Re-statement of Bhar el Ghazal Region Customary Law Act, 1984).

Arueth literally means: 'I feed him/her with milk.' After the payment of the bride-wealth by the husband and his relatives to the in-laws, they are deemed to have been exhausted or deprived of cattle and therefore to have no milk to drink. It therefore becomes the responsibility of the in-laws to pay a number of cattle (or property), in a specific proportion to the bride-wealth, to the husband and his relatives so that they are able to continue to feed on milk. *Arueth* is sometimes described as reverse payment in relation to the bride-wealth.

Aruok When a girl or an unmarried woman has been made pregnant without being married by the man who has impregnated her, or when divorce or dissolution of marriage occurs, the relatives of the girl or woman have the power to retain or take the children into their custody. If the father wants to obtain his child or children, he is required under the customary law to pay to the girl's or woman's relatives a specific number of cows for each child. *Aruok* therefore is the payment of cattle for the redemption of children (s.10 of the Re-statement of the Bhar el Ghazal Regional Customary Law Act, 1984).

Awac (or Awuoc) Wrong; offence; crime; mistake or anything bad in general.

Awec Appeasement; reparation; making good the wrong, with the objective of restoring good social relations; for example, where a married woman does some wrong which hurts the feelings of her husband, as when she commits adultery, her relatives (with intent to preserve the marriage) may decide to offer a cow or more, according to the gravity of the wrong, to her husband in order to appease him and alternatively to prevent him from taking any drastic measures which may threaten the continued existence of the marriage.

The objective of *awec* is always the preservation of social and legal relations (in certain matters) between people, where some wrong has been done to a person or to a group of persons and there is fear that existing relations may collapse, due to the commission of that wrong.

Awec also signifies apology or apologetic attitude.

Bai This term has several meanings; for example, it means the territory of a community, which is equivalent to 'country'. It may also mean the 'community' itself. Further, it may mean 'home' or the land or territory, which the people use for settlement (or homes) and for agriculture. This last meaning is the meaning in which the term is used in this book.

Banybith (singular) Banybiith (plural) A Spiritual Leader; a Spearsmaster; a Prophet. *Banybith* differs from a magician in that he (the *Banybith*) does not believe in medicine, diagnosis of diseases or causes of illnesses, like the magician. He does not, in other words, use esoteric medicine. He derives his divine authority from God. He communicates through God's guidance. God rules the spiritual lives of the people through him. His divine authority is hereditary.

Bany-wut (singular) Bany-wuot (plural) Literally, chief of the cattle-camp. He is the bailiff, a person whose duty is to execute decrees and judicial orders.

Beer Inheritance or succession.

Beer-kang Connotes appoinment, by the will of the deceased, of a person as a trustee to the estate or family of the deceased.

Beeré-lukic Revision or review of judicial decision or order.

Bere-pinyé luok Renewal of cases which have been finally decided by the court or courts.

Bil A black cow with a white patch on its side or on both sides.

Cien (or acien) A will (of the deceased) made by the deceased at the time of his death; e.g. *ciené-kang*: the making of a will by appointing a trustee. *Cien* or *acien* also means 'curse'.

Corpus (Latin word; Roman Law): physical control or detention of property or thing.

Cuat-ka ukum 'Pass the judgement or court's decision.' It is an order or a command made by Agam-long. (see page 248 – glossary).

Dané-weré-piu *Dan* comes from the word *dou* which means heifer or calf. *weré-piu* means ceremonious sprinkling with water when a husband is invited to eat food which belongs to his in-laws. He does not do so unless he is given (by his in-laws) a heifer: *dané-wereé-piu*. The ceremony is conducted by the elderly men of his wife's family.

Diing (Refers to colour): a cow with a mixed colour of white and brown, usually in large patches.

Dit Maturity

Dooc Ownership

Ekedie 'It is mine.'

Gasima (Arabic-Islamic term). A document which contains a legal contract of marriage between a Muslim couple. The document is signed by two adult Muslim men as witnesses before a 'Mazun' or religious man (Muslim).

Gemé-ruai Consent to marriage.

Guen-jang A greenish cylindrical type of bead which is now very old and very rare. It was imported to Southern Sudan during the Turkish rule in the Sudan. Because of its rarity, it has become very precious and valuable. It is a very important ornament worn on special occasions; e.g. when a marriage ceremony is about to take place or is taking place, the beads are worn for decoration.

Hok-thieek Bride-wealth cattle (or property).

Ke long dan theer 'The rule has been part of our law from time immemorial.'

Keny (singular) Kany (plural) Debt: obligation, liability.

Kittabiya (From Kitab, Arabic-Islamic terminology for the 'Book'.) The 'Book' is the Bible which a true believer in Islamic religion must respect. *Kittabiya* is a girl or

Glossary

a woman who is a believer in the Bible or Jewish religion. Christians and Jews are the people of the revealed Book.

Kol The deeper or deepest part of a river or lake. Fish prefer to live in this part of the water and this gives it more importance, apart from the fact that it stores plenty of water upon which people and animals depend during periods of long drought.

Kuei Trust.

Kujur An Arabic term for a magician, witch or any person who claims or possesses spiritual powers.

Lát; lét (Lat-guop or leté-guop) Defamation or insult.

Levirate A system by which a widow or the wife of a deceased man cohabits with the latter's kisman for the purpose of procreation. The widow and the offspring of this cohabitation belong to the deceased man. The corresponding term in Dinka is '*Lo-hôt*'.

Lo-Hôt Literally, the term means 'entering someone's house'. Legally, it is a system whereby a man is permitted to maintain sexual cohabitation with the wife of a deceased relative or the wife of an impotent relative, or the wife married to another woman who is a relative, for the purpose of procreation of children. The children of such a union legally belong to the relatives of the deceased man or the impotent or the woman married to another woman, as the case may be.

Long Rule of law; law; order (i.e. legal order).

Long-de-kede (or Longé-kede) Law of property.

Luk Suit; case; litigation.

Make-piny (or dom-riel or yuit, as in, yuité-nya or yuité-tik Rape

Muōk Possession or having the physical control or custody of a thing or property.

Muta A temporary marriage in Islamic law. It may be arranged for a few weeks, months or years according to the contract.

Nhiem-cie Literally, it means, 'my hair'. Legally, it means 'my original property which I am entitled to trace into the hands of anyone who is in possession of it.'

Nyanyom (Refers to colour): a red or brown heifer with a white patch on the head.

Oor (or, oor-dom) System whereby an individual person may be permitted by an owner of agricultural land to cultivate the land on a temporary basis. The person permitted to cultivate the land does not own or have the possession of the land which he cultivates by permission. He enjoys only the produce of his labour on the land.

Puoké-ruāi Divorce; dissolution of marriage.

Peeth Means the same as *wuuth* (see below). Among the Western Dinka, namely, Rek, Malual and Tuic, *peeth* has an additional meaning, which is: clever or intelligent. It also means cleverness or intelligence.

Raan ci bar-kang A person who has been appointed as trustee (or successor) to a deceased's estate.

Raan-koony Debter.

Rak A tree which bears large sweet fruits. Its nuts are very rich in oil. It is the *lulu* tree in Arabic.

Rôôth The power of a roth, i.e. of a sorcerer. Again, among the Western Dinka, the word *roth* or *rooth* is synonymous with *wuth* or *wuuth*.

Rôth Sorcerer or a person who has supernatural power to inflict skin diseases on people, or who causes sickness through physical contact.

Ruai Marriage; blood-relationship; marriage ceremony or marriage festival.

Tak Oval type of large bead, which the Turks imported into the Sudan before the Condominium Rule.

Thakha A Venda (tribe) term for bride-wealth.

Theer Time immemorial; a long time in the past.
Thieek This term means 'marriage' only.
Thieeké-diar-juec Polygamy
Thienyé-cil A precious stick made from the horn of a rhino. It is a weapon as well as an instrument to be carried on prestigeous occasions.
Toc A low land with open planes which are seasonally flooded, while the lowest parts may remain swampy throughout the year or for a considerable period in the year. The Sudd region, along the Nile, is a typical example of *toc*.
Tong Fight; war; battle. It also means a spear. It may also mean anger; e.g. *aci tong luel*: he is very angry and ready to fight.
Tung-akoon Elephant tusk. *Tung* means horn of an animal, while *akoon* means elephant. An elephant tusk is shaped in the form of a cylinder and is used as an armlet. It is an ornament worn on special occasions, or for prestigeous purposes.
Wakfs An Islamic term for a religious property or property dedicated to a mosque for sacred or religious purposes and for the benefit of the poor.
Wuntheer (singular) Wuot-theer (plural) The word comes from *wut* which means cattle camp. *Wuntheer* means ancient cattle camp. These places, which are known as *wuot-theer*, are ancient mounds believed to have been built by the Luo (Gel or Jur-Luel) in the past when they were the masters of the present Dinka toc (land).
Wut (singular) Wuot (plural) Apart from the meaning given above, *wut* may also mean the tribe or community as an administrative unit. It may be led by a chief or a single administrative leader assisted by a number of chiefs and sub-chiefs. If a *wut* grows very large, it may break up into many autonomous administrative units, where each unit is led by a chief or leader who is assisted by sub-chiefs.
Wuth The meaning is the same as in *peeth* above; an evil-eyed person; a person who has supernatural power to kill or cause the death of other people by look.
Wuuth While *wuth* is a person, *wuuth* is the power itself.
Yin aca pat 'I have moved out of your way. You can now move forward to trace your original property into the hands of the person who is still in possession of it.'

Appendix

THE RE-STATEMENT OF BAHR EL—GAZAL REGION CUSTOMARY LAW (AMENDED) ACT 1984
BHAR EL-GHAZAL REGION ACT NO. 1, 1984

In accordance with the provisions of Section 55, 57 of the Presidential Order No. 1, 1983 and Regulation 35(1) of the People's Regional Assembly, Conduct of Business Regulations, 1983, the People's Regional Assembly, Bhar El-Ghazal Region, hereby pass the following amended Act:

PART 1
CHAPTER 1

S.1 *Title and Commencement*

This amended Act shall be called the RE-STATEMENT OF BHAR EL-GHAZAL REGION CUSTOMARY LAW (Amended) ACT 1984, and shall come into operation as an Act, on the date of its signature by the Governor of the Region.

S.2 *Repeal*

The Bhar El-Ghazal Province Local Order No. 1 of 18th December, 1975 is repealed.

S.3 *The Law to apply in certain cases*

(i) Whenever a conflict arises between any Customary Law embodied in this amended Act and the provisions of the general territorial State Law, the State Law shall prevail.[1]

---

[1] The State Law in this context does not include any personal law of another community.

(ii) Whenever a Court does not find an appropriate customary rule applicable to a case before it, in this Act, recourse shall be made to any appropriate Customary Rule in existance.

S.4 *Penalty, Damages or Compensation*
(i) Damages or compensation awarded under this amended Act shall not prevent the Court from imposing any other penalty authorised by law, provided damages or compensaton recoverable shall be taken into account in assessing the other penalty.
(ii) Where the award is in cattle, goats, spears and so forth, the Court making the order for payment, or the Court executing it, or the parties themselves, may assess current market value of the property awarded and proceed to execute payment in money or in any other property.

S.5 *Court*
'Court' means the Local Courts and State Courts.

PART 2

CHAPTER 2

THE CODE OF DINKA CUSTOMARY LAW

S.6 *Title*
This law shall be called the Code of the Dinka Customary Law.

S.7 *Application*
The provisions of this Regional Code shall apply throughout the Region of Bhar El-Ghazal to the following types of persons and situations:
(a) All Dinkas of Bhar El-Ghazal Regions.
(b) All persons involved in sexual offences or acts with Dinka girls, wives or women of Bhar El-Ghazal Regions.
(c) All persons who have adopted the Dinka way of life or have accepted to be bound by Dinka Customary Law as practised in this Region.
(d) Personal disputes connected with marriages, divorce, custody of children and their redemption, provided the woman in respect of whom such claims arise comes from a family subject to the Dinka Customary Law as applied in Bhar El-Ghazal Region.
(e) Tortious acts committed within this Region against a Dinka of Bhar El-Ghazal Region by non-Dinka or Dinkas outside the Region, provided that such actors are subject to customs similar to those of the Dinka in the field of compensation, or homicide and personal injuries, provided also that such acts are not already regulated by some border Agreements.
(f) Gifts and intestate or testate succession where the donor or the deceased is subject to the Dinka Customary Law of this Region.

Glossary

GENERAL EXPLANATIONS AND DEFINITIONS

S.8 *'Hok-thiek' – Bride-wealth'*

The term 'hok-thiek' means the cattle payable by a bride-groom or husband and his relatives to the relatives of the bride or wife as consideration for the marriage.

S.9 *'Arueth'*

'Arueth' means the property or cattle payable to the husband and his relatives, in a certain proportion to the bride-wealth cattle or property, after the conclusion of marriage.

S.10 *'Aruok' of Children*

When a girl or an unmarried woman has been pregnant without being married by the man who has impregnated her, or when divorce or dissolution of marriage takes place between a man and a woman, the relatives of the impregnated girl or unmarried woman, or the woman whose marriage has been dissolved, have the power to retain the child or children into their custody. If the father intends to obtain his child or children, he shall pay to the girl's or woman's relatives a specific number of cows for the child or each child. This payment of cattle for the redemption of a child or children by the father is called 'Aruok'.

S.11 *'Akor' (Adultery)*

(a) The word 'Akor' means adultery with a married woman. It further means cattle or property payable as damages by the man who commits adultery with a married woman, to the husband or his successor or agent or trustee.

(b) 'Akor', in the sense of adultery, means commission of sexual intercourse between a married woman and another man without the husband's consent.

S.12 (i) *'Awac'*

The word 'Awac' literally means a mistake or offence. It also means cattle or property payable to a party aggrived by the breach of marriage relations, or damages payable by a person who impregnates, rapes or elopes with a girl or woman or any party whose reputation has been injured by the publication of a defamatory material. 'Awac' has a penal feature.

(ii) *'Awec'*

It means a payment for a conciliation or an appeasement. It is civil in nature.

S.13 *'Tiop'*

It means the number of cattle payable by a man whose wife is dead to her relatives when the marriage is treated as dissolved by such death.

S.14 *'Akeeth' (Incest)*

'Akeeth' means the commission of sexual intercourse between a man and a woman who have blood relationship either from the paternal or maternal side. Sexual intercourse of this nature is believed to affect the health of the woman afterwards and the health of the children she will produce, unless some religious purification is undertaken after she has confessed the identity of all the relatives who have had sexual intercourse with her.

S.15 *Relative*

The word 'relative' in this Code (Act, Part II) includes parents, brothers and sisters, guardians, maternal uncles and paternal uncles who are bound, when there is marriage, to contribute some cattle towards the bride-wealth, or contribute by paying some cattle for 'apuk' when another person is killed, or who are entitled to share in bride-wealth property when a girl is married or share in 'apuk' cattle, when a person of one blood has been killed by another person.

S.16 *Parents and step brothers*

'Parents includes 'step-fathers' and 'brothers' includes 'step-brothers'.

S.17 *'Apuk'*

'Apuk' means the act of paying cattle or other property as damages by the accused or the accused and his relatives to the relatives of the person whom he has killed or the person whom he has injured.

S.18 *'Werpiu' or 'Lok-thok'*

(a) When a Dinka man marries, he is bound by a customary rule to abstain from eating any food or drinking anything that belongs to or which has been prepared by his in-laws. After the conclusion of such marriage, his in-laws must give him a heifer. When he receives the heifer, the elders among his in-laws carry out a religious ceremony by sprinkling him with water. This process of sprinkling with water before he can drink or ear from his in-laws is called 'Werpiu' or 'Lok-thok'. The heifer which is given to him by his in-laws for this purpose is called 'Dan-werpiu' or 'Lok-thok'.

(b) For the purpose of this law, a person or an animal dies naturally or a thing or property is destroyed or damaged naturally when he/it is not killed or damaged or destroyed by a human being.

CHAPTER 3

PERSONAL LAW

RUAI – (MARRIAGE)

S.19 *Definition of Ruai (marriage)*

Subject to other provisions of this Law, a Dinka ruai or marriage is a union between one man, or his successor, or his trustee and one or more women for their lives for the purpose of sexual cohabitation, procreation of the young and maintenance of the homestead, provided that such a union may take place between one barren or childless woman and another for whom male consorts are provided; provided also that such a union may take place between a deceased male and one or more women through his successor or trustee.

S.20 *Consent (Game-ruai)*

(a) The only consent which is material for the conclusion of a valid ruai or marriage is that of the parents, brothers and close paternal uncles of the spouses.

Appendix

(b) When a man and a woman have taken each other as husband and wife without the consent of their relatives, such a union may be dissolved or confirmed by such relatives.

S.21 *Capacity (Dit)*

(a) No marriage shall be consummated between a boy and a girl until both of them have attained maturity.

(b) *Determination of maturity*

For a girl, the beginning of maturity age is marked by the first period of menstruation, while for the boy, it is marked by certain physical or biological changes, such as vocal change, growth of hair in the arm-pits or loin or by traditional marks designed to mark the end of the period of boyhood.

S.22 *'Hok-thiek' (Bride-wealth)*

The relatives of both parties to a marriage shall be free to fix the number of cattle or amount of property payable as 'Hok-thiek' – bride-wealth. They shall also be free to fix the manner and time of delivery of such cattle or payment of such property.

S.23 *Form of marriage*

(a) A formal marriage is established by undertaking the procedure of (i) engagement (thuot), (ii) agreement (luele-ruai) and (iii) ceremony accompanying the delivery (atoc) of the bride (apuoc-thiaak) to her bride-groom (ame-thiek).

(b) Failure to follow the stages mentioned in (a) above except (ii) does not affect the marriage validity.[2]

Explanation: The agreement referred to in (a) (ii) above refers to the agreement between the relatives of the spouses.

S.24 *When the Court fixes the number of bride-wealth cattle*

When a man takes a woman as his wife but neglects or refuses or otherwise fails to pay any bride-wealth cattle or property to her relatives, or when the whole marriage is in dispute, the Court may enforce the marriage. When the Court enforces the marriage, it shall order the man, together with his relatives to pay thirty cows and six bulls as bride-wealth (Hok-thiek), provided that the Court shall always have the power to over-ride the will of the relatives of both spouses.

S.25 *The following rights accrue from the outset of the marriage to the husband and relatives.*

(i) Delivery of the bride to the bride-groom by her relatives.

(ii) Payment of 'Arueth' cattle by the bride's relatives to the husband and his relatives.

(iii) Payment of a heifer (or a cow) for 'werpiu' or 'lok-thok' to the bride-groom.

(iv) Payment of a heifer for 'Wan' or 'Ahoth' to the bride-groom.

---

[2] All the three stages do not necessarily need to be followed always. Engagement and the *atoc* are procedural. Sometimes a short-cut may be made by dropping one or two of them, if there are good reasons for that. But agreement is essential for the validity of marriage.

(v) Claim of a share in the bride-wealth of the bride-groom's younger sister-in-law or sisters-in-laws who is or are subsequently married.

S.26 *Rights accruing to the family of the bride*

Payment of the bride-wealth or property to them by the relatives of the bride-groom.

S.27 *'Akor' or Adultery*

Presumption of marriage Any Dinka who is not a girl is presumed to be a married woman and any man who commits sexual intercourse with such a woman does so at his own risk.

S.28 *Number of 'Akor' cattle*

When a man commits adultery with a married woman, he shall pay six cows and one bull to the husband or his successor as 'akor' or 'aruok' and no penalty may be passed against him by the Local Court, but if he has no cattle to pay as 'akor', he shall be punished with imprisonment or fine or with both as prescribed by the Sudan Penal Code.

S.29 *No payment of 'Akor' cattle, if adultery is committed for a second time.*

When a married woman commits adultery for a second time with another man after the 'akor' cattle have been paid for the first act of adultery, the husband or his successor or trustee is not entitled to claim any 'akor' cattle again, but the man who commits the offence shall be punished with imprisonment or fine or both in accordance with the provisions of the Sudan Penal Code.

S.30 *The party to sue in adultery cases*

The husband, or if he is dead, his successor is the only competent party to sue in the case of adultery.

S.31 *Adultery committed by a married woman with the husband's relative.*

Whenever a woman commits adultery with a relative of her husband who has contributed a cow or some cows during her marriage as part of the bride-wealth, the relative who commits the offence is only bound to pay a cow to the husband or his successor or trustee as 'awec', but if such relative never paid any cow or some cows as his contribution to the bride-wealth, he is bound to pay six (6) cows and one bull as 'akor' (or 'aruok') to the husband or his successor.

S.32 *Child who is the product of adultery*

The child who is the product of a sexual intercourse between a married woman and another man belongs to the legal father. But, if the legal father elects to divorce his wife and disowns the child, his wife's relatives will be entitled to have the child.

S.33 *When a husband is compellable to sue for 'Akor' cattle*

When a man whose wife has committed adultery with another person elects to divorce her, he is bound or compelled by the Court to sue the offender in order to obtain 'akor' cattle before the divorce or the dissolution of the marriage is granted.

Appendix

S.34 *Passing of the title to adultery cattle where divorce takes place*

When a woman who has committed adultery with another man is divorced after the 'akor' cattle have been obtained by the husband, the title to the cattle shall pass to her relatives, provided that the Court may allow the husband to retain them by way of a set-off where he is exerting a claim for the recovery of the bride-wealth cattle or property from her relatives.

S.35 *Puokē-ruāi (Divorce)*

A valid divorce shall always be granted by the Court with the consent of all or more interested parties to the marriage contract.

S.36 *Grounds for granting divorce (Puokē-ruāi)*

A Court may grant divorce, if requested, on any one of the following grounds:
(1) Barrenness of the wife.
(2) Impotence of the husband.
(3) Death of all or more children of the spouses.
(4) Akeeth (Incest).
(5) Woman's gross misconduct.
(6) Cruelty to the wife by her husband or his relatives.
(7) Infectious or venereal disease passed on to the complaining spouse by the other.
(8) Deterioration of relations between the relatives of the spouses.

S.37 *When a Court may refuse to grant 'puokē-ruāi' (divorce)*

A Court may refuse to grant divorce, if it is of the opinion that the marriage relationship has been established for a long period or on account of the number of children born during the union of the spouses.

S.38 *When death may terminate marriage relations*

Death of the wife may terminate the marriage relations between the spouses, but the death of the husband has no such effect.

S.39 *Parties to divorce suit*

The following parties may sue for divorce before the Court:
(1) The husband or his successor or consort or trustee.
(2) The wife or her parents or guardian, provided that the Court seeks before it, the attendance of all or more parties who are bound by the marriage contract to give their consent to the divorce.

S.40 *Valid divorce or dissolution of marriage to take place in Court*

No valid divorce or dissolution of marriage relationship shall take place outside the Court through:
(1) Mutual agreement of the relatives of the spouses.
(2) Mutual agreement of the spouses.
(3) Unilateral decision of any one of the spouses, but if the parties have adopted outside the Court any of the above methods, the Court shall not lend its aid or authority to any one of the parties who fails to obtain his or her rights against the other party thereafter.[3]

---

[3] The Court in certain circumstances may accept puoke-ruai (divorce) which takes place outside the Court and enforce the parties' claims.

260 The Customary Law of the Dinka People of Sudan

S.41 *Effects of the dissolution of marriage or divorce (puokē-ruāi)*

The following are the legal effects of divorce or dissolution of marriage:
(1) Relief of the spouses of their marital relationships.
(2) Freedom of the woman to marry another man.
(3) Recovery of bride-wealth cattle or property and offspring and all other rights due to the husband from his wife's relatives.
(4) Recovery of 'arueth' and all other rights due to the relatives of the divorced woman from the husband and his relatives.
(5) Right of the husband to take the children, provided that he pays 'aruok' cattle to the relatives of his divorce wife.

S.42 *Liēnyē-Nya (Impregnation of a girl)*

(a) Whenever a girl is impregnated, the man who has committed the offence is bound to pay a heifer as 'aruok' to her relatives or parents, if he refuses to marry her, provided that the heifer shall not be paid by him as 'aruok', when her relatives refuse to marry her to him, while he is able and ready to satisfy their demand by paying a number of cattle as bride-wealth.
(b) Possession of the heifer, which has been obtained as 'aruok', for the impregnation of the girl is vested in her relatives, provided that they shall transfer it, together with the girl, to any man who subsequently marries her.

S.43 *Payment of Aruok for a child when a girl is impregnated*

When a man impregnates a girl, he shall be given an opportunity to redeem the child, who is the product of such impregnation by paying 'aruok' cattle to the girl's relatives, otherwise she and her child will be given to any man who will marry her.

S.44 *Elopement with a girl (jôtē-nye)*

A man who elopes with a girl is bound to pay one heifer to her relatives as 'awac', if he refuses to marry her, provided that he shall not be bound to pay a heifer as 'awac' if he is rejected from marrying her by her relatives on grounds other than failure to pay a sufficient number of cattle as bride-wealth.

S.45 *Penalty where a girl is eloped with for the second time*

When a man elopes with a girl for the second time after he has been rejected from marrying her for failure to pay a sufficient number of cattle demanded by her relatives or for some other reasons, he shall only be liable to any penalty provided by the Sudan Penal Code.

S.46 *Transfer of 'awac' heifer to a subsequent husband*

The title to any heifer which has been obtained by relatives as 'awac' for the elopement with their girl shall be transferred, together with the girl, to any man who will subsequently marry her.

S.47 *Payment of cows for 'tiop' for the death of a married woman*

(a) A man whose wife dies naturally shall pay to her relatives or parents two cows and one bull as 'tiop', when the marriage is deemed to have been dissolved by such death.
(b) The basis for the payment of cattle as 'tiop' is the consolation of her parents or relatives.

Appendix

S.48 *Make-piny (Rape)*[4]

When a man rapes:
(a) a girl who is
   (i) under age, he is bound to pay to her relatives five cows as 'aruok' and he shall also be liable to any penalty which is prescribed by the Sudan Penal Code;
   (ii) mature, he is bound to pay only one heifer to her relatives as 'aruok' and he shall also be liable to any penalty prescribed by the Sudan Penal Code;
(b) a married woman, he is bound to pay six cows and one bull as 'aruok' to the husband or his successor and he shall be liable to any penalty prescribed by the Sudan Penal Code;
(c) a free woman, he shall be liable to any penalty prescribed by the Sudan Penal Code.

S.49 *Where a girl or a free woman is impregnated through rape (Lienye-nyan ci makpiny ku ting ci makpiny)*

When a girl or a free woman becomes pregnant through rape, the child, born as a result, may belong to the biological father, provided that he redeems him or her by payment of 'aruok' cattle to the girl's or woman's relatives, otherwise the child may be delivered together with the girl or woman to any man who will formally marry her or marry her with the consent of her parents or relatives at any time afterwards.

S.50 *Rape cattle transferable to a subsequent husband*

The title to the cattle paid by the offender as 'aruok' for raping a girl or free woman, shall be transferred with her to a man who will afterwards formally marry her or marry her with the consent of her parents or relatives.

S.51 *Succession*

Where a person, who owns property, dies intestate the following persons shall be the heirs or successors:
(1) wife and children;
(2) parents or brothers, if there are no wife and children.

S.52 Where the person who dies intestate has no wife, children, parents nor brothers, his paternal uncle, if no maternal uncle, shall hold the possession of the property as a trustee. He shall use this property in marrying a woman for the deceased and transfer any balance of the said property to the deceased's newly married woman, who shall also hold it partly as a trustee for her children.

CHAPTER 4

THE LAW OF PROPERTY

S.53 *Tracing of cattle or property*

When divorce or dissolution of marriage takes place, the husband is entitled to trace his cattle or property into the hands of anyone who has acquired

---
[4] Or yuite-nya or yuite-tik.

possession or title to them from his in-laws through subsequent marriages, provided that he shall only be entitled to recover damages from his in-laws for any cattle or property delivered by them to the third parties through sale or discharge of certain obligations while the marriage was still valid.

S.54 *Damages for cattle which naturally died after transfer to third parties*

Where a dissolution of a marriage or divorce or other relationship takes place, the husband is entitled to recover damages from his in-laws or transferee for any of the bride-wealth or other cattle which naturally died, after the transfer of title or possession to any third party by way of sale of discharge of certain obligations or debts, while the marriage or the relationship was still valid. But he is not entitled to recover any damages for any cattle which naturally died in possession of the in-laws or the transferee before the dissolution of the marriage.

S.55 *Tracing of cattle includes their off-spring*

Tracing of cattle into the hands of anyone, who has acquired possession or title to them, includes their off-spring, but it excludes the off-spring which dies through premature birth (athorbei).

S.56 *Transfer of title to property*

The true owner is not deprived of his title when possession of such property has been transferred through:
(1) theft;
(2) robbery;
(3) breach of trust;
(4) deceit or fraud; and
(5) any other wrongful means.

S.57 *Tracing of property wrongfully transferred*

The true owner is entitled to trace any property which has been transferred to any person through one of the ways mentioned in section 56, sub-sections one to five, above.

S.58 *Recovery of damages where property is wrongfully transferred*

If the property which has been transferred in any one of the ways mentioned in section 56 (1–5), above, has been destroyed or has perished or got damaged or injured, the true owner is entitled to recover damages against the person who made the wrongful transfer or acquired possession from him.

S.59 *Tracing of title by way of gift*

The title to any property which has been transferred to another by way of gift or donation is not traceable, provided that the giver or the donor had a better title against anyone else at the time of the transfer to the donee.

S.60 *Title to gift property reverts to donor on revocation*

The title to any property which has been transferred to another by way of gift or donation reverts to the original owner (donor) when revocation of the gift is effected.

S.61 *No tracing of gift property into the hands of third parties*

Where revocation of a gift takes place, the donor or the giver is not entitled to trace the property given or donated into the hands of anyone who lawfully or in good faith acquires possession or title to it before the revocation is effected, but he is only entitled to recover damages from the donor or the receiver of the gift.

S.62 *Tracing of property transferred to a third party by a finder*

The true owner is entitled to trace his property into the hands of anyone who acquires possession whether in good faith or bad faith through a finder.

S.63 *Tracing of property transferred by non-owner*

The owner is entitled to trace his property into the hands of anyone who acquires possession in good faith or bad faith from anyone who has no title to it.

S.64 *Amuk or Amec (Pledge)*

(a) 'Amuk' or 'Amec' (pledge) is any property delivered by a debtor to a creditor as a form of security or guarantee for the repayment of a debt or discharge of an existing obligation.

(b) If the debtor fails completely to repay the debt at the time fixed or at the period which the Court may consider to be reasonably long in the circumstances where no fixed period for the discharge of the debt was agreed upon at the time of the contract, the secured creditor is entitled to own the property he possesses as 'amuk'.

Examples of Amuk

(1) 'A' takes a loan of Ls.30 (or a cow) from 'B'. But 'B' insists that a bull or a cow or some other property should be transferred into his possession temporarily as a guarantee for the repayment of the loan or discharge of the obligation on 'A'. 'A' delivers a cow or any property to 'B' to be held by 'B' till the debt is discharged. This cow or property is called 'Amuk'.

(2) Or, 'A' takes a bull from 'B' and promises to give a heifer to 'B' in the near future. However, in order to assure 'B' that the promise shall ultimately be fulfilled, 'A' may deliver a cow into the possession of 'B' on condition that he will recover it after he has fulfilled his obligation by paying a heifer to 'B'.

S.65 *Lien (retention of property for 'ariop')*

When a person does some work on another's property on the ground that he shall be paid, he is entitled to retain that property till the owner pays him for the work done on it.

Example: 'A' delivers a hoe to 'B', a blacksmith, to sharpen it. 'A' and 'B' agree that 'A' shall pay 'B' ten piasters for his work. When 'B' has sharpened the hoe, he is entitled to retain it till he is paid for his work.

S.66 *Ran-amuk (Pledge or secured creditor or lienee to exercise reasonable care)*

Any person who retains possession of a cow or other property as 'amuk' (pledge) or any property for the work done on it (lien) is bound to exercise reasonable care for it. If such a cow or property perishes or disappears through his negligence or the negligence of his successor or agent, he is bound to pay damages to the owner, in case of the property held for work done on it;

and in case of 'amuk', the property or cow which has perished or disappeared in his possession through such negligence shall be deemed as full satisfaction of his claim against the debtor.

Illustration (in case of 'amuk') 'A' takes a bull from 'B' on condition that he will pay a heifer to 'B' in the near future. 'A' secures the debt by delivering a cow to 'B'. Both 'A' and 'B' agree that the cow will be taken back to 'A' when 'A' delivers a heifer to 'B' in satisfaction of 'B's claim.

The cow placed into the possession of 'B' is afterwards killed by a crocodile through 'B's negligence. 'B' is not entitled to claim the heifer for the bull which 'A' has taken from him because 'A' has been discharged from his obligation by the death of his cow through 'B's negligence.

CHAPTER 5

TORTS

S.67 *Damages for personal injuries*

The Court or Chiefs' Court shall award damages as follows for the loss of:
- One eye — Seven (7) cows.
- Two eyes — Twenty (20) cows.
- One leg — Ten (10) cows.
- Two legs — Twenty (20) cows.
- One arm — Ten (10) cows.
- Two arms — Twenty (20) cows.
- One toe — One (1) cow.
- Grevous hurt — one cow or more according to the gravity of the injury inflicted.
- One tooth — One (1) bull.
- Four front teeth — One (1) cow.
- One molar — One (1) cow.
- Complete loss of hearing — Ten (10) cows.

S.68 (i) *Damages for personal injury caused by one class of domestic animals*

When a cow or bull or goat or ram or sheep causes injury to a person, who is not a trespasser, the cow or bull or goat or ram or sheep, which has caused such injury, shall be awarded to the person as damages.

(ii) *Damages for personal injuries caused by another class of domestic animals*

When an injury is caused to another person, who is not a trespasser, by a cat or dog or horse or donkey or any domestic animal other than those mentioned in paragraph (i) above, the owner is not bound to pay any damages to the victim, unless he knows that the animal has previously shown a dangerous character.

S.69 *Nake-raan or Homicide cases*

'Apuk' or compensation for killing a person while helping a maternal uncle. Where a person kills another in a fight while helping his maternal uncle or uncles, he and his paternal uncles are bound to pay 'apuk' of thirty (30) head of cattle to the relatives of the deceased. But, if the killer lives as the child of his maternal uncles on the ground that his father did not redeem him by the payment of 'aruok' cattle, where divorce had taken place or where marriage had failed to take place in the case of an impregnated girl or girl eloped with, it is the sole duty of his maternal uncles to pay 'apuk' for him.

S.70 *When 'apuk' is payable by killer's relatives or by the whole tribe.*

When two tribes or more enter into a fight and some people get killed on either side, the payment of 'apuk' to the relatives of the deceased person or persons shall be confined to the killers and their relatives, but where the killer is unknown, the tribe involved in the fight against the deceased's tribe is bound to pay 'apuk'. 'Apuk' or compensation is 30 cows for causing the death of a person.

S.71 *Self-defence is no excuse for avoiding payment of 'apuk'*

A person who has caused the death of another is bound with his relatives on the paternal side to pay 'apuk' of thirty (30) cows to the relatives of the deceased, although death might have been caused while the killer was exercising the right of self-defence.

S.72 *'Apuk and bride-wealth property payable to the husband's relatives when killed by his wife.*

If a woman intentionally causes the death of her husband, the marriage is automatically dissolved and the relatives of the deceased are entitled to obtain 'apuk' cattle together with the cattle they had paid for bride-wealth during the marriage from her relatives, provided that, if there are children, the deceased relatives are bound to pay 'aruok' cattle to her relatives for each child, otherwise her parents or relatives shall be entitled to take the children.

S.73 *Bride-wealth cattle convertible into 'apuk' cattle when husband kills his wife*

When a husband intentionally kills his wife, the marriage is dissolved and the cattle which he had paid to her relatives as bride-wealth cattle shall be converted into 'apuk' cattle, but if the number of the bride-wealth cattle he had paid was less than thirty (30) head of cattle, he and his relatives are bound to fill the gap by paying more cattle. However, if the number of bride-wealth cattle was more than thirty (30) head of cattle, he or his successor is entitled to recover the surplus from the deceased's relatives, provided that he or his successor shall pay 'aruok' cattle for each child together with the 'arueth' cattle or any rightful claims to the relatives of the deceased.

S.74 *'Apuk' is ten (10) cows when a person is killed through mistake of fact*

Where a person kills another through a mistake of fact (rol), he is bound to pay ten (10) cows as 'apuk' to the relatives of the deceased.

S.75 *'Apuk' is ten (10) cows where a person is killed by one who lacks capacity or who is insane*

Where a person is killed by another who is insane or lunatic, or a child who lacks capacity, the relatives of the killer are bound to pay ten (10) cows as 'apuk' to the relatives of the deceased.

S.76 *'Apuk' is thirty (30) head of cattle when a relative other than a member of the same family is killed*

Where a person intentionally causes the death of his relative other than a member of his family, he is bound to pay thirty (30) head of cattle as 'apuk' to the relatives of the deceased, unless the members of the deceased's family waive their rights.

S.77 *'Apuk' is payable by the husband and his relatives if his wife kills another person*

Where a married woman kills another person, who is not her husband's relative, 'apuk' must be paid to the relatives of the deceased by her husband and his relatives. But if the marriage between such a woman and her husband is afterwards dissolved, the husband shall be entitled to recover from her relatives the cattle he had paid as bride-wealth together with damages for the thirty (30) head of cattle he had paid for the 'apuk' provided that he shall at the same time be bound to settle all other rights claimed against him by her relatives.

S.78 *Damages for Defamation (Lete-guop, yor-guop, buol or yuop-buol)*

Any person whose reputation is affected or is likely to be affected by the publication of a defamatory statement or injurious falsehood is entitled to recover damages from the wrongdoer as follows:
(i) if the defamatory statement or injurious falsehood is published in an ordinary conversation or talking, he is entitled to obtain one heifer;
(ii) if the falsehood or defamatory statement is published in a song, he is entitled to obtain one pregnant heifer, provided that the Court may pass, in addition, an appropriate sentence of imprisonment or fine or both against him, in accordance with the provisions of the Sudan Penal Code.

S.79 *Damage to property*

When the property of anyone is damaged by (i) a cow or bull, or (ii) a goat or a he-goat, or (iii) a sheep or a ram, which belongs to another person, the owner of the property is entitled to obtain damages from the owner of such animal in the form of money calculated according to the degree of damage done.

S.80 When a cow or bull or goat or he-goat or sheep or ram dies owing to the injury caused, while it was within the owner's premises, by another trespassing or wandering cow or bull or goat or sheep or ram or he-goat that belongs to another person, the animal that inflicted the injury which caused the death shall be awarded to the owner of the animal which has been killed as damages, but no damages shall be awarded if the injury was caused while both animals were wandering outside the premises of their owners or when trespassing in the premises of a third party.

S.81 *Property destroyed by fire caused by another person*

When the property of anyone is destroyed by fire caused by another person, damages shall be awarded to the owner against the tortfeasor in the form of money or a bull or heifer or cow or more, according to the value of the property destroyed or damaged.

PART 3

THE CODE OF LUO CUSTOMARY LAW

PRELIMINARY AND APPLICATION

S.82　*Title*

This Law shall be called the Code of the Luo Customary Law.

S.83　*The provisions of Part 3 shall apply throughout Bhar El-Ghazal Region to*
(1) All Jo-Luo of Bhar El-Ghazal Region.
(2) All persons involved in sexual wrongs with Luo girls, women or wives of Bhar El-Ghazal Region.
(3) Matters connected with marriage, divorce, custody and redemption of children of a Luo woman.
(4) Tortious acts committed within Bhar El-Ghazal Region against a Nga-Luo by a non-Luo or by a Nga-Luo outside this Region against a Luo.

CHAPTER 6

S.84　*General explanations and definitions; sense of expression once explained*

Every expression, which is explained in any part of this Code, is used in every part of this Code in conformity with the explanation, unless the subject or sense of the context otherwise requires.

S.85　*'Jogo'*

'Jogo' or bride-wealth is the property payable by the bride-groom and his family to the family of the bride in consideration of her marriage.

S.86　*'Arueth' or reciprocal payment*

'Arueth' means the cattle payable by the family of the bride to the bride-groom in a certain proportion to the bride-wealth.

S.87　*'Per' or 'Aruok'*

'Per' or 'Aruok' is the compensation payable by the male offender in sexual wrongs, namely adultery, fornication, rape and failed elopement.

S.88　*'Cimonyo'*

'Cimonyo' is the personal token gift made by the bride-groom to the eldest paternal uncle and aunt and eldest sister of the bride, and is currently Ls.20 each. This practice prevails only among the Luo of East Bank of River Jur.

S.89　*'Family'*

'Family' is what is known in Luo as 'dho uot'.

S.90　*'Brothers and Sisters'*

The terms 'brothers' and 'sisters' include step-brothers and step-sisters.

S.91 *'Nyakou' or girl or woman*

The term 'nyakou' or girl or woman means an unmarried female of any age.

S.92 *'Dhango' or wife*

'Dhango' or wife means a married woman within the provisions of this Code.

S.93 *'Husband'*

'Husband' means the person married to a woman within the provisions of this Code.

S.94 *'Court'*

'Court' carries the same meaning as is defined in Part 1 of this Act.

CHAPTER 7

PERSONAL LAW

S.95 *Marriage – Definition*

(i) Marriage is a union between one man or his successor on his behalf and one or more women for their lives for the purpose of sexual co-habitation, procreation of the young and maintenance of the homestead.

(ii) It shall also be considered marriage, where a parent or a childless woman takes another woman for the purpose of procreation of the young in her name by a consort of her choice.

S.96 *Consent in marriage*

The only consent which is material and essential for the conclusion of a valid marriage is that of the families of the spouses. Wherever a man and a woman have taken each other as husband and wife without the prior consent of their families, such a union may be dissolved or confirmed by such families.

S.97 *Consummation of marriage*

No marriage shall be consummated between a boy and a girl until both of them have attained maturity.

S.98 *Bride-wealth*

(1) The families of both parties to a marriage shall be free to fix the amount, number and kind of bride wealth as well as the manner and time of delivery.

(2) Provided that where the Court marries the parties irrespective of family consent the bride-wealth shall be:

(a) among the Luo of the East Bank of River Jur, 5 cows, 3 bulls, Ls.600, 15 goats and 12 spears, and 'arueth' is payable;

(b) among the Luo who have adopted the tradition of marrying in cattle, 30 head of cows and 6 bulls.

S.99 *Contribution to bride-wealth*

The father, and in his absence, the eldest brother or paternal uncle of the bride-groom is liable to contribute to the payment of bride-wealth.

Appendix

S.100 *Share in bride-wealth*
  (1) The bride-wealth goes to the family of the girl to be used as the family thinks fit.
  (2) Provided that among the Luo of the East Bank of River Jur, the eldest paternal uncle and aunt and the eldest sister are entitled to 'cimonyo' which is Ls.20.
  (3) Provided that among the Luo of the West Bank of River Jur, the eldest maternal uncle is entitled to a cow and the mothers of the parents-in-law are each entitled to one big he-goat.

S.101 *Forms of marriage*
  (1) Open courting, engagement to marry, agreement to the marriage and the bride going to live in the house of the bride-groom after the delivery of the bride-wealth.
  (2) Registration in Court that an agreement has been made to marry the parties and part of the bride-wealth has been delivered.
  (3) Taking of the woman by the man after an agreement to marry has been made and part of bride-wealth delivered.
  (4) Elopement which is confirmed.

S.102 *Rights accruing to the man upon marriage*
  The following rights shall accrue at the outset of the marriage to the husband:
  (a) right to children born during the subsistence of his marriage;
  (b) right to children born out of any wedlock before his marriage;
  (c) right to compensation for fornication by his wife;
  (d) right to compensation for adultery by his wife.

S.103 *Obligations of the husband*
  The husband is vicariously liable for the torts of his wife and minor children.

S.104 *Sexual wrongs*
  Adultery: Definition and compensation
  (1) Sexual intercourse with a married woman is adultery.
  (2) Compensation payable by the adulterer shall be Ls.100.000 m/ms.
  (3) Compensation for adultery shall be payable to the husband, his agent or successor.

S.105 *Fornication: definition and compensation*
  (1) Sexual intercourse with an unmarried woman is fornication.
  (2) Compensation for fornication payable by the fornicator shall be Ls.50.
  (3) Compensation for fornication is payable to the father of the woman in trust for her subsequent husband or her subsequent husband, his agent or successor.

S.106 *Elopement: definition and its results*
  (1) Elopement is the taking of an unmarried woman with a genuine intention to marry her.
  (2) The families of the parties may dissolve or confirm the marriage by elopement.
  (3) Where the marriage by elopement is confirmed, the husband shall pay to the family of his wife damages known as 'awaja' to be fixed by the family of the woman.

(4) Where the marriage by elopement is dissolved the man shall pay compensation as that for adultery.
(5) The Court may confirm the marriage by elopement, irrespective of the opinions of the families of the parties, where it thinks fit and, here, bride-wealth is as provided in section 98(2) of the Code.

S.107 *Rape: definition and compensation*

(1) Whoever has sexual intercourse with an immature girl or a woman without her consent or against her will is said to have committed rape.
(2) Compensation payable by the rapist shall be:
    (a) in the case of an immature girl, the same as that for an unmarried woman;
    (b) in the case of an unmarried woman, Ls.150;
    (c) in the case of a married woman, Ls.200.
(3) Compensation payable for raping an immature girl or unmarried woman shall be recoverable by her father in trust for the subsequent husband of the girl or woman.
(4) Compensation for raping a married woman shall be recoverable by her husband, his agent or successor.

S.108 *Incest: definition and its results*

(1) Sexual intercourse with a blood relative is incest.
(2) No compensation is payable for incest, but the offender shall be liable to punishment.

S.109 *Impregnation of a girl*

(1) Compensation for impregnating a girl shall be Ls.100.
(2) The compensation shall be recoverable by her father or guardian in trust for her subsequent husband.

S.110 *Divorce*

When it takes effect
(1) Divorce takes effect upon pronouncement by the Court; or
(2) when the wife leaves her husband and her family returns to the family of the husband the bride-wealth, less deductions.

S.111 *Grounds for divorce*

The Court may, if it thinks fit, grant divorce on any of the following grounds:
(1) barrenness of the wife;
(2) repeated infedility of the wife;
(3) neglect of duties by the wife;
(4) gross misconduct by the wife;
(5) impotence of the husband;
(6) gross misconduct by the husband and neglect of his duties.
(7) total breakdown of the marriage relationship.

S.112 *Parties to divorce suit*

The parties to a divorce suit shall be the husband on the one hand, and the wife and her family as co-parties on the other hand.

S.113 *Effects of divorce*

(1) Upon divorce the husband shall be entitled to recover the bride-wealth paid
   (a) where there are no children, all the bride-wealth, less an amount equal to compensation for adultery;
   (b) among the Luo of the East Bank of River Jur: where there is only one child, only one (1) cow and cash payment;
   (c) among the Luo of East Bank of River Jur: (i) where there is a girl, four (4) cows and (2) bulls are deducted; (ii) where there is a boy, three (3) cows and one (1) bull are deducted;
   (d) where the marriage was according to cattle marriage tradition, the Code of the Dinka Customary Law shall apply;
   (e) where there are more than two children, no bride-wealth is recoverable.

(2) Upon divorce the family of the woman shall be entitled to:
   (a) recover any compensation received by the husband for rape or fornication or adultery by the wife;
   (b) the right to the children until redeemed by the father where the bride-wealth paid is not enough to cover the compensation for co-habitation and deducations for the children.

(3) Upon divorce the wife shall have the right to custody of the children until each one attains the age of seven, provided the husband shall be entitled to their custody at an earlier age, if the interest of the children so requires.

S.114 *Liability of husband for children raised by the family of the wife*

Where the children are raised by the family of their mother owing to the neglect of their father to redeem or raise them, the father shall be liable to pay one cow for each child, upon redeeming or collecting them.

S.115 *Effect of death of husband or wife upon marriage*

(1) The death of the husband has no effect on the marriage.
(2) The family of the husband may dissolve the marriage upon the death of the wife.
(3) Where the marriage is dissolved due to the death of the wife:
   (a) the family of the husband shall be liable to pay to the family of the wife one cow as compensation;
   (b) the bride-wealth shall be recoverable as upon divorce.

S.116 *Testate succession*

A man may, by oral or written will, distribute his property within the family.

S.117 *Intestate succession*

(1) The subjects of succession are:
   (a) wife or wives;
   (b) children;
   (c) property.
(2) The closest male relatives inherit the deceased's property generally.
(3) The wives shall be taken over by the male members of the family as they think fit.
(4) Where the deceased left no son or wife his property shall be held in trust by his successor with a view to marrying for him.

CHAPTER 8

THE LAW OF PROPERTY

S.118 *Interest in land and the right of cultivation*
The family has the exclusive right of cultivation on traditional family habitats.

S.119 *Hunting right*
The right of the first person to spear an animal:
The first person to spear an animal is the lawful owner of the animal even if killed eventually by another person, provided the person who kills the animal eventually shall be entitled to one of the animal's front legs.

S.120 *Tracing of cattle*
Same as in Section 53 of Part 2.

S.121 *Damages for cattle which die naturally after their transfer to a third party*
Same as in Section 54 of Part 2.

S.122 *Tracing of off-spring of cattle*
Same as in Section 55 of Part 2.

S.123 *Transfer of title to property*
Same as in Section 56 of Part 2.

S.124 *Tracing of property wrongfully transferred*
Same as in Section 57 of Part 2.

S.125 *Recovery of damages where property is wrongfully transferred*
Same as in Section 58 of Part 2.

S.126 *Transfer of property by way of gift*
Same as in Section 59 of Part 2.

S.127 *Title to gift property reverts to donor on revocation*
Same as in Section 60 of Part 2.

S.128 *No tracing of gift property into the hands of third parties*
Same as in Section 61 of Part 2.

S.129 *Tracing of property transferred to a third party by finder*
Same as in Section 62 of Part 2.

S.130 *Tracing of property transferred by non-owner*
Same as in Section 63 of Part 2.

S.131 *Pledge*
Same as in Section 64 of Part 2.

S.132 *Lien*
Same as in Section 65 of Part 2.

S.133 *Pledge and lienee to exercise reasonable care*
Same as in Section 66 of Part 2.

CHAPTER 10

TORTS

S.134 *Damages for personal injuries*
(1) Damages recoverable for the loss of:
    (a) One eye — two cows and one bull.
    (b) Both eyes – three cows, two bulls and Ls.300.
    (c) One leg — two cows and one bull.
    (d) Both legs — three cows and one bull.
    (e) One arm — two cows and one bull.
    (f) Both arms — three cows and one bull.
    (g) Hearing — two cows and one bull.
(2) Damages recoverable for other personal injuries shall be in accordance with the gravity of the injury inflicted.

S.135 *Damages for personal injury caused by domestic animals*
Same as in Section 68 of Part 2.

S.136 *Compensation for causing death*
Compensation shall be payable in all cases of causing the death of any person.

S.137 *To whom compensation for causing death shall be payable*
    (a) The family of the deceased.
    (b) The family of his mother, where:
        (i) his mother is not married;
        (ii) he has not been redeemed by his father.

S.138 *Persons liable to pay compensation for causing death*
Compensation for causing death shall be payable by
(1) the family of the killer;
(2) the family or clan of the family that was fighting the family or clan of the deceased where the killer is unknown;
(3) the family of the mother of the killer, where:
    (a) his mother is not married;
    (b) he has not been redeemed by his father;
(4) the family of a married woman who has killed and the family of her husband.

S.139 *Compensation payable for causing death by accident or negligence, causing death by a minor or person of unsound mind*
(1) Compensation for causing death, unless otherwise provided for herein-

after, shall be:
(a) for a childless person, five (5) cows, four (4) bulls and Ls.500;
(b) for a person who has a son, three (3) cows, two (2) bulls and Ls.300.
(2) Compensation for causing death by accident or negligence or by a minor or person of unsound mind shall be two (2) cows and one (1) bull and Ls.250.

S.140 *Effects of wife killing*
Where the husband intentionally kills his wife, he shall be liable:
(a) to complete payment of bride wealth, if not paid in full;
(b) to pay compensation for the death.

S.141 *Where the wife kills the husband intentionally*
Where the wife kills the husband intentionally:
(a) the marriage is dissolved;
(b) the family of the wife pays the family of the husband the compensation for causing death.

S.142 *Damages for defamation*
Damages are recoverable for a defamation published other than in the form of a song.

S.143 *Damage to property by domestic animals*
Same as in Section 79 and 80 of Part 2.

S.144 *Damage to property by fire*
Where property is destroyed or damaged by fire caused by another, the owner shall be entitled to damages payable by the person who caused the fire.

PART 4

THE CODE OF FERTIT CUSTOMARY LAW

CHAPTER 9

PRELIMINARY

S.145 *Title*
This Law shall be called the Code of Fertit Customary Law.

S.146 *Application*
The provisions of Part 4 shall apply throughout Bahr El-Ghazal Region to:
(a) All Fertit of Bahr El-Ghazal Region.
(b) All persons involved in sexual wrongs with Fertit girls, women or wives in Bhar El-Ghazal Region.

(c) Matters connected with marriage, divorce, custody and redemption of children of a Fertit woman.

CHAPTER 10

GENERAL EXPLANATIONS AND DEFINITIONS

S.147 *Sense of expression once explained*

Every expression, which is explained in this Code is used in every part of this Code in conformity with the explanation, unless the subject or sense of the content otherwise requires.

S.148 *'Mbo ni' or 'Mali ni (Ndogo) vili ni (Balanda)'*

'Mbo ni' or bride-wealth is the property payable by the bride-groom and his family to the family of the bride in consideration of her marriage.

S.149 *'Ba si co'*

'Ba si co' is the compensation payable by the male offender in sexual wrong, namely adultery, fornication and rape.

S.150 *Family*

'Brother' and 'sister'
 (i) The terms 'brother' and 'sister' include step-brother and step-sister.
 (ii) 'Vi ni' means unmarried female up to the age of 18 years.
 (iii) 'Ni' includes married or unmarried woman.
 (iv) 'Ni dako' means a married woman within the provisions of this Code.
 (v) 'Mgbanga' Court carries the same meaning as is defined in Part 1 of this amended Act.

CHAPTER 11

PERSONAL LAW

S.151 *Marriage*

Definition of marriage
Marriage is a union between the families of the spouses for the life of each spouse for the purpose of sexual co-habitation, procreation of the young and maintenance of the homestead.

S.152 *Consent in Marriage*

The only consent which is material and essential for the conclusion of a valid marriage is that of the families of the spouses, as well as that of the spouses themselves.

Explanation: It must be noted that if the girl does not consent to the marriage or is forced to marry the man she does not want, the marriage is very likely to break down, that is why 'kaa' is always put before the elders and the spouse is asked to take it; if she takes it, this symbolizes that she accepts to marry the bride-groom; if she refuses to take it, it means that she does not want him.

S.153 *Consummation of marriage*

No marriage shall be consummated between a boy and a girl until both of them have attained maturity.

S.154 *Bride-wealth*

(a) The relatives of the two parties shall be free to fix the bride-wealth to be paid by the relatives of the bride-groom to the relatives of the bride.

Explanation:

(i) The bride-wealth is always difficult to fix. It is always the family of the bride who say they want such and such amount to be paid for their girl, and the family of the bride-groom will try to persuade them to reduce it until they eventually agree on what the family of the bride-groom have to pay.

(ii) The current tendency has been that parents of the girls demand high bride-wealth. It has been noticed with alarm that this discourages marriages, thus leaving a large number of unmarried men and women in the community. Therefore the parents should revert to the age-old practice of demanding low bride-wealth.

(b) Bride-wealth or 'mali ni' shall be paid by the bride-groom or his father or brother or by the maternal uncle, if he is not a redeemed child, to the bride.

(c) Where a man and a woman agree to cohabit as husband and wife, regardless of the consent of their parents, the father of the girl shall be entitled to sue the man for the bride-wealth.

S.155 *Forms of marriage*

(1) Open courting.
(2) Sending of 'kaa' by the bride-groom to the family of the spouse to see if the spouse accepts to be married to him or not.
(3) Bride-groom goes openly to his in-law's house and performs any work he may be required to do.
(4) The bride is taken to the house of the bride-groom where a feast for the marriage takes place.

S.156 *Rights accruing to the husband upon marriage*

The following rights shall accrue at the outset of the marriage to the husband:
(a) right to children born during the subsistence of the marriage;
(b) right to compensation for the adultery of his wife.

S.157 *Sexual wrongs*

Adultery: definition

(a) Sexual intercourse with a married woman is adultery.
(b) Compensation payable by the adulterer shall be Ls.150 payable to the husband.

S.158 Rape

Definition and compensation

Whoever has sexual intercourse with an immatured girl or a matured girl or woman without her consent is said to have committed rape.

Compensation payable by the rapist shall be as follows:
(i) For a married woman, Ls.200 payable to her husband.
(ii) For an unmarried woman, Ls.150 payable to her family.
(iii) For an immatured girl, Ls.300 payable to her parents.
(iv) For a wife of a blood friend 'Muka' or 'Bakure', one head of tobacco, one white cock and one bow and arrows.

Explanation: It is the custom of the Fertit that money, 'molodo', 'kaa', etc., should never be paid between blood friends, because this has been cursed at the time of drinking of blood between the two parties concerned.

Note: The use of tobacco, arrows, bow and white cock is for swearing the two parties, man and woman, not to repeat this again.

S.159 Divorce

When divorce takes effect
(a) Divorce takes effect upon pronouncement by the Court.
(b) The parties to the divorce suit are the husband and his wife.

S.160 Ground for divorce

The Court, if it thinks fit, grants divorce on any of the following grounds:
(1) Repeated infidelity of the wife.
(2) Neglect of duties by the wife.
(3) Gross misconduct by the wife.
(4) Gross misconduct by the husband and neglect of his duties to the family.
(5) Impotence of the husband.
(6) Total breakdown of the marriage relationship.

S.161 Effect of divorce

(1) Where there are no children, and if the husband is the cause of the divorce, he is returned only his 'kaa' and the bride-wealth is retained by the family of the woman.
(2) Where the cause of the divorce is from the wife, and if they have children, the husband is returned half of the bride-wealth, all his children plus his 'kaa'.
(3) The woman is returned to her relatives.
(4) Upon divorce the wife shall have the right of custody of the children until they attain the age of seven, provided that the husband shall be entitled to their custody at an earlier age, if the interest of the children so require.

S.162 Effect of death of husband or wife upon marriage

(1) When the husband dies his wife may remain within the family, provided that she is married by one of his relatives.
(2) When the wife dies, the husband is still bound to contribute to the unpaid part or balance of the bride-wealth to her family.

S.163 *Testate and intestate succession*

(1) A man may, by oral or written will, distribute his properties within the family.
(2) Where a man dies without making a will, his estate passes to his children or his brothers or close relatives in that order.

CHAPTER 12

THE LAW OF PROPERTY INTEREST IN LAND

S.164 *Right of cultivation*

The family has the exclusive right of cultivation and dwelling on traditional family habitats.

S.165 *Hunting right*

The person who spears an animal first is the lawful owner of that animal, even if it is eventually killed by another person, provided that the person who eventually kills it is entitled to one front leg of that animal.

S.166 *Transfer of title to property*

Same as in Section 56 of Part 2.

S.167 *Tracing of property wrongfully transferred*

Same as in Section 57 of Part 2.

S.168 *Recovery of damages where property is wrongfully transferred*

Same as in Section 58 of Part 2.

S.169 *Transfer of title by way of gift*

Same as in Section 59 of Part 2.

S.170 *Transfer of property to a third party by finder*

Same as in Section 62 of Part 2.

S.171 *Tracing of property transferred by non-owner*

Same as in Section 63 of Part 2.

S.172 *Lien or retention of property for work done on it*

Same as in Section 65 of Part 2.

CERTIFICATE OF AUTHENTICITY

1. In accordance with the provisions of Section 51 of the Presidential Order No.1/1983, I hereby certify that this is the authentic Act of the People's Regional Assembly, Bahr El-Ghazal Region, amending THE RE-STATEMENT OF BAHR EL-GHAZAL REGION CUSTOMARY LAW (AMENDED) ACT, 1984, which was passed at its Sitting No.23 on the Seventh Day of August, 1984.

John Wuol Makec,
Speaker, People's Regional
Assembly, Bhar El-Ghazal Region,
Wau.

2. I *assent*

Dr Lawrence Wol Wol Majok,
Governor, Bhar El-Ghazal Region,
Wau.

Wau,
18/9/1984

Index

(*Note:* the suffix 'n' indicates that the reference appears in a footnote).

Acts of God, 133
Adjectival Law
   distinguished from Substantive Law, *see* Substantive Law
Adultery
   compensation for *(akor), see under* Compensation; seriousness of, as an offence, 38, 67–8; belief that adulterer/ess carries sickness, 49; public criticism of, 51; definition of, 67; sanctions against, 68, 70, 77; law supports husband in cases of, 68; multiple, 70; and divorce, 70, 72–5; in 'ghost marriages', 70–2, 73; in polygamous marriages, 72; right to sue for, vested in husband, 72–3, 230; and paternity of children, *see* Paternity; with husband's relative, 75–7; in disputed remarriage, 83–5; other references, 33, 39, 43, 61, 62, 89
Adversary System, 218
African legal systems
   objectives of, 35–6, compared with European legal systems, 35, 53, 86, 101–2; positive nature of, 36, 46, 198–9; apparent absence of legal sanctions in, 45–6, religious sanctions in, 47–9, 52; deterrent objective of, 53; and concept of *mens rea*, 206–7
Agam-long (court orator), 234–7
Agar Dinka, the, 68–9, 154–5, 182, 183
Age of maturity, 63
Agriculture, 153, 161, 162, 170, 178
   prevented by drought, 47
Akeeth, see Incest
Akolawin, Natale O., 23n, 116n
Akor, see Compensation: for adultery
Alau, 124
Aliab, 39
Aliamtooc Regional Court, 82n
Alien cultures
   adverse effects on Dinka and other African personal law, 26–7, 221, 241

Allen, Sir Carleton, 24
Amakiir people, the, 181–2
Ameth Wet-Duang area, 184
Amuk or *Amec* (security for loan), 187–91
Amuol people, the, 184–5
Ancestors
   in religious ceremony, 48; disrespect to, 48; and family property, 143; and land tenure, 156
Anderson, Norman, 101n
Animals
   statements of wisdom attributed to, 47; non-domestic, 166, 168–9; tortious acts by, 192–8; straying or trespassing, 193, 194, 196; classification of, 192–3, 195–6, domestic *(see also* Cattle), 193–8; dangerous, 193, 196, 197, 198
Animals Act, 1971, The, 193
Anyanya war, 72n, 85
Apaak area, 39
Appeals
   for restoration of dissolved marriage, 83, 88; for revision of maintenance order, 109; against rejection of claim for title to stolen cattle, 121; against recovery of cows from innocent third party, 129; against award of stolen cow to thief, 130–1; in land dispute, 174–7, in debt disputes, 189–91, court hierarchy in, 238–40, changes in system, 238–40; time limits for, 240–1; grounds for, 241; compared with request for revision, 242
Appeasement, *see* Awec
Apuk (compensation; also act of paying compensation for causing death or injury), *see* Compensation
Arueth (reverse payment to bridegroom's family), *see also* Cattle: as *arueth*: 39, 65, 67, 104; recovery of, 90, 91, 98
Arungara people, *see* Zande people
Aruok (redemption of children), *see* Children,

280

redemption of
Aryamba, Wilson, J., 116
Ashton, H., 210
Athoi people, the, 183
Atkin, L. J., 122
Atuot people, the, 39, 132
Awan people, the, 180, 184–5
Awec ('appeasement')
    for pre-marital impregnation, 61; for adultery by husband's relative, 75, 76, 77; in marital disputes, 87, 89; for mitigated homicide, 208, 209
Aweil Dinka and district, 49n, 84, 158, 184

Baai (upland/farm and residential land), *see under* Land
Banybith (pl. *Banybiith*) (spiritual leader)
    traditional roles of, 33, 47–9; decisions of, regarded as having divine force, 33, 48–9, 238; religious duties of, 47, 48; respect accorded to, 49; mistakenly associated with magic by foreigners, 49; oaths taken before, 51, 212; judicial decisions by, 238; other references, 35
Bari customary law, 106
Barrenness (of women), 58, 60, 88
Bennet, Chief Justice, 22
Bhar el Ghazal Province, 39, 76, 105, 112, 212n, 224–5
Bhar el Ghazal Province Council, 40
Bhar el Ghazal Province Court, 98–9
Bhar el Ghazal Region Customary Law Act, 1984, *see* Restatement of Bhar el Ghazal Region Customary Law Act, 1984
Blackburn, J., 120
Border disputes, 33, 227
Breach of the peace, 68, 169n, 213–4
'Bride-price', *see also* Bride-wealth, 58, 63, 65–6
Bride-wealth, see also Cattle: as bride-wealth
    recovery of, after dissolution of marriage, 59, 71, 75, 83–4, 88, 90–1, 97–8, 128, 134–5; inaccurately called 'bride-price', 63, 65–6; generally paid in cattle, 63; in inter-communal marriages, 63–4; legal importance of, 64–5, 95; regarded as compensation, 64–5; stabilises the marriage, 65; involves prestige, 65; and *arueth* (reverse payment), *see* Arueth *and* Cattle: as *arueth*; not a commercial transaction, 65–7; and paternity of children, 95–6; woman's family suspending right to, 97; paid by Muslim men, 110; relatives claiming, in mixed marriage, 111; paid in money, 128; and damages in event of divorce, if bride-wealth cattle were slaughtered, 133; other references, 39, 76–7, 104, 203n
Busia, K. A. 143n

Cattle
    as *awac* compensation (for impregnation), 33, 38; as *akor* (adultery) compensation (*see also* Compensation: for adultery), 33, 38, 61, 62, 69, 73, 74–7; as *apuk* (death or injury) compensation (*see also* Homicide: compensation for), 33, 199, 201, 204–5, 207, 208–9; killed in purification ceremony after homicide, 36; as compensation for sexual offences, 38; as *arueth* (reverse payment to bridegroom's family (*see also* Arueth), 39, 67, 91, 98–9, 126, 133; as bride-wealth (*see also* Bride-wealth), 39, 59, 63–4, 65, 67, 75, 76, 83–4, 85, 90–1, 95, 97–8, 129, 133, 134, 209, 212n; sacrificed after moving to new place, 47–8; in religious ceremony, 48; as compensation for rape, 61; as *awec* (appeasement), 61, 75, 87, 89, 208, 209; shared between wives in polygamous marriages, 66; as *aruok* (redemption of children), *see* Children, redemption of; given to bridegroom by in-laws as symbol of hospitality, 104; is most important movable property, 104, 146, 150, 151; theft of, 120–1, 124–5, 130–1; tracing of, 129–32, 134–5; as security for loan (*amuk*), 126–7, 188–92; damages for, after divorce, 127, 133–4; ownership of, 156, 172; of strangers, 180; injuring or killing people, 197; other references, 89, 193, 235
Cattle camps, 48, 132, 176, 179
Cause of action, *see under* Procedure
Central Dinka, the, 170
Chiefs' Conferences, 39, 169
Chiefs' Courts, 33, 107, 108, 109, 112–3, 114, 115, 116, 121, 232, 239–41, 242, 243
    Constitution of, 222–3; jurisdiction of, 223–7; Branch, 223, 227, 239; Main, 125, 223, 239; Regional, 82n, 126, 130, 173–7, 223, 227, 239; Special, 182, 223, 226
Chiefs' Courts Ordinance, 1931, 19, 33, 222, 224, 226–7, 229, 233, 238–9, 240–3
Chief Justice of the Sudan, the, 108, 112, 223, 224, 233
Children, *see also* Procreation of children
    redemption of *(aruok)*, 39, 83n, 90, 91, 93–7, 98–9, 102–3, 111–2, 115; of 'ghost marriages', *see under* 'Ghost marriages'; uniting two families, 61, 88; as potential fighters, 61; bride-wealth a consideration for, 65; and right to share in family cattle, 66; paternity of, in cases of adultery, *see* Paternity; and divorce of parents (*see also* Custody *and* Maintenance), 82–3, 89, 90–2; custody of, *see* Custody of children; maintenance of, *see under* Maintenance; of mixed marriage, 110; and inheritance, *see under* Succession
Christians
    Dinka, 107–9; non-Sudanese, domiciled in Sudan, 19, 108; Sudanese, 108–9
Civil Justice Act, 1983, 19, 20, 22, 23
Civil Justice Ordinance, 1929, 20, 22n, 110n, 113, 241
Civil law
    differentiated from criminal law, 34; more developed than criminal law in Dinka society, 34–8, 45
Civil Procedure Acts, 1974 and 1983, 22n, 240
Civil Transactions Act, 1983, 150n, 228
Civil Wrong
    definition of a, 34; *awac* or *awuoc* Dinka term for, 37
Communal rights, *see* Rights, communal

Compensation (or damages, or *apuk*) (*see also* under Cattle)
claimed as chief aim of African law, 35, 36; for homicide, *see* Homicide: compensation for; punitive element in, 37–8; for adultery (*akor*), 33, 38–9, 61, 62, 69, 70, 71–7, 84; for rape, 38, 61; for extra-marital pregnancy, 33, 38, 61; for trespass, 40; for dead or untraceable cattle, 98; for irrecoverable property, 122, 129, 132–4, 135; for death or injury caused to livestock, 193; for tortious acts by animals, 169, 194–8; for tortious acts by humans, 199–205; for defamation, *see under* Defamation; for grevious injury, 201, 203n; other references, 34

Conciliation, *see under* Procedure

Condominium rule in Sudan, 221

Contempt of court, 231, 237

Contract, law of, 186–7, 191–2

Contract of sale, 191

Cory, H., 86–7, 104

Court of Appeal, the, 19–20, 22n, 108–9, 110, 223, 240

Courts
of Appeal, *see* Court of Appeal; Branch, Chiefs', Main, Regional, and Special, *see under* Chiefs' Courts; district, 129, 232; inter-district, 33; Province (formerly Civil High Court), 19, 94, 98–9, 107, 109, 121; Sharia, 108, 111–2, 114–5, 116; Supreme, *see* Supreme Court; public's role in, 83, 85–6, 234–5, 236–7; procedure in, *see under* Procedure; President of, 231, 232, 233–4, 235, 237–8; clerk of the, 232, 234, 238; employees and retainers of, 232, 234, 237, 243–4; court police, 234; seating arrangements in, *see under* Procedure, court orator (*Agam-long*), 234, 235, 236, 237

Crime, definition of a, 34

Criminal Justice Act, 1967, 193

Criminal law
differentiated from civil law, 34; less developed than civil law, 34–8, 41, 45; requires law enforcement agencies, 34–5; untrue that Dinka do not have it, 37–8; *awac* an element in, 38; moral principles fill gaps in, 52

Crops, *see* Agriculture

Custody of children (*see also* Maintenance), 90–103;
and payment of *aruok* cattle, 90–1, 93–7, 98, 111; and rights of father, 91, 93–6; and powers of mother's relatives, 91, 93–6; where bride-wealth has not been paid, 96; in English Law, *see* English Law; in Islamic Law, *see* Islamic Law; differences between African and other legal systems, 101–2; in Venda Law, 102–3; after dissolution of mixed marriage, 111–3, 116; in Sukuna Law, 91n

Custom
as a major source of state law, 18–20; conditions for acquiring a binding force of law, 21–5; controversy over definition of, 22–4; antiquity of, 23, 24, 31–2; restricted to its locality, 25; common among different tribes, 25; inferior to territorial or state law, 25, 172; tests of a, 26–30; Muslim (marriage), 27; Hindu, 29; social value attached to a, 29; and sacred beliefs, 29; ascertained from decisions of elders, 167

Damage to property, caused by animal, 194, 196

Damages, *see* Compensation

Debt, 126–7, 133, 134, 135, 187–92;
security for repayment of (amuk), 187–92; failure to discharge, 189–91

Defamation, 40, 201, 209–15;
compensation for, 201, 210, 211; and the family name, 210, gravity of, as an offence, 210; definition of, 210; in conversation or discussion, 211; in songs, 211, 213–4; and imputation of supernatural powers, 211–3; morally corrective element in, 213–4; element of prestige in, 213; distinguished from insult, 214–5

Defence of territory, 61, 205

Deng, Dr Francis, 17n, 67n, 72, 74, 75–7, 143n, 151n, 152n, 156–7, 161, 170, 172, 210n

Dias, R. W. M., 24, 25, 26, 32n, 92n, 159, 166

Dinka Customary Law
need for development of, 20–1; civil law more developed than criminal law, *see under* Civil law or Criminal Law; non-existence of law enforcement agencies in, 34–5, 36, 38, 44, 53; lack of uniformity in, 38–9; variations between districts overcome through Chiefs' Conferences, 39; codified and unified at Bhar el Ghazal Conference, 1975, 39–40, 106–7, 138; Code becomes Part II of the Restatement of the Bhar el Ghazal Region Customary Law Act, 1984, 39–40, 106–7, 213n; authorities' lack of initiative in developing, 17, 40; a recognised source of state or territorial law, 18–20, 40; administrators' efforts to develop, 40; apparent absence of legal sanctions in, 45–6; sources of, 31–3, 47, 165; religious and mystical sanctions in, 47–9, 49–50; public opinion a sanction in, 51; Code of the (Part II of the Restatement of Bhar el Ghazal Region Customary Law Act, 1984), 40, 62; similarity to Nuer Law, 71; aims to restore social equilibrium, 36, 46, 198, 206, 215, 220

Dissolution of marriage or Divorce (puokë-ruai), 77–116;
in Islamic Law, 27; by death of spouse, 39, 78; and recovery of bride-wealth, 39, 75, 83–4; in English Law, 57; after death of childless wife, 58–9; bride-wealth a protection against, 65; and adultery, 70–5; in 'ghost marriages', 71–2, 82–3; difficult to obtain against a widow, 72; and the husband's family, 73–4; and paternity of children, 74–6; made difficult by birth of children, 61; after brutal treatment by husband, 67; differences between Western and African concepts, 77–81; undermines society, 81; importance of taking place in court, 82–6; out of court, 82, 83; conflicting court decisions, 84–5; grounds for, 86, 88–9; among Sukuna tribe, 86–7; rare to obtain in African Dinka societies, 86–8; legal effects of, 90; and custody and maintenance of children, *see* Custody of children *and* Maintenance; all claims settled in single suit, 97; procedure, 97–8; distribution of property after, 103–5; between Christians, 107–9; between non-Muslims and Muslims, 109–16; and tracing of property, 127–8, 134; after homicide against spouse, 209

Index

District Commissioners, 39, 109, 112, 113, 115, 182, 225, 239, 241–2, 243
District judges, *see under* Judges
Divorce, *see* Dissolution of marriage or Divorce
Dogs (Protection of Livestock) Act, 1953, 193
Dribert, J. H., 36n, 46, 48, 206–7
Dundas, 36n, 204

Elders
 decisions acquire force of law, 32; forming ad hoc courts, 33; religious duties, 47, 48; giving approval to fights, 48; at Wanh-alel Conference, 1975, 39, 73; intervening in adultery cases, 77, 89; resisting divorces, 87; role in making rules of custom, 167; adjudicating disputes, 207, 221, 238; advising in court, 237; other references, 35
Elias, T. O., 35–6, 207
Elopement, damages for, 38
Employment, 56
English Law
 applied to cases where both parties had Dinka Customary Law, 21; influence over Sudanese judges, *see* Judges, Sudanese; matrimonial, 57, 78–81, 99–101; contrasted with African customary law by Western writers, 86; of custody and maintenance, 99–101; whether to be applied in marriage disputes/divorce between Sudanese Christians, 107–9; of personal property, *see under* Property; of land, 150; other references, 31–2, 192, 195, 228
Equatoria Province, 224
Esher, Lord, 34n
Evidence
 rules of, 50, 217; false, 219
Excepted Communities, 19

False oath, consequences of, 50–1
Family(ies)
 ties loosened by modernisation, 55–6; and marriage, 56–9, 73–4, 90; importance of children in creating family ties, 58, 61, 88; large, attract respect, 61–2; distribution of labour within, 62; and bride-wealth, 63–5, 76–7; respect for dead kinsmen, 71; communal ownership of property within, *see under* Property; tortious acts by kinsmen, 76; adultery within, 75–7; and marital disputes or divorce, 71–4, 83–91, 106–7; strength of, contrasted with Western societies, 102–3; and succession, *see* Succession; 'African conception of', (K. A. Busia), 143; and collective responsibility, *see under* Homicide *and* Tort; disputes within, 204, 220, collectively party to legal suits, 229–30
Farming, *see* Agriculture
Farran, Prof. C. d'Olivier, 17n, 20n, 27–8, 105–6, 107–8, 109, 114
Fights, inter-tribal, 201–2, 204
Fines
 in Dinka and African law, 37, 38; in foreign legal systems, 37; for defamation, 211
Fishing and fishing rights, 66, 149, 153, 157, 166, 168–9, 179, 180, 182–3
Ford, D., 56–7
Foreign ideas, as corrupting force, 50–1

Forests, 149, 150, 153, 158, 180

'Ghost marriages' (or Levirate or *Lo-hot*) (marriages conducted for deceased persons), 58–60, 141, 143–4, 145–6; characteristics summarised, 59; divorce from 71–2, 82–3; children of, 59–60; 71, 82–3, 88, 141, 144, 145, 149, 199; and succession, 141–2, 143–4, 145, 148–9; and compensation for homicide, 199
God, *see also* Religious beliefs *and* Sanctions, religious
 fear of, as a sanction in African law, 47–9, 235n; as the source of justice, 47; God's protection sought, 48; deemed to recognise fights approved by elders, 48; Will of, that a person's lineage continues, 60; Acts of, *see* Acts of God; invoked in court, 235
Gogrial District, 39, 72n, 184
Government intervention in disputes, 182
Governor-General, the, 223n, 239
Grand Kadi, the, 112
Grazing rights, 149, 157, 179, 183

Health care, 56
Hobbes, Thomas, 41, 43
Homicide
 confession of, 50; purification rites connected with, 36, 50, 202; compensation for *(apuk)*, 36, 50, 51–2, 134, 148, 199–209; classified as tort, 198–9; family's collective responsibility for, 199–205, 208; in inter-tribal fighting, 201–4; among the Nuer, 203; mental element *(mens rea)* in, 205–7, 208; in self-defence, 205–6; through accident or mental incapacity, 207; of a relative, 209; of a spouse, 209; other references, 187
Housing conditions, 56
Howell, P. P., 17n, 59, 70, 71, 74, 199n
Hunting and hunting rights, 66, 153, 168–9, 179, 185

Ijong, Chief Macar, 169
Impotence of husband, 60, 88
Incest *(akeeth)*
 believed to be fatal or weakening to offspring, 50, 88; purification rites connected with, 50, 88n; confession of, 50; not punishable in Sudan Penal Code, 52–3; as grounds for divorce, 88n; other references, 33
Inheritance, *see* Succession *and* Wills
Inspectors of Local Government, 232
Inter-tribal fights, *see* Fights, inter-tribal
Islamic Law
 content primarily personal, 23n; of divorce, 27, 110; immutability of, 27; punishments in, 44; of custody and maintenance, 101–2; of marriage, 109–17; conflicting with Dinka Customary Law, 112–6; example other Arab states have set by reforming, 117; of land, 150

Jewellery, *see* Ornaments
Jok, Chief Deng, 169
Judges (*see also* Judges, District; Judges, English; Judges, Province; Judges, South

African; Judges, Zimbabwean)
    making arbitrary decisions at variance with custom, 21; subjectively determining 'reasonableness' of a custom, 26–30; influenced by English Law, 26; author's advice to, in considering admissibility of a custom, 29–30; absence of professional judges in Dinka Customary Law, 45; confronted with conflict of laws arising from mixed marriages, 110–6, task to interpret intentions of legislators, 165; functional role in trials, 218–20
Judges, District, 121, 130–1, 174, 177, 190, 225, 232, 240, 241
Judges, English
    working in Sudan, 26, 108; influence on post-Independence Sudanese judges, 26–7; antipathy to Mohamedan Law of marriage, 27; decisions made by, in Sudan, 108–9
Judges, Province, 109, 223n, 226, 239n, 241
Judges, South African, 108
Judges, Zimbabwean (pre-Independence), 108
Jur-beli people, the, 154–5

Kacoul, Chief Arol, 125
Kinship groups (kinsgroups), 56, 58, 73, 76, 87, 200–5
Kittabiya women, 110
Kuei Reginal Court, 126

Lakes, *see* Rivers, lakes and pools
Lakes District, 39
Lal, Dr Nand, 222n, 224
Land, *see also* Land Law
    scarcity of, 56, 147, 161, 170, 178, 179; defence of, *see* Defence of territory; and succession, 146–7; arable or farmland (*see also* baai under this heading), 146–7, 155, 156, 157, 160, 162, 164–5, 166, 170, 179; abandoned, 147, 156, 157, 161, 167–8, 170–1, 172, 173, 174; unoccupied, 150, 154, 156–7, 161, 170, 172–3, 177, 178; communal usage or ownership of, *see under* Land Law; Government-owned, 150, 162n, 172; *toc* (lowland/communal grazing land), 152–3, 155n, 157, 170, 179, 180, 181–2; *baai* (upland/farm and residential land), 152–3, 180, 181; and ancestral spirits, 156; residential (*see also* baai under this heading), 157, 160–1, 164–5, 169–70, 180; rivers, lakes and pools, *see* Rivers, lakes and pools; migration from, 20, 170–3, 178–9, 181–2, 183–5; infertility of, 170, 178; other references, 119
Land Law, 150–85;
    not embodied in the Restatement of the Bhar el Ghazal Region Customary Law Act, 1984, 150; statutory provisions of, 150–1; and unoccupied land, *see* Land, unoccupied; rights in, regulated by custom, 150; differences from English Law, 150; qualifications to right of ownership in, 150–1; in urban communities, 151; slow development of, 151–2; communal usage or ownership, 151, 153, 156, 157–8, 160, 172, 174, 178–80, 182; modes of acquisition of title, 154 (by occupation, 154, 160; by conquest, 154, 160, 163; by gift, 154–5, 160, 172, 181–2); individual interests and ownership, 150–1, 153, 154–66, 171–3, 178–9; inheritance of land, 157, 163, 172, 177, 181–2; usufruct, 158, 159, 162–3; abandoned land, *see* Land, abandoned; ownership of things on or under land, 166–9; loss of title to land, 169–79; migration, *see under* Land; eviction, 170, 172; disputes, 172–7; partition by court order, 174, 176; land use extended to strangers, 179–80, 182; inter-tribal disputes, 180–2, 183–5; exclusive fishing rights, *see* Fishing and fishing rights; exclusive grazing rights, *see* Grazing rights
Land Settlement and Registration Act, 1925, 150
Langan, P. St J., and Lawrence, D. G., 216n, 217n
Law
    society's need for, 43; civil, *see* Civil law; criminal, *see* Criminal law; penal, 44; Dinka Customary, *see* Dinka Customary Law; English, *see* English Law; Islamic (or Sharia or Mohamedan), *see* Islamic Law: Mosaic, 44; Roman, *see* Roman Law; Syrian, 101
Law enforcement agencies, 44, 53;
    non-existence of, in Dinka society, 34–5, 36, 38, 45
Legal sanctions
    apparent absence of, in Dinka Customary Law, 45–6; necessity of, 42, 44–5
Levirate, *see also* 'Ghost marriages' *and* Lo-hot
    regarded by many Westerners as 'unreasonable', 27; Farran's advice to judges on, 28; Muslim shock at, 28; sacred aspects of, 30; A. Philips' definition, 58
Liability, definition of, 186
Lindsay, Chief Justice, 22, 23, 25
Livestock, *see* Cattle *and* Property
Lo-hot, see also 'Ghost marriages' and Levirate, 80, 88;
    definition of, 60
Luac people, the, 173, 177, 182
Lual people, the, 181
Luo people, the, 25, 154, 155n, 181;
    customs in common with Dinka, 25, 116

McDowell, J., 113, 114, 115
Mabor, Isaiah Kulang (Province Commissioner, Bhar el Ghazal; Chairman, Bhar el Ghazal Conference, 1975), 39
Maintenance, *see also* Custody of children
    of children, 99–100, 103, 109; in English Law, *see under* English Law
Malual Dinka and country, 170, 181
Manual of Nuer Law, 59, 199n
Marriage
    inter-communal, 20, 63; between persons with a common custom, 20; disputes arising from, 20, 105–16; mixed, *see* Mixed marriages; Muslim, 27, 109–16; defined by the Restatement of the Bhar el Ghazal Region Customary Law Act, 1984, 54; polygamous, *see* Polygamy; monogamous, *see* Monogamy; a union between two families, 56–7, 58–9, 61, 78, 81, 88, 89, 90; African, contrasted

with English, 57; conditions of legality, 57, 95; a lifelong union (for women), 57–8; continuing after death of spouse, 58–9, 78; dissolution of, *see* Dissolution of marriage; of barren or childless woman to another woman, 60; conducted for deceased persons, *see* 'Ghost marriages' *and* Levirate; objectives of, 61–2; consent of relatives a requirement of, 62, 109–10, 110n, 114, 115; irregular, 62–3; maturity of partners a requirement of, 63; imperfect if bride-wealth not paid in cattle, 63; ceremony, 65; as a social, not commercial, contract, 65–7; duties of husband within, 66; rights of wife within, 66; without payment of bride-wealth, 67, 95–6, 97; wife's relatives' role within, 67; husband's absolute sexual right, 76; a sacred institution, 82; and bride-wealth, *see* Bride-wealth; among Dinka Christians, 107–9; and transfer of property, 127–9, 133, 136, 148; sons marrying in order of age, 147; and symbolic wearing of ornaments, 148

Maturity, age of, *see* Age of maturity
Meek, C. K., 178
Men, duties of, in Dinka society, 62
Mens rea
and homicide, *see under* Homicide; and defamation, 215
Metallic ore, right to, 168
Migration, *see under* Land
Miscarriages of justice
in marital cases, 21; in cases of tort, 21; in cases of crime, 21; where a time limit is set for appeals, 241
Mixed marriages
between Muslims and non-Muslims, 21, 109–16; divorce and disputes arising from, 105–16; personal law of woman governs marriage and divorce, 106, 110, 116; children of, 110, 112–3; and the courts, 110–6; and bride-wealth, 111; author's view on legal system governing, 116
Mohamedan Law, *see* Islamic Law
Monogamy, 55
Muslims, *see also* Islamic Law
married to non-Muslims, *see under* Mixed marriages; shock at customs of other communities, 28

Native Courts Ordinance, 1932, 19, 239n
Negligence, 188, 205
Ngok Dinka, the, 170
Nilotes Dinka, the, 156
Non-Mohamedan Marriage Act, 1926, 108, 109
Non-Mohamedan Marriage Ordinance, 19, 20
Nuer land, 120
Nuer people and law
customs in common with Dinka, 25, 71; custom of 'ghost marriage', 59; married to Muslims, 113; and damages for adultery, 74; and homicide, 203
Nuer Law, Manual of, *see* Manual of Nuer Law

Oaths, swearing of
before a *Banybith*, 50–1, 212; in court, 235, 236
Obligations and Law of Obligations
definition of, 186; contractual, *see* Contract, Law of; tortious, *see* Tort and tortious acts; debt, *see* Debt; liability for homicide, *see* Homicide
Offences, previous, 237n
Olwak, Natale, 26, 27n
Original Communities, the, 18
Ornaments (jewellery), 105, 148, 167
Osborn's Concise Law Dictionary, 23, 79n, 92n, 162n, 186, 218n, 223n
Ownership and possession
definitions of, 163–4, 171; of land, *see under* Land Law; and property, *see under* Property

Pakam area and people, 174–7, 182
Pakam Regional Court, 174–7
Panyon people, the, 183
Paternity
in cases of adultery, 74–5, 84; and bride-wealth, 95
Pathuon, 181
Penalties, reasons for imposition of, 34
People's Local Courts Act, 1977, 19
Perjury, *see also* False oath, 235n
Philips, A., 55n, 56, 58, 64
Plants and herbs, medicinal, 166
Police, 35, 44, 132;
absence of, in Dinka Customary Law, 45
Police posts, 184
Polygamy
regarded by many Westerners as 'unreasonable', 27; in Islamic Law, 27; a main feature of Dinka marriage, 54–5; universal in most of Africa, 55; and Christianity, 55; threatened by modernisation, 55–6; and procreation of children, 61; and adultery, 72; and distribution or inheritance of family property, 144, 146, 147; in urban communities, 147
Population increases, 56
Power(s)
defined, 92; distinguished from right(s), *see* Right(s); balanced by liability(ies), 92, 94
Pre-marital sex, pregnancy resulting from, 38, 61
Prescription and Limitation Ordinance, 1928, 162n, 228
Previous offences, *see* Offences, previous
Prisons, absence of in Dinka Customary Law, 35, 38, 45
Procedure
rules of, distinguished from rules of substantive law, 216–8, 222; objectives of, 217; hearings in camera, 217; functional role of judge or court, 218–20; court investigatory system, 218–20, 235–6; conciliation principle, 36, 220–2; out of court settlement, 221–2; simplicity of, 222; cause of action and right of action, 227–9, 231, 232, non-renewal of decided cases *(res judicata)*, 229; families collectively party to cases, 229–30; survival of actions after death of parties, 230; production or seizure of property subject to litigation, 230–1, 232–3, 243; of court hearing, 231–8; seating arrangements and personnel, 233–4; appeals, *see* Appeals; execution of decrees and orders, 243–5

Procreation of children, see also *Children*
man's need for, 42; main objective of marriage, 58, 61–2, 76, 88, 145; in 'ghost marriages', 58–9, 71, 88, 141–2, 143–4, 145–6, 148–9

Property
transfer of title to, *see* Transfer of title to property; damages for trespass to, 40; man's need for, 42, 118; conflict over, 42–3; communal ownership of, within family, 73, 77, 142, 144, 147–8, 201; right to tracing of, by original owner, 40, 98, 119, 121–3, 127–35; 136–7; distribution of, after divorce, 103–5; and ownership, Dinka liguistic distinction between, 118; in English Law, 118, 119–20, 121–2, 125–6; differences between English Law and Dinka Law of, 118–9, 121–2, 125–6; rights of innocent third parties, 119, 122, 124, 125–6, 130–1, 132–4, 135–9, 190; theft of, *see also* Theft, 123, 130, 138, 139; received knowingly as stolen, *see under* Theft; traced following divorce, 127–9, 134–5; tracing of, includes offspring or produce, 128–9, 130–1, 132, 137; damages for, if irrecoverable, 122, 129, 130–1, 132–4, 135, 137, 138, 140; lost and found, 130, 131, 132, 139–40, 167–8; rights of intermediary parties, 136–7, used for discharging obligations, 142, 143, 147–8; must remain inside family, 142–4; and ancestors, *see* Ancestors; and polygamy, *see* Polygamy, Livestock most important part of, 146, 150, 151; land as, *see* Land *and* Land Law; on or under land, *see under* Land Law; rights over another person's, 185

Prostitution, 69
Province Courts, *see* Courts, Province
Province Governors, 223n, 239, 241–2, 243
Province Judges, *see* Judges, Province
Punishments, *see* Legal Sanctions *and* Penalties, reasons for imposition of Purification rites, *see under* Ritual

Radcliffe-Brown, A. R., 56–7, 64
Rape, 43, 61;
damages for, 38, 61; gravity of, as an offence, 38,
Redemption of children, *see* Children, redemption of
Rek Dinka, the, 154, 170
Relatives, *see* Family(ies)
Religious beliefs, *see also* God *and* Sanctions, religious
as a source of Dinka Customary Law, 33, 47–9; and land tenure, 155–6, 178
Remarriage, 84–6
Rent Restriction Act, 1953, 217
Resident Magistrates, 225, 239, 241
Restatement of the Bhar el Ghazal Region Customary Law Act, 1984
Part II (Code of the Dinka Customary Law), 40, 62; Part III (Code of the Luo Customary Law), 106; section 7(a): marriages between Dinka and non-Dinka, 110n; section 7(b): personal law of woman governing marriage, 106; section 20: definition of marriage, 54; section 21(i): consent to marry, 62; sections 25 and 26: marital rights and obligations, 62, 65, 66, 83n; sections 27 and 29: marital rights, 62; section 27: adultery, 68; section 28: adultery, 68n; section 29: adultery, 69n; section 30: right to sue in cases of adultery, 70n, 73, 75n; section 31: adultery with husband's relative, 76, 77; section 32: paternity, 74; section 34: compensation for adultery, 75; section 36: divorce, 81n; section 38: death of husband, 57; section 40: divorce, 82n; section 41: divorce, 90; section 48: rape, 61; section 51: legal heirs defined, 141; section 52: appointing trustees, 141, 146; section 53: reversion of property to original owner following divorce, 136, 137; section 54: exceptions to right to trace property, 133n, 134, *and* acquisition of property paid as compensation, 137; section 55: right to trace offspring or produce of property, 128n; sections 56 and 57: ownership of property, 123, 130, 131, 138; section 58: damages in lieu of irrecoverable property, 131, 133n, 138; section 59: transfer of property by gift, 128; section 60: revocation of gift, 128, 129; section 61: no right of tracing property to innocent third party, 129, 135n; section 62: right to trace property, 131n, 139; section 63: tracing of property, 123; section 64: law of contract, 187, 190n; section 66: care of security for debt, 187–8; section 67: liability for personal injury, 198n; section 68: tortious acts by animals, 193n, 198n; section 70: death caused by inter-tribal fighting, 202; section 71: killing in self-defence, 205; section 75: killing of wife by husband, 209; section 76: defamation, 211; section 79: damage caused by animals, 194, 196; section 80: liability of animal-keepers, 194; and marriage, 81; and transfer of title to property, 123; some rules of property not embodied in, 131n, 137, 138; and 'ghost marriages' *(Lo-hot)*, 143; Land Law not embodied in, 150; General Explanations and Definitions (re. custody of children), 91

Rewards, 139
Revenge
fear of, as a sanction in African law, 46, 51–2; prevention of, by compensation, 50, 205; for homicide, 51–2, 205; family responsibility for, 51–2; and insulting publication, 214
Riau, 184
Right(s)
defined, 92–3; distinguished from power(s), 92–5; balanced by duty(ies), 92–4, 169; and property, *see under* Property; and land, see under Land *and* Land Law; communal and public, 149, 178–81; of way, 149, 153n, 180, 185; fishing, *see* Fishing and fishing rights; grazing, *see* Grazing rights; hunting, *see* Hunting and hunting rights; of action, *see under* Procedure; of appeal, *see* Appeals.
Ritual
purification, 36, 47, 50, 88n, 202; sacrifice of cattle, 47, 48; fishing ceremonies, 183; following killing through accident or mental incapacity, 207; oath-taking in court, 235
Rivers, lakes and pools, 66, 149, 152, 157, 168, 180, 183, 185
Roman Law, 192, 195
Rumbek District, 39, 107, 120, 126, 154, 182n

Index

Rumbek town, 124, 155, 174

Sacrifice, 47, 48
Saed Mohamed Ahmed El Mahdi Dr, 150n, 151n, 163
Salmond, 160n, 164, 171
Sanctions
   legal, *see* Legal sanctions; religious, 47–9, 50, 52–3, 235; modern, 52; traditional, strength of, 52–3
Self-Government Statute, 1956, 223n
Sexual offences, *see also* Adultery, Incest, Rape; and Pre-marital sex, pregnancy resulting from: 38, 200, 203–4
Sharia Courts, *see* Courts, Sharia
Sharia Kadi or Gadi, 101, 112–3, 116
Sharia Law, *see* Islamic Law
Shilluk people, the, 156
Songs
   as a social or moral sanction, 51; defamatory, 211, 213–4
Southern Sudan, re-division of, 106
State Government, 61
State Law (Territorial Law), 18–19, 110, 240–1
State Penal Code, *see* Sudan Penal Code
Stubbs, Captain Cook, 49n, 50n, 52, 158
Substantive Law, distinguished from Adjectival Law, 217
Succession, *see also* Property
   law codified, 40; intestate, 140, 141, 144–5, 146, 149; testamentary, 140, 143, 146; and legal heirs, 140–1, 145–6, 149, 172, 173, 230; and trustees, 140–1, 143–4, 145–6, 148–9; and importance of the family, 141–6; and 'ghost marriage', *see* 'Ghost marriages'; limitations upon freedom of bequest, 143; exclusion of daughters from inheritance, 144; exclusion of divorced wives from inheritance, 144; and polygamy, 144, 146, 147; in Islamic Law, *see* Islamic Law
Sudan, British rule in, 72n, 115
Sudan Criminal Code, 77
Sudan, Independence of, 115
Sudan Penal Code, 1983
   and incest, 52–3; and sexual cohabitation, 61; and adultery, 68, 69, 70, 77; and recovering stolen property, 124–5; and defamation, 211
Sukuna Law, 103–4
Sukuna tribe, 68
Summons, 232–3
Supernatural powers
   fear of, as a sanction in African law, 49–50; and defamation, 211–3
Supreme Court, the, 110, 116, 240
Suttee (Hindu custom), other communities' condemnation of, 28

Taylor, Jeremy, 41
Territorial Law, *see* State Law
Theft, 43, 120–1, 123–6, 130–1, 133–4, 135, 217;
   and receiving of stolen property, 124–5
Thompson, Cliff F., 17n

Toc (lowland/communal grazing land), *see under* Land
Tonj District, 39, 182, 214
Tort and tortious acts
   miscarriages of justice in cases of, *see* Miscarriages of justice; committed by animals, *see under* Animals; law of, 186–7; distinguished from contract, 186–7; homicide classified as, *see under* Homicide; collective responsibility for, by family, 199–205
Towns and urban communities, 20, 69, 147, 151
Tracing of property, *see under* Property
Transfer of title, *see under* Property
Trees, 166
Trespass, 40, 193, 195, 197;
   by animals, 193, 194, 198
Trustees of the deceased
   Marrying a woman for him, *see* 'Ghost marriages'; rights of, 60; in adultery suits, 70–1, 76; differing degrees of status, 71; duties towards estate, 140–1, 143–4, 145; caring for family, 148–9; other references, 229
Trustees of property
   creditors as, 188; which is subject to litigation, 231
Tswana people, the, 86
Turkish rule in Sudan, 148
Twic people, the, 170, 184–5

Unregistered Land Act, 1970, 150, 151, 171–2
Upper Nile Province, 224
Urban communities, *see* Towns and urban communities

Venda Law, 102–3, 104

Wanh-alel, conferences held at, 39, 73, 106–7, 214
Warmelo, J. J. Van, and Plophi, W. M. D., 90n, 102–3, 104n
Warrants of Establishment of Courts, 223, 224, 226, 233
Wau, 94, 107
Wautown, 39
Western Dinka, the, 170
Western Nuer (Bentiu), 112
Wet-Duang people, the, 180, 184
White Nile, 154
Widows, 58, 70–2
'Widow concubines' (cf. P. P. Howell), 70–1
Wills, *see also* Succession: testamentary, 140, 144–5, 146, 148
Witnesses (in court), 217, 219, 232, 234, 235–6
Women, duties of, 62
Wylds, Major (former District Commissioner, Yambio), 109

Yambio District, 109
Yirol District, 37, 39, 112
Yirol Town Court, 37n

Zande people, the, 28